Rangers on a Scout in the Big Bend Country, western Texas.

SIX YEARS WITH
THE TEXAS RANGERS

1875 TO 1881

BY

JAMES B. GILLETT

EDITED, WITH AN INTRODUCTION, BY
M. M. QUAIFE

FOREWORD BY OLIVER KNIGHT

UNIVERSITY OF NEBRASKA PRESS
Lincoln and London

First Bison Book printing: 1976

Library of Congress Cataloging in Publication Data
Gillett, James B   1856–1937.
  Six years with the Texas Rangers, 1875 to 1881.

  Reprint of the ed. published by Yale University
Press, New Haven.
  1. Texas rangers. 2. Frontier and pioneer life
—Texas. 3. Texas—History—1846–1950. 4. Gillett,
James B.,   1856–1937. I. Title.
F391.G473 1976   363.2'092'4   76–4495
ISBN 0–8032–0889–8
ISBN 0–8032–5844–5 pbk.

⊛

Bison Book edition reproduced by arrangement with
Yale University Press.

TO
MY OLD RANGER COMRADES
WHEREVER THEY MAY BE

CONTENTS

ILLUSTRATIONS

FOREWORD
by Oliver Knight

"Arrived here Saturday with company. All quiet."[1]

That laconic report by a Texas Ranger captain probably comes closer than any other single statement to summarizing the nature, purpose, and function of the Texas Rangers — a state law enforcement agency of mobile trouble shooters whose job was and is to maintain law and order when a local situation gets out of hand, when local police resources are insufficient, when criminal activities spread beyond local jurisdiction, when a major crime calls for state intervention and assistance.

Around the Rangers, as around any other colorful body of fighting men, has grown a reputation for tenacity, firmness, and quick-triggered summary justice when necessary. The Rangers built that reputation because they had to build it—because Texas was niggardly in maintaining the Rangers, and upon the shoulders of relatively few men fell a heavy responsibility: in the earlier years, of fighting Texas' inveterate enemies, the Indian and the Mexican; in later years, of combating the toughest and most desperate criminals in the state.

To recount the evolution of the tradition would require a full history of the Rangers, and of Texas as well, and can here only be suggested. It was the Rangers who rid Southwest Texas of the swaggering ruffians who were running things to please themselves. It was the Rangers who maintained law and order in the explosive railroad towns as the Texas and Pacific built across West Texas,

1. Report of Captain Bryan Marsh, Feb. 28, 1881, quoted in J. Evetts Haley, *Jeff Milton, A Good Man with A Gun* (Norman, University of Oklahoma Press, 1948), p. 88. Punctuation has been modernized for clarity.

Foreword

and who, on occasion, had to pay their own defense counsel when charged with murder after shooting down lawbreakers in self-defense. It was the Rangers who later kept the lid on rip-roaring oil boom towns in both East and West Texas. It was the Rangers who guarded the Mexican border against bandits, cattle thieves, rumrunners, dope smugglers, and German spies during World War I.

Captain Bill McDonald—a hell-for-leather sort—was called to Brownsville in 1906 when some Negro soldiers from Fort Brown had raided the town. Marching melodramatically into the Fort with an automatic shotgun in his hand and one Ranger at his side, McDonald found himself looking into the business ends of rifles held by twenty defiant Negro soldiers. "Put them guns down!" he barked. That he exceeded himself in trying to boss the Army around was shown when the governor and local judges cut the ground from under him, but his cheek illustrates something of the hardness and disregard for protocol that has marked the Ranger. Indeed, McDonald's disregard for any distinction between state and federal authority, if state laws had been violated, is of a piece with a long history of action along the Mexican border. The Texas Rangers would thumb their noses at international comity by weaving back and forth across the Rio Grande in pacifying — permanently — Mexican bravados who raided Texas ranches to steal and kill.

The story is that of Lieutenant J. B. Armstrong, who traced and captured, in Florida, John Wesley Hardin, a frontier gunman of the type police now designate as mad-dog killers; of the relentless pursuit and killing of Sam Bass; of the facing down of mobs and potential mobs in more instances than can be recounted here. The name-

Foreword

less Ranger who said, simply, "We had a little shooting and he lost," was typical. So was another's "I have been accused once. We were camped out on the Pecos. A norther came up, I pulled the cover off, and he froze to death."[2]

Because of the Ranger tradition—magnified by movie accounts as accurate as such accounts are—a young lady tingled with excitement one evening a few years ago. She was trying her luck in a gambling house situated between Fort Worth and Dallas. Somebody yelled, "The Rangers!" Her fellow players dived for doors and windows. Not she. She wanted to see the booted, spurred, two-gun men in big hats and chaps. But she was terribly disappointed. The business-like Rangers simply wore business suits. And, if I recall the story correctly, they added insult to injury by wearing *shoes*.

All too sketchily, these incidents symbolize the spirit, the activities, the tradition, the dangers, the high sense of purpose, and the prosaic daily routine of the Texas Rangers, whose early years are described here by James B. Gillett. (Incidentally, he was not responsible for being called Captain Gillett. He was a sergeant in the Rangers, not a captain.) His account might well be entitled "The First Six Years of the Modern Texas Rangers," for the present force had had only a halting beginning during the year before he, as an adventurous eighteen-year-old, enlisted.

Gillett's book really is one of the better first-person frontier narratives. Because it is written with such understatement, one has to get into it before his excitement

2. Walter Prescott Webb, *The Texas Rangers: A Century of Frontier Defense* (New York, 1935), passim. Except where otherwise noted, the internal history of the Texas Rangers up to 1935, as here given, is based upon Webb.

Foreword

quickens with the realization that here is both depth and probity. Here is the story not only of a man who loved adventure but of a man who loved the out-of-doors—what he calls the grand frontier before it was marred by the hand of man. In this book can be seen the quick passage of a stage of frontier development, as well as a sense of what it meant to a young man to be alive and kicking on that part of the Texas frontier during the turbulent 1870s, when the emerging cattle kingdom clashed with the nomadic Indian and then with lawless whites, before the foundation for civilization in the broad reaches of West Texas could be laid. Then, too, there is the feeling and experience of a perceptive young man who saw and loved the land.

In common with most such first-person accounts written from memory, Gillett's story can be given credence for what he personally saw and experienced but becomes less reliable in description of pertinent incidents that he did not actually witness. His account of the Salt Lake War near El Paso, which occurred before he reached El Paso, is at variance with the more carefully researched version in Walter Prescott Webb's *The Texas Rangers*. However, such criticism is picayunish, because Gillett presents a historically valuable account and, of equal importance, a highly readable one.

The Texas Rangers, which Gillett joined in 1875, had had an off and on existence ever since 1823, when Stephen F. Austin formed a band of ten rangers to protect the first American settlements from Indians. A formally organized force of Texas Rangers did not appear, however, until the outbreak of the Texas Revolution in 1835, at which time they were formed as an irregular military body. From that time on—throughout all their ups and

Foreword

downs, disappearances and reappearances—the Rangers were irregulars. They were irregular as hell, in everything except getting the job done.

As established during the revolution, the Rangers were also a mounted body, each man furnishing his own horse and his own weapons. After the revolution, when Texas was responsible for its own destiny as a republic, the impoverished nation had to defend its borders from the deadly, mounted plains Indians, principally the Comanches, but there was not money enough to maintain a regular army. However, rangers could be raised for periods of three to six months. Because of the shortage of money, Texas relied upon them, ultimately making them an institution.

The earliest members of the force— that established by Austin and enlarged in the next few years—were not known as Texas Rangers. They usually were designated as mounted volunteers, mounted gunmen, spies, and rangers. Just as they were distinct from a regular army, they were distinct from the Texas militia and local police. Their organization was almost primitive, resembling that of the roaming bands of Comanches, simple and informal. The smallness of the force and the nature of its work made ordinary military discipline impossible. Moreover, the earliest rangers were frontiersmen—and frontiersmen were never noted for obedience to anybody.

In protecting the settlements near the Gulf Coast from roaming bands of savages farther inland, the Texas Ranger assumed one of the characteristics that marks the plainsman from a woodland man—he was mounted. He had to be mounted, because his enemy was mounted. Indeed, the Comanches had a reputation for being one of the best light cavalry forces the world has ever seen. Prior

Foreword

to the 1840s the Comanche cavalry had a decided and distinct advantage over their white opponents. Using bows and arrows, they could fire volley after volley at their enemy, whereas the white man had to fire and then reload.

This disadvantage was ultimately overcome with another major instrument distinguishing the plainsman from the woodsman—the six-shooter. In 1836 a young eastern inventor, Samuel Colt, began manufacturing revolving pistols, which the Texans used to good advantage. The first Colt revolvers were not suited to the heavy service demanded in Indian warfare; besides being light and fragile, the whole pistol had to be taken apart in three pieces before it could be reloaded. But in 1839 Colt, at the urging of Ranger Captain Samuel H. Walker, came out with a much heavier revolver known as the Walker Colt. During the Mexican War, Colt designed still another revolver for the Texas Rangers, which became known as the Old Army Type. It was the six-shooter, made to specifications of the Texas Rangers, that tamed the Great Plains.

The Rangers were not known as such to the contemporary writers until the Mexican War. They served—with debatable distinction—in Mexico, but General Zachary Taylor sent Captain Jack Hays' Rangers back home.

Shortly thereafter, with Texas a state in the Union, the role of the Rangers faded. Through annexation the federal government had assumed a responsibility for protecting the Texas frontier from hostile Indians. Sometimes the Rangers were called into service for an emergency, but only as short-term volunteers. Texas wanted the federal government to pay the Rangers, which Wash-

Foreword

ington was not willing to do. On the other hand, Texas could not make the Rangers a regular force without representing the United States Army as incompetent, which Austin was not willing to do. Between annexation in 1846 and the outbreak of the Civil War, the Texas Rangers existed almost in name only, although they had a flamboyant revival on the eve of the Civil War, when Governor Sam Houston—who had not been at all enthusiastic about them during his two terms as president of the republic, pursuing a pacific policy toward the Indians—suddenly placed about 1,000 Rangers in active service. One explanation for this sudden flurry is that Houston intended to invade Mexico, creating a diversion that would abort the threatened Civil War (he was a Unionist) and perhaps catapult him into the White House.

And then came the Civil War, during which the Texas Rangers again faded almost into oblivion. With the iron heel of Reconstruction upon Texas, the Rangers did in fact disappear, their place being taken by the state police of hated memory.

When Texas regained control of her political destiny in 1874, the legislature wiped out these oppressive and tyrannical state police, supplanting them with a new body of Rangers. It is from that reorganization in 1874 that the present Rangers date. Actually, two distinct Ranger forces were created. One was the Frontier Battalion, commanded by Major John B. Jones, whose six Ranger companies were to guard the frontier from the Red River to the Nueces River—a frontier that extended along a line that is slightly west of present central Texas. It is of this Frontier Battalion that Gillett writes. The other force was a special Ranger force in southwest Texas, com-

Foreword

manded by the legendary Captain L. H. McNelly. Whereas Jones' Frontier Battalion was designed initially mostly to guard against Indian incursions, McNelly was charged with suppressing lawlessness in a giant-sized chunk of country bounded roughly by a line running from Corpus Christi to San Antonio to Eagle Pass. McNelly's job was to fight and subdue a number of lawless bands of white men in the then emerging cattle country of southwest Texas, and also to fight Mexican bandits.

Paradoxically, or perhaps perversely, the Texas Rangers of the Frontier Battalion were placed on station because the state of Texas disliked and did not have confidence in the United States Army, which also maintained a frontier force in forts stretching across West Texas. The paradox comes about because, before the Civil War, Texas had been unwilling to establish a regular state force for frontier defense, relying upon the federal government. The Civil War, which at least in theory had established the supremacy of the federal government, left such antagonism that Texas at last was willing to foot the bill for its own frontier defense. Not only were the troopers on West Texas station Yankees but, in the years during and immediately after Reconstruction, many were Negroes— the "buffalo soldiers," as they were known to the Indians, who likened the kinky black hair of Negroes to the curly hair on buffalo.

The attitude of Texas in regard to the efficiency of the army on the frontier coincides, however, with a rather general frontier view of the army. Erroneously, frontiersmen almost always considered that they knew a lot more than the United States Army about fighting Indians, and they thought they could do a better job of it.

Jones took command of the Frontier Battalion with the

Foreword

view of a commanding general rather than that of a Ranger captain like McNelly, Rip Ford, Ben McCulloch, or Jack Hays. As a commanding general, he regularly traveled up and down his line of frontier outposts on a border that was about four hundred miles long and one hundred miles wide. In contrast with the Army, which established its men in forts and permanent cantonments, the Rangers of the Frontier Battalion lived in tent camps.

During the first six months, the Rangers fought Indians fifteen times, killing fifteen Indians, wounding ten, capturing one, and recovering two hundred head of stolen livestock valued at $5,000. During this same time they followed twenty-eight trails of Indians who had raided Texas settlements. Approximately forty war parties entered Texas in this period—about the average for some years previously. In the second six months the number of war parties was reduced to twenty, and Rangers met them in five fights, again killing one Indian per fight. Then, during the third six months, only six war parties came. It was in this latter period, in August 1875, that Gillett first smelled powder smoke in an Indian fight. Thereafter, between September 1875 and February 1876, no Indians at all were reported in the area guarded by the Frontier Battalion.

However tempting it might be to credit the Rangers with this desirable change, the fact of the matter is that the Indian raiding was stopped by the United States Army. In 1874, the very year in which the Frontier Battalion was organized, the federal government became exasperated with the warlike conduct of Indians on reservations in what is now Oklahoma. For some years the government had been trying to congregate Southern Plains Indians on reservations in the western part of the Indian Terri-

Foreword

tory. To a large extent it had succeeded. It had managed to bring into the reservation some of the most warlike of the Southern Plains Indians, especially the Kiowas—a small band which, in proportion to its size, probably killed more white men than any other group of Indians in North America—and some bands of the loosely organized Comanches, who were the wildest and most dangerous of all the raiders on the Texas frontier. But the Indians on the reservation, especially around Fort Sill, lived rather comfortably at government expense, and then amused themselves by slipping off the reservation, crossing the Red River, and hunting Texans for breakfast. Exasperated by these Indian activities, the government in 1874 authorized the War Department to pacify them, taking the Indians from under control of the Bureau of Indian Affairs, at that time a corruptly managed arm of the Interior Department.

As a result, the Army drove a three-fingered campaign into West Texas, especially the Staked Plains. With one force of troops moving north from Fort Concho near San Angelo, a smaller force moving west from New Mexico, and a much larger force moving westward out of the Kansas forts, the campaign broke the back of Indian resistance on the Southern Plains. After the campaign was finished, only one band of warlike Indians was still off the reservation. That was the Quahadi band of Comanches, under the half-white Quanah Parker, whose mother, Cynthia Ann Parker, had been stolen as a little girl from a settler's fort in central Texas.

Because of the Army's 1874 campaign, Indian fighting was a practically nonexistent function of the Frontier Battalion after young Gillett joined the Rangers. Indeed, in March 1877 the Rangers were ordered not to make

Foreword

further westward scouts after Indians, unless they defi-
nitely were following a fresh trail or acting upon verified
information of an Indian raid. The job of the Frontier
Battalion consequently became one of subduing lawless
white men, a story Gillett tells very well.

What young Gillett witnessed and participated in was
the sudden eruption and equally sudden subsidence of the
frontier along the eastern edges of West Texas. To be
sure, there remained much roughness, lawlessness, and
six-gun justice in the cattle kingdom that immediately
thereafter spread all across western Texas, but the frontier—in the sense of a line between civilization and sav-
agery—passed very quickly in that part of the country. It
is astonishing, in a way, that the experience of one man
should have encompassed not only the passage of that
frontier and sequence of events in that part of the state,
but also an almost exact duplication of the same thing
when he later moved out to El Paso. There, too, he saw—
but did not get much chance to participate in—the last
fights against the murderous Apache Indians, their final
conquest, and then the eruption of white lawlessness along
the border, to which was added the constant theme of warfare with Mexicans. The last Indian fight on Texas soil
was the battle against a small band of Apaches in southwest Texas in 1881—which Gillett recounts, although he
had been left behind to guard the Ranger camp at Ysleta.

The history of the Texas Rangers throughout this
period also illustrates in large measure why Texas has the
fierce state pride, actually a form of nationalism, which
many outlanders either do not understand or misunder-
stand. From its admission to the Union in 1846 until Oklahoma became a state in 1907, Texas had a contiguous
border with only one other state of the United States—

Foreword

Louisiana plus a chip of Arkansas. The rest of its borders were infested by the ancient enemies of the Texans—Indians on the north and west, Indians and Mexicans on the west, and Mexicans on the south. By and large, Texas for a great many years had to fight those enemies itself. True, the Army did more in subduing the plains Indians than contemporary Texas frontiersmen were willing to admit, but still the scattered nature of settlements and the constant invasion by Mexican banditti forced Texans to do a lot of their own fighting. This was especially true along the border where the United States Army did not participate in fighting Mexican—or white—cattle thieves. Naturally, there developed in Texas a spirit of oneness and a sense of self-reliance, as well as a spirit of independence.

Taking the long view, one must give credit to the Texas Rangers for suppressing the lawlessness and wanton killing that characterized the cow country in the form of such outlaws and gunmen as Sam Bass, John Wesley Hardin, and King Fisher. The Rangers, however, were not always looked upon as staunch and true defenders of law, order, and a fair and open trial. As a matter of fact, they acquired a reputation as men who would shoot a man first and then tell him to put up his hands.

Gillett refers only obliquely to this aspect of the public attitude toward the Rangers, but it is made even clearer in another incident. In 1884 Jim Courtright, who had been a frontier marshal in Fort Worth, was arrested there by two Texas Rangers and a New Mexico officer in connection with the murder of some Mexicans at Silver City, New Mexico. When his friends in Fort Worth learned that Courtright had been arrested by Rangers, a mob formed in an effort to free him, some of the men in the

Foreword

mob loudly protesting that the Rangers would murder him.[3] There is a story in my own family of a Ranger, a distant relative, who walked into a large house stacked to the rafters with Mexicans, and was carried out dead. According to the family story, the other men in his company thereupon killed every human being in the house including women and children; and the story was passed down in the family with quite a bit of shock—the Rangers should not have killed the women and children. Yes, family traditions undoubtedly are the most unreliable of all forms of historical information, and I don't even know *whether* this happened, let alone *when* and *where*. But the existence of the story, and its passage down through the family, at least serves to illustrate the point made here— that the Rangers were not always looked upon as "white hats."

After Gillett left the Rangers, he remained in police work for a time, a story which he tells in the concluding chapter, and then devoted his attention to ranching, first as a manager for the Estado Land and Cattle Company near Alpine. Later he managed his own ranch near Marfa and then acquired another near Alpine, which he ran until 1900. He sold that ranch and bought another near Roswell, New Mexico, where he remained until 1907. Then he returned to the Marfa section and bought the Barrell Springs Ranch, which he operated until 1923, at which time he sold his cattle and leased the ranch to his son, Milton E. Gillett. Gillett died at his home in Temple in 1937.

In the years immediately after Gillett left the service, the Rangers continued the functions with which he had been associated. They remained essentially a mounted

3. *Fort Worth Gazette*, Oct. 19, 1884.

Foreword

police force charged with enforcing the law in a lawless land of cattle kings and rustlers, of small-time and ruffianly cowmen who sought to burn out and drive out the so-called nesters, and who cut the barbed-wire fences that were being put up across Texas, as the white man finally learned how to live with, and make his living from, the once forbidding Great Plains.

During the 1880s the Rangers who were charged with this task still operated as an irregular body, each man largely self-supporting and still required to furnish his own equipment—saddle, ropes, guns, bedding, horses, and clothing. The state only paid him a small salary, fed him, and supplied him with a monthly ration of ammunition. As in the past, the Ranger was clothed in the large white hat of the Texas cowboy, which he could use for shade from the sun, protection from a driving blizzard or pelting rainstorm, as a water bucket for himself and his horse, and for signaling. On his feet he wore shopmade boots, which the Ranger of that day wore knee high and cut round at the top, not quite like the cowboy boots that have become pretty much standard in later years. On his boots the Ranger favored the Petmecky spurs, which were made in Austin, or Mexican Chihuahua spurs. In between his hat and his boots, he wore whatever he dang well pleased. While mounted, he seated himself firmly in a saddle made by the Padget Brothers of Waco, the largest saddle makers in the state. Being a sensible man and one who had to spend long hours in the saddle, the Ranger naturally favored the western or stock saddle, in which he could seat himself comfortably, lean his weight against the stirrups, and thus actually help his horse on long rides across desolate country. To him, the traditional cavalry saddle or the regular riding saddle made a man look like

Foreword

"a frog on a shovel." During these years, the Texas Ranger was essentially a cowboy with a commission.[4]

The Frontier Battalion continued in existence until 1901, when a smart lawyer discovered that the original law said that each *officer* of the Rangers was entitled to make arrests, and the construction placed upon the law was that *only* the commissioned officers of a Ranger company could arrest a citizen, that the privates could not. As a result, a new Ranger force was constituted, composed of four companies of twenty men each—only eighty men for the whole state of Texas—and they were placed on station either in far western Texas or along the always turbulent Rio Grande. Gradually, from then until the mid-1930s, the reputation of the Rangers was somewhat tarnished through political manipulation by various governors.

The result was that in 1935 the Rangers, who had always been under the Adjutant General of Texas, were transferred to the newly created Department of Public Safety. At the time there was considerable apprehension that the Rangers would pass out of existence altogether, but this did not happen. Today they number sixty-two men, organized in six companies, with their headquarters in Houston, Dallas, Lubbock, Corpus Christi, Midland, and Waco. A captain, sergeant, and one or two Rangers are stationed in each company headquarters. The other Rangers of each company are scattered around the state, sometimes on single-man stations.

The Texas Rangers today are charged with four major duties: protection of life and property through enforcement of the criminal laws of Texas; suppression of riots and insurrections; the investigation of major crimes, such

4. Haley, p. 29.

Foreword

as murder, rape, robbery, burglary, cattle theft, felonious assault, etc.; and the apprehension of fugitives and transportation of prisoners. Their duties are varied within each of these four areas. They might be called upon to save lives in disaster areas, to recover drowning victims, to guard against looting in disaster areas, suppress a prison riot, or keep a mob under control.

Today the Texas Rangers have a reputation of being composed of the cream of Texas peace officers. Recruited from the ranks of officers in the Texas Department of Safety and other police agencies, a Ranger must be at least twenty-seven years old, a resident of Texas for at least one year, in excellent physical condition, and have an outstanding record of at least five years experience with a law enforcement agency engaged principally in investigating major crimes. This means, in essence, that a Texas Ranger is chosen from among veteran officers who have demonstrated their ability as criminal investigators.

After being chosen for the Rangers, a man receives special training at various departmental schools, such as the School for Criminal Investigators. He later works with other Rangers, gaining experience in their various duties, particularly in criminal investigation, raids, and mob and riot control.

The Ranger is still a mobile trouble shooter, using modern police equipment, which he has simply added to his role of a mounted policeman. He may travel about the state in an automobile equipped with a three-way radio; he might be flown in a Texas Ranger plane to some outlying part of the state; he might have to throw a Ranger jeep into gear to go across rough country; he might go afoot into the same country and remain in touch with other officers by means of a walkie-talkie; or he might have to use

Foreword

one of the light armored cars, one of which is maintained at each Ranger company headquarters for use particularly in capturing barricaded criminals. Although, as in the past, Texas does not furnish him with horse or equipment, he is required to have a horse, saddle, and other gear available for use in inaccessible areas.

The Ranger dress continues to be a matter of individual choice. Although he varies his apparel according to the area in which he is working and the nature of the assignment, he usually wears tan gabardine trousers, a short western jacket, a tan shirt with black tie, a Texas hat, and boots. When so dressed, the Texas Ranger badge is worn on the left breast, but when the Ranger wears a business suit, the badge is concealed beneath the coat. Although he may sometimes strap on two pearl-handled pistols for effect during a parade or other ceremony, the Texas Ranger on duty ordinarily carries one side arm. Here again he can exercise personal choice. Some still favor the old Colt frontier model single-action .45, but others will carry .38 Colt automatics or .357 Magnums.

With the tradition of the Texas Rangers behind him, a modern Ranger—or even the reported near presence of a Ranger—can and does strike fear into the hearts of lawbreakers who might otherwise be able to intimidate local officers. One reason for this tradition, and the Rangers' reputation among the Texas underworld, was fairly well summarized by Bill McDonald when he said, "No man in the wrong can stand up against a man in the right who keeps on a-comin'." An official publication describing the work of the Texas Rangers says that that statement perhaps comes as close as any other to stating their basic creed.[5]

5. *The Texas Ranger*, Texas Department of Public Safety, 1961.

Foreword

More laconically and more typically, the status and effectiveness of the Ranger was summed up by another famous Ranger captain, Tom Hickman, who said in explaining his success in maintaining order in oil boom towns: "The name Texas Ranger, you know, has a lot of weight behind it."[6]

That weight began to be attached to the name Texas Ranger during the years of which you are now about to read.

6. Quoted in C. L. Douglas, *The Gentlemen in the White Hats* (Dallas, 1934), p. 185.

INTRODUCTION

THE story of the Texas Rangers has never been told in its entirety, nor can it be told without recounting the history of Texas itself. The modest volume of Sergeant James B. Gillett, here presented to the reader, does not undertake to recount the history of the ranger organization, but merely to present a cross section of that history during the picturesque, lurid years of Sergeant Gillett's service as a ranger.

The term *ranger* carries the tang of the old American frontier, and as applied to the Texas state police it embodies a wealth of historical association. Probably the most notable ranger force in American annals was the organization of irregular partisan warriors led by Major Robert Rogers in the French and Indian War. Rogers' Rangers and the Texas Rangers share in common the quality of being composed of picked men trained to the use of arms and ready at all times to engage in any enterprise however hazardous it might be: but while the earlier organization was of but temporary duration, created for service in a foreign war, the more recent one is permanent, having existed almost a hundred years.

The history of the Texas Rangers is coeval with that of the republic itself. "Before the first gun of the Texas Revolution was fired at Gonzales in December, 1835, before the Declaration of Texan Independence was adopted, before the heroes of the Alamo laid down their lives for freedom, and before the Mexican Army under Santa Anna was destroyed by Sam Houston at San Jacinto, a ranger force was organized in Texas." Thus spoke Chief Justice Fly of the Texas Civil Court of

Introduction

Appeals in a recent decision upholding the constitutionality of the ranger law. Even before an army was raised, the ranger force was established, consisting of three companies of fifty-six men each. Although the force has varied in size from time to time its existence has been continuous from its first organization until the present moment.

To guard the frontier against the Indian and the Mexican was the original task of the rangers. At the end of half a century the Indian menace had practically disappeared, and that presented by the Mexican from across the Rio Grande had measurably diminished in intensity. Meantime, the rangers had assumed the added duty of repressing domestic foes of the peace of the commonwealth throughout the far-flung Texan borders. Thereby the force began to assume the character of a mounted state police whose activities were directed to supplementing and reinforcing the efforts of sheriffs and other local officials in the maintenance of peace and order. And there was plenty of work of this character to do, for most of the huge area of Texas was still a frontier region forty or fifty years ago, wherein banditry flourished and crimes of violence were committed with appalling frequency.

In the discharge of their onerous and dangerous duties the Texas Rangers long since attained widespread and well-deserved renown. The utility of such an organization began to be perceived by other commonwealths, and New York, Pennsylvania, Michigan, and a number of others now maintain forces of state police. Already some of these organizations, notably the state police of New York and Pennsylvania, have begun to achieve a renown of their own. Compared with

Introduction

the Texas Rangers, however, all other state-police organizations are still in their infancy, and from the widely changed character of the problems which confront them, none can ever have a career comparable to that which lies behind the rangers.

Today, as of old, the rangers maintain vigilant watch and ward over the peace and welfare of the commonwealth of Texas. Owing to fiscal considerations the force has in recent months been reduced until it constitutes but little more than a skeleton organization, with a total force, for the five companies now existing, of less than thirty men. There is nothing particularly new in this, for Sergeant Gillett recounts in his narrative crises of like character almost half a century ago. To some extent the gas-chariot has replaced the mustang as a vehicle of transportation for the force. Despite these changes the rangers yet remain a powerful influence in the maintenance of peace and order; and still, as of old, their arrival brings a sense of relief and security to the law-abiding and a corresponding depression of spirit to the law-breaker.

To edit such a narrative as Sergeant Gillett's *Six Years with the Texas Rangers* is both a privilege and a pleasure. His is a great story, simply and modestly told. The age of opportunity for Americans will not be closed so long as careers such as his are possible; and there need be no fear for the welfare of the republic while men of his stamp comprise the majority of her citizenry.

It seems proper, in concluding, to inform the reader how the narrative came to assume its present form. In the nature of things men of action cannot ordinarily become masters of the art of literary composition. Nor is

Introduction

the man of university training commonly able to arrange his manuscript in form suitable for publication without the assistance of a competent editor. When preparing his story for publication several years ago, Captain Gillett invoked the aid of an editor to assist him in putting it into its final literary form. The book as then published has been subjected to a further careful revision by the present editor; certain corrections have been made and considerable additional information has been supplied by Captain Gillett; and the work as revised has been submitted to his final scrutiny and approval.

M. M. QUAIFE.

Burton Historical Collection,
Detroit.

May 4, 1925

PREFACE

TO write a complete history of the Texas Rangers as a state organization would require much time and an able historian. I am not an historian and could not undertake an exhaustive treatise, and it is only at the earnest solicitation of my children, frontier friends, and old comrades that I have undertaken to write a short history of the rangers during the years I served with them. This little volume, then, has only the modest aim of picturing the life of the Texas Rangers during the years 1875-1881. I cannot at this late date recount in detail all the scouts that were made while I was in the service. I have, therefore, confined myself principally to the description of those in which I was a participant. Naturally, I remember these the best.

It has been said that truth never makes very interesting reading. Of the accuracy of this dictum I leave my readers to judge, for I have told my story just as I remember it, to the best of my ability and without any effort to embroider it with imagination. If I can interest any of my old ranger comrades or even one little boy who likes to read about a real frontier, I shall feel amply repaid for all the labor and expense involved in preparing this work.

I wish sincerely to thank Miss Mary Baylor for placing at my disposal the books and papers of her distinguished father, Captain G. W. Baylor. And I would be an ingrate, indeed, did I fail here to record my obligation to my wife, without whose inspiration and sympathetic encouragement this book would never have been written.

Preface

That I might show the training of the typical Texas Ranger, I have ventured to include a short account of my own life up to the time I became a ranger, June 1, 1875.

JAMES B. GILLETT.

SIX YEARS WITH
THE TEXAS RANGERS

CHAPTER I

THE MAKING OF A RANGER

THE greatest shaping force in human life is heredity, and from my father I inherited my love of the open frontier and its life of danger and excitement. This inheritance was further strengthened by environment and training, and finally led me to embrace the life of the Texas Ranger. My father, James S. Gillett, was himself a frontiersman, though born in the quieter, more settled east. When he was very young his parents migrated from his birthplace in Kentucky to Missouri. Here, after a short time, they died and the young orphan lived with a brother-in-law. When still quite a youth my father, with three other adventurous Missourians, set out on an expedition to Santa Fé, New Mexico. While passing through Indian Territory, now the state of Oklahoma, the little party was captured by the Osage Indians. Fortunately for the youngsters, their captors did them no harm, but turned them loose after two weeks' imprisonment in the redskin camp.

Despite this first setback my father persevered and reached Santa Fé. Here he lived several years and mastered the Spanish language. Not long afterward the emigrating fever again seized him and he journeyed to Van Buren, Arkansas. While living there he studied law and was admitted to the bar. Shortly thereafter he removed to Paris, Texas, where he was elected to the legislature as representative for Lamar and adjoining counties.

When Texas entered the Union and brought on the Mexican War, my father enlisted in 1846 and rose to the rank of major. In 1854 he was adjutant general of Texas. In 1859-1860, during the governorship of Sam Houston, my father was quartermaster of a battalion of rangers, thus making it natural that I should also feel drawn toward this famous organization.

At the time of the Civil War my father was beyond military age,—he was born in 1810—but as the South became hard-pressed for men he enlisted in the spring of 1864 and served in Captain Carington's company until the end of the war.

In 1850, a few years before he became adjutant general, my father married Miss Bettie Harper, then a resident of Washington County, Texas. My mother's father, Captain Harper, was a southern planter who had emigrated from North Carolina between 1846 and 1848, and, settling in Washington County, established a Dixie plantation with a hundred slaves. My mother was a cultivated and refined woman. On her marriage she brought several negro servants with her to her new home in Austin. Of her union with my father five children were born. The first two, both boys, died in infancy. I was the fourth child born to my parents, and first saw the light of day in Austin, Texas, on November 4, 1856. An older sister, Mary, and a younger, Eva, survived to maturity.

At the close of the Civil War my father returned to his family pretty well broken in health and spirit. His slaves had been freed and his landholdings, about two

The Making of a Ranger

hundred acres of cedar land, some five or six miles from Austin, and a tract of pineland in Grimes County, Texas, were not very productive. There was not much law-practice in Austin following the close of the war, but my father set to work resolutely to provide for his family. Though I did not realize it then, I now know that he had a hard struggle. I was only eight and a half years old when he returned from the Confederate army, but I remember he used to amuse himself by relating to us vivid accounts of his Indian fighting and frontier adventures. What heredity gave me a predilection for was strengthened by these narratives, and I early conceived a passionate desire to become a frontiersman and live a life of adventure.

In those early days there were no free schools in Austin, so my father sent the three of us, Mary, Eva, and myself, to the pay schools. None of these was very good, and I lost nearly two years at a German school, trying to mix German and English. I have never been of a studious nature—the great out-of-doors always called to me, and I found the confinement of school particularly irksome. When school closed in the early summer of 1868 I went fishing, and never attended school an hour thereafter. For books I substituted the wide-open volume of nature and began the life of sport and freedom that was to prepare me later for service with the rangers.

Poor as he was, my father always kept a pony, and I learned to ride almost before I could walk. Raised on the banks of the Colorado River, I learned to swim and fish so long ago that I cannot now remember when I was unable to do either. I fished along the river with a few hand-lines and used to catch quantities of gasper-

3

gou or drums. These were fine fish and sold readily on the streets of Austin, so I soon saved money enough to buy a small skiff or fishing boat. I now bought a trot-line with a hundred hooks and began fishing in real earnest. About five or six miles below Austin on the Colorado was Mathews' mill. Just below the mill-dam the fishing was always good, and here I made my fishing grounds. I had a large dry-goods box with inch auger-holes bored in it. This box, sunk in the river and secured by a rope tied to a stake driven in the ground, made a capital trap, and into it I˜dropped my fish as they were caught. In this way I kept them alive and fresh until I had enough to take to town.

Many free negroes were farming along the banks of the Colorado, and I would hire a pony of them for twenty-five cents a trip when I was ready to take my catch into town. Many times I left the river by star-light, reached the old Market House at Austin at dawn, spread out a gunny sack, and bunched my fish in readi-ness for the early marketers. I kept up my fishing until the fish stopped biting in the fall of 1868.

Many Confederate soldiers returning home from the war brought with them old Enfield muskets. These were smooth-bore and chambered one large ball and three buckshot. These old guns, loaded with small shot, were fine for use on birds and squirrels, but they had one serious objection—they would kick like a mule. As the boys used to say, they would "get meat at both ends." A day's shooting with one of these muskets would leave one's shoulder and arm black and blue for a week.

When fishing failed I decided to become a hunter, and bought one of these old guns for $3.50. It was al-

The Making of a Ranger

most as long as a fence rail, and at my age I could not begin to hold it out and shoot off-hand, so I had to use a rest. The Enfield musket had the longest barrel I have ever seen on a gun, and the hammer was as long as a man's hand. I could cock my gun with both hands, but if I failed to get a shot I was not strong enough to let the hammer down without letting it get away, so I had to carry it cocked. To keep from losing the cap, I would take it off the tube and put it in my pocket until I had a chance for another shot. I remember once when I cocked my musket I could see no cap on the tube and, thinking it had fallen off, I pulled the trigger. The cap had stuck up in the hammer and the gun roared like a cannon. I was always sure to look for the cap after this. I did not make much headway using this kind of weapon, but it taught me the use and danger of firearms, a knowledge I was to find very useful in later years.

In the spring of 1869 I returned to my fishing lines, and in the fall I bought a double-barrel shotgun for $12. With it I killed quail, ducks, and other small game, all of which I sold on the streets of Austin. By the fall of 1870 I was fourteen years old and could handle a gun rather well for one of my age.

Early that winter wild geese came south by the hundreds. I used to hunt them down the Colorado River, ten or twelve miles below Austin. The birds would feed in the cornfields in the early morning, then flock to the sandbars in the river during the middle of the day. There was nothing silly about those geese, for they were smart enough to frequent only the big islands, three or four hundred yards from any cover. It was impossible to reach them with any kind of a shotgun. I used to slip up to them as close as I could and watch them for hours, trying to think of some plan to get within gunshot of them. I saw as many as a thousand geese on those bars at a single time. I have thought regretfully of these birds many times since, and have wished I could have shot into one of the flocks with a modern rifle—I could have killed a dozen geese at a shot.

In the spring of 1871 I had my first trip to the frontier of Texas. My father traded some of his Grimes County pineland for a bunch of cattle in Brown County, and took me with him when he went to receive the herd. This was the first time I had ever been twenty-five miles from Austin. I was delighted with the trip, the people, and the country. Those big, fine frontiersmen, each wearing a pair of revolvers and most of them carrying a Winchester, fired my boyish imagination. Their accounts of frontier life and their Indian tales fascinated me. I wanted to stay there with them and lost all interest in ever living in town again. During the same year my father drove several bunches of cattle to Austin and I helped him on these drives. Thus I began to be a cowboy—my first step toward the life of the open, upon which I had set my heart.

In the summer of 1872 my mother's health began to fail and my father took her to Lampasas Springs. The water seemed to help her so much that he decided to make Lampasas our home. At that time Lampasas County was strictly a cattle country, but there was not much cow-hunting during the winter. The cattlemen and the cowboys spent a good deal of time in town just having a good time. During this period I became well acquainted with them. In the spring of 1873 my father made a trip back to Austin on some business. The fron-

The Making of a Ranger

tier had been calling to me ever since my first visit there, and I now took advantage of his absence to slip out to Coleman County, at that time on the frontier of Texas.

Monroe Cooksey and Jack Clayton had bought a brand of cattle in Coleman County and I saw the outfit when it left Lampasas. I was slightly acquainted with most of the men in this outfit, so I decided to follow it and try to get work. It was an Indian country every step of the way, and I was afraid to make the trip alone. In a day or two I met a man named Bob McCollum. He was hauling a load of flour to Camp Colorado and let me travel with him. I bade my mother and sisters good-bye and did not see them again until the next December.

We reached old Camp Colorado without mishap in about five days. Clayton and Cooksey's outfit was there loading up supplies for the spring work. I stood around watching the cowboys making their preparations, but lacked the courage to ask them for work. Finally, the outfit started down on Jim Ned Creek to camp for dinner. I went with the men and at last got up spunk enough to ask Monroe Cooksey for a job. He looked at me for a minute and then asked, "What kind of work can a boy of your size do?"

I told him I was willing to do anything a boy of my age could do. He made no reply, and we went on and camped for dinner. After dinner the men made ready to go over on Hoard's Creek to camp for the night. The boys made a rope corral and began to catch their mounts. I just stood there like an orphan watching them. Presently Mr. Cooksey threw his rope on a heavy-set bay horse. The animal showed the whites of

7

his eyes, made a rattling noise in his nose, and struggled so violently that it took three men on the rope to hold him. Mr. Cooksey then turned to me and said, "Here, boy, if you can ride this —— you have a job cinched."

I turned, grabbed my saddle, bridle, and blanket and started to the animal. An elderly man in the outfit headed me off.

"Young man," he said, "this is an old, spoiled horse, and unless you are a mighty good rider you had better not get on him."

I brushed him aside.

"Pshaw, I'm hunting work, and while I'm not a broncho buster, I will make a try at riding him if he kills me."

By this time one of the boys had caught the horse by both ears and was holding him fast. They threw my saddle on him, tightened up the cinch, and finally, after much trouble, got the bridle on him and lifted me into the saddle. When I had fixed myself as best I could they let the animal go. He made two or three revolving leaps forward and fell with his feet all doubled up under him.

Mr. Cooksey seemed to realize the danger I was in, and shouted to me to jump off. Before I could shake myself loose the horse had scrambled to his feet and dashed off in a run. I circled him around to the remuda (bunch of surplus saddle horses), and rode him until night without further trouble. I had won my job, but it was a dirty trick for a lot of men to play on a boy, and a small boy at that. However, to their credit, I wish to say they never put me on a bad horse again, but gave me the best of gentle ponies to ride.

The Making of a Ranger

Our first work was to gather and deliver a herd of cattle to the Horrell boys, then camped on Home Creek. We worked down to the Colorado River, and when we were near old Flat Top Ranch the men with the outfit left me to drive the remuda down the road after the mess wagon while they tried to find a beef. I had gone only a mile or two when I saw a man approaching me from the rear. As he came up I thought he was the finest specimen of a frontiersman I had ever seen. He was probably six feet tall, with dark hair and beard. He was heavily armed, wearing two six-shooters and carrying a Winchester in front of him, and was riding a splendid horse with a wonderful California saddle. He rode up to me and asked whose outfit it was I was driving. I told him Cooksey and Clayton's. He then inquired my name. When I told him he said, "Oh, yes; I saw your father in Lampasas a few days ago and he told me to tell you to come home and go to school."

I made no reply, but kept my horses moving. The stranger then told me his name was Sam Gholston. He said it was dangerous for one so young to be in a bad Indian country and unarmed, that the outfit should not have left me alone, and counseled me to go back to my parents. I would not talk to him, so he finally bade me good-bye and galloped off. His advice was good, but I had not the least idea of going home—I had embraced the frontier life.

Cooksey and Clayton did not stay in business long. After filling their contract with the Horrell boys they sold out to Joe Franks. I suppose I was sold along with the outfit, at least I continued to work for Mr. Franks. A kinder heart than that of Joe Franks never beat in a human breast. He was big of stature and big of soul.

Six Years with the Texas Rangers

He seemed to take an interest in his youthful cow-puncher, and asked me where I was raised and how I came to be away out on the frontier. When cold weather came on that fall he gave me one of his top-coats. It made a pretty good overcoat for me and came down quite to my knees. The sleeves were so long I could double them up and hold my bridle reins, and in one garment I had both coat and gloves.

During the summer of 1873 John Hitsons, Sam Gholston, and Joe Franks were all delivering cattle to old John Chislom, whose outfit was camped on the south side of the Concho River, about where the town of Paint Rock now stands. The other outfits were scattered along down the river about half a mile apart. There were probably seventy-five or a hundred men in the four camps, and at least five hundred horses. One evening just after dark the Indians ran into Gholston's outfit, captured about sixty head of horses, and got away with them. The redskins and the cowboys had a regular pitched battle for a few minutes, firing two hundred shots. This fight was in plain view of our camp, and I saw the flash of every gun and heard the Indians and the cowboys yelling. One of Mr. Gholston's men received a flesh wound in the leg and several horses were killed.

Two nights later the Indians ran upon Franks' outfit and tried to take our horses. Bob Whitehead and Pete Peck were on guard at the time, and I was sleeping on a pallet near by. When the Indians began shooting and yelling I sat up in my bed. As I did so an Indian, mounted on his pony, almost ran over me, firing his pistol as he ran at Whitehead and Peck, who followed in hot pursuit. I was wide-awake by this time

The Making of a Ranger

and ran for a thicket barefooted and in my undergarments.

Mr. Franks and the boys drove our horses back to camp and held them in a pen for the remainder of the night. I was beginning to get a taste of frontier life early in the game.

For years cattle had drifted south into Menard and Kimble counties, and Joe Franks was one of the first of the Coleman County outfits to go south into the San Saba and Llano country. He worked the Big and Little Saline creeks, and the Llano and San Saba rivers, and found many of his cattle down there. By the last of November he had about finished work for the year, and, gathering three hundred fat cows to drive to Calvert, Texas, he left John Banister down on the Big Saline to winter the horses.

I passed through Lampasas with these cows, and saw my mother and sisters for the first time in nine months. When we reached Bell County a cow buyer met us and bought the cows at $10 per head. He got down off his horse, lifted a pair of saddlebags off, and counted out $3,000 in twenty-dollar gold pieces, and hired some of the boys to help him drive the cattle into Calvert. Mr. Franks, with most of the outfit, turned back to Lampasas. When he settled with me, Mr. Franks owed me just $200, and he handed me ten twenty-dollar gold pieces. It was the most money I had ever earned, and almost the greatest amount I had seen in my life.

I spent December and January at home, and early in February, 1874, I started back to Menard County with Mr. Franks, as he was anxious to begin work as early in the spring as possible. When we reached Parsons' Ranch on the Big Saline we learned that the

Indians had stolen all his horses, seventy-five or eighty head, and he had left only eight or ten old ponies. Mr. Franks sent Will Banister and myself back to Coleman County to pick up ten or twelve horses he had left there the year before, while he himself returned to Lampasas and Williamson counties to buy horses.

This trip from Menard County to Coleman County, a distance of about one hundred and fifty miles, was rather a hazardous trip for two boys to make alone. However, we were both armed with new Winchesters and would have been able to put up a stiff fight if cornered. Our ponies were poor and weak, so that it would have been impossible for us to have escaped had we met a band of Indians, a thing we came very near doing.

There was no road from Menard to Coleman at that time, so we just traveled north. I had cow-hunted over most of that country the year before and knew by landmarks pretty well how to go. We reached the head of Big Brady Creek one evening while a cold north wind was blowing. We camped for the night in the bed of a dry creek to get out of the wind. We saddled up next morning and had not gone more than a hundred and fifty yards from camp when we discovered where sixteen or seventeen Indians had just gone along—at least there was that number of pony tracks. These redskins had hopped a skunk and killed it with a chunk of wood. When we found the body it had scarcely quit bleeding. We saw moccasin tracks, as if the savages had all got off their ponies for a few moments. Banister and I made the trip safely, and returned to Menard County early in March. Mr. Franks soon came with a new bunch of horses, and we went to work gathering and delivering cattle.

The Making of a Ranger

About the first of June, Bee Clayton came to the outfit from Lampasas County and told me my father had been dead more than a month. Mr. Franks settled with me and I started for home the next day. Upon reaching Lampasas I began work with Barrett and Nicholls' outfit. They were the biggest cattle owners in that country and ran three large outfits, one in Llano County, one in San Saba County, and another in Lampasas. I worked with the last-mentioned outfit that I might be near my mother and sisters.

I had now become familiar with most aspects of frontier life. I had cow-punched and seen Indian raids, but I had not yet met the Texas "bad man"—the murderer and the bandit. My education was not long neglected, for it was while working with Barrett and Nicholls that I made my acquaintance with gentry of that ilk. One day five or six of our boys were sitting down in a circle, eating on a side of broiled calf-ribs. One of the men, Jack Perkins, suddenly became involved in an altercation with Levi Dunbar, and, without warning, jerked out his six-shooter and shot him to death. In rising to my feet I had my right shoulder powder-burned by Perkins' shot.

I stayed with Barrett and Nicholls until they quit work, about December 1, 1874. In those days cattle were not worked much in the winter months, so I spent the winter at home. By spring I had become as restless as a bear and longed to get back to the frontier. Finally, I could stand the idleness no longer and told my mother I was going back to Menard County to work for Mr. Franks. I reached the town of Menardville early in March, 1875. There I learned that Joe Franks was then at work on South Llano in Kimble County, about sixty miles from Menard. Wess Ellis had just bought the Rufe Winn stock of cattle and was ready to start on a cow-hunt. He wanted me to work for him, declaring he could pay me as much as Joe Franks or anybody else, so I hired to him for $30 a month, the top wages for a cowboy at that time.

During the year I was at home a company of Texas Rangers commanded by Captain Dan W. Roberts had been stationed over on Little Saline. This company received its mail at Menardville, and I became acquainted with this famous organization. Their free, open life along the frontier had fired me with longing to become one of them and join in their adventurous lives. In the spring of 1875 the governor of Texas authorized Captain Roberts to increase his command to fifty men. Almost immediately Captain Roberts announced in Menardville and vicinity that he would enlist twenty good men on June first to bring his company to full strength. Here was my opportunity, and I decided I would be one of those twenty recruits.

CHAPTER II

THE TEXAS RANGERS

THE Texas Rangers, as an organization, dates from the spring of 1836. When the Alamo had fallen before the onslaught of the Mexican troops, and the frightful massacre had occurred, General Sam Houston organized among the settlers in the territory a troop of sixteen hundred mounted riflemen. This company, formed for the defense of the Texan borders, was the original Texas Ranger unit, and it is interesting to note that from its very inception to the present moment the organization has never swerved from that purpose—the protection of Texan borders, whether such protection be against the Indian, the bandit, or marauding Mexicans from beyond the Rio Grande.

When the republic of Texas was organized in December, 1837, the new state found herself with an enormous frontier to protect. To the south were the hostile Mexicans, while to the west and northwest roved the Indian and the bandit. To furnish protection against these enemies and to form the nucleus of a national standing army the ranger troop was retained. During the seven years that Texas had to maintain her own independence before she was admitted into the American Union, the rangers repelled hordes of Mexicans, fought the murderous Apaches, Comanches, and Kiowas, and administered justice on a wholesale plan to numbers of outlaws and ruffians who had flocked into the new republic from the less attractive parts of the United States.

15

Six Years with the Texas Rangers

So vital was the service rendered by the rangers in protecting the lives and property of the settlers along the frontiers of the state that twelve hundred rangers were retained as mounted police for patrolling the Mexican border and as a safeguard against the savages of the Southwest. When the Civil War broke out between the North and the South, Texas was drawn into the conflict on the side of the Confederacy. General Con Terry, an old ranger, organized the famous body of men known as Terry's Texas Rangers. This command was composed almost exclusively of ex-rangers and frontiersmen. From Bull Run to Appomattox this organization rendered gallant service, and lost seventy-five per cent of its original muster roll. General Sherman, in his memoirs, speaks admiringly of the bravery of the rangers at the battle of Shiloh.

The return to peace, and the days of reconstruction, did not do away with the necessity for the service which only the ranger could render. Indian uprisings, banditry, and cattle thievery all flourished, for the bad man confidently expected the post-war turmoil would protect him from punishment for his misdeeds. He was to be undeceived, for the rangers effectively taught him that their duty was the protection of lives and property, and right loyally did they perform it. From 1868 to 1873 the ranger companies were gradually reduced from one thousand to about three hundred men.

The federal government adopted a most unfortunate policy toward the Indians after the war. The tribes were removed to reservations and rationed as public charges. Unscrupulous dealers, in their desire for gain, illegally sold firearms to the Indians, and whenever a redskin massacred a frontiersman he was

16

sure to capture good weapons, so that they soon became well armed and very expert in handling their new weapons. As no attempt was made to confine them to the reservation limits, the redskins, under their native chiefs, were continually sneaking off and raiding western Texas. They stole thousands of horses and cattle, and did not hesitate to murder and scalp the defenseless people along the frontier. Numbers of women and children were carried off as captives, only a very small proportion of whom were subsequently ransomed. Repeated complaints to Washington brought no redress. Indeed, some of the government officials calmly declared that the Indians were doing no harm—it was white men disguised as redskins that caused the trouble!

In 1874 conditions along the frontier had become so acute that the need for an organized mounted police for the protection of the settlers against the continued Indian raids became apparent. As in the past, the state looked again to her rangers. Early in 1874, during the administration of Richard Coke, the first Democratic governor since secession, the legislature appropriated $300,000 for frontier defense, thus authorizing the formation of the Texas Rangers as now constituted. The governor immediately issued a call for four hundred and fifty volunteers. These were formed into six companies of seventy-five men each. Each of these units was officered by a captain and a first and second lieutenant. The companies were designated A, B, C, D, E, and F, and received the official name of the Frontier Battalion of Texas Rangers. John B. Jones of Corsicana, Texas, was commissioned major of the command. At this time the captains received a salary of $100 per month, lieutenants $75, sergeants $50, and corporals and privates $40. Subsequently, as the legislature continually sliced into the ranger appropriation, the pay of privates was reduced to $30 a month, a mere pittance for the hazardous service demanded of them.

Early in 1874 the force took the field, and each company was assigned a definite territory along the frontier. Company A, being the northernmost company, was camped on the main fork of the Brazos River; Company F, the southernmost, was stationed on the Nueces River. The four remaining companies were posted along the line between these two commands about one hundred and twenty-five miles apart, so that the battalion of four hundred and fifty men was required to cover a frontier of between five and six hundred miles.

Major Jones was a very able commander, and he quickly won the confidence of his men and of the people along the border he was sent to protect. The frontiersmen coöperated with him in every way possible, sending runners to the various ranger camps whenever an Indian trail was found or a bunch of horses stolen. During the first six months of service nearly every company in the battalion had an Indian fight, and some of them two or three. The battalion finally cleared the Texas frontier of the redskins and then turned its attention to the other pests of the state—thieves, bandits, and fugitives from justice. In this work the rangers rendered service second to none, and became in an incredibly short time perhaps the most famous and efficient body of mounted police in the world.

In the eighteen years from 1865 to 1883 the Texas Rangers followed one hundred and twenty-eight In-

Ready to Take the Field. From a photograph of Company D, Captain Frank Jones, taken in 1889. Captain Jones (seen at right of picture) and one-third of his men were subsequently killed in action.

The Texas Rangers

dian raiding parties, and fought the redskins in eighty-four pitched battles. During this same period they recovered six thousand stolen horses and cattle and rescued three citizens carried off by Indians. In this period twelve rangers were killed. Despite this record of service, the legislature at Austin could not always be made to see the advantage—nay, the necessity—of a ranger force, and it was continually tinkering with the appropriations for the support of the battalion. When the appropriation was small the command was reduced to keep within the expenditure doled out by the parsimonious solons; whenever the lawmakers could be prevailed upon to increase the annual ranger budget, it was recruited to full strength.

By 1885 conditions had changed. Texas was no longer endangered by Indians, for the rangers had done much to convert the red devils into good Indians—that is, into dead ones. Although the Indians had disappeared from the state, the activities of the rangers did not cease. The white "bad man" who had stirred up the first Indian troubles now began to plunder and murder his own race and indulge in every form of lawlessness. From hunting the murderous redskins the rangers became now stalkers of the man-killers and those who despoiled their neighbors of their property. The local legal authorities could not or would not handle this task themselves, so the rangers were made peace officers and given the right of arrest without warrant in any part of the state. They then became mounted constables to quell disorder, prevent crime, and bring criminals to justice and assist the duly constituted authorities in every way possible. This new work was less romantic than the old Indian warfare, but it was every bit as dangerous and as necessary in the building up of the fast-developing state. As in every other task assigned him the ranger did his duty fearlessly and well. In the years 1889-1890 the rangers arrested five hundred and seventy-nine persons, among them seventy-six murderers. With the coming of the railroads the rangers began to use them, as they permitted more speed and the covering of greater distances than was possible on horseback. Moreover, commands could be dispatched from one part of the state to another as occasion demanded. This greater mobility led to larger usefulness and an increasing number of arrests by the ranger forces.

The outbreak of the war with Spain found the rangers ready and anxious for service in the defense of the Union. Many enlisted in Roosevelt's famous Rough Riders.

"I have heard from the lips of reliable rangers," declared General Miles, in speaking of the ranger service in Cuba, "tales of daring that are incomparable. It is, indeed, too bad that the world knows so little about those marvelous men. There have been hosts of men among the Texas Rangers who were just as nervy as Davy Crockett, Travis, or Bowie at the Alamo."

Sketchy as has been this history, it discloses a record of continuous duty throughout the half century of the ranger battalion's existence in guarding the lives, the liberty, and the property of Texas citizens. And the ranger has been content to perform this duty unheralded and almost unsung. Performance of duty, it matters not where it may lead him, into whatever desperate situation or howsoever dangerous the thing demanded, has always been the slogan of the organiza-

The Texas Rangers

tion. For courage, patriotic devotion, instant obedience, and efficiency, the record of the Texas Rangers has been excelled by no body of constabulary ever mustered.

Though formed into military units and officered as a soldier, the ranger is not a military man, for scant attention is paid to military law and precedent. The state furnishes food for the men, forage for their horses, ammunition, and medical attendance. The ranger himself must furnish his horse, his accoutrements, and his arms. There is, then, no uniformity in the matter of dress, for each ranger is free to dress as he pleases and in the garb experience has taught him most convenient for utility and comfort. A ranger, as any other frontiersman or cowboy, usually wears heavy woolen clothes of any color that strikes his fancy. Some are partial to corduroy suits, while others prefer buckskin. A felt hat of any make and color completes his outfit. While riding, a ranger always wears spurs and very high-heeled boots to prevent his foot from slipping through the stirrup, for both the ranger and the cowboy ride with the stirrup in the middle of the foot. For arms, the ranger after 1877 carried a Winchester rifle or carbine, a Colt's .45 revolver, and a bowie knife. Two cartridge belts, one for Winchester and one for revolver ammunition, completed his equipment, and thus armed he was ready to mount and ride.

"We live in the saddle and the sky is our roof," say the old rangers, and this is literally true. The rangers are perfect centaurs and almost live in the saddle. They take horse where they will and may arrest or search in any part of the state. There is very little of what a West Point graduate would call drill. A ranger is expected to be a good rider and a quick and accurate shot. No crack cavalryman in any army can mount a horse more quickly or more expertly than a ranger, and he can keep a constant stream of fire pouring from his carbine when his horse is going at top speed, and hit the mark nine times out of ten. Should a ranger drop on the ground anything that he wants he does not even check the speed of his horse, but, bending from the saddle as if he were made of India rubber, he picks up the object in full gallop.

When not on active duty the rangers amuse themselves in various ways. Some play cards, others hunt, while the studious spend their time over books and good literature. Horse-racing is popular, and the fastest horse in the company is soon spotted, for the rangers match their mounts one against the other. At night around their camp-fires the men are constantly telling stories of adventures that put to shame all the inventions of the writers of imaginative fiction. But when on duty all this is changed. No pace is too quick, no task too difficult or too hazardous for them. Night and day will the ranger trail his prey, through rain and shine, until the criminal is located and put behind the bars where he will not again molest or disturb peaceful citizens. For bravery, endurance, and steadfast adherence to duty at all times the ranger is in a class by himself. Such was the old ranger, and such is the ranger of today.

CHAPTER III

I JOIN THE RANGERS

THE fame of the rangers had, of course, become common knowledge among all Texans. Their deeds of adventure and their open, attractive life along the frontier appealed to me, and I had conceived the desire to enlist in the battalion. But the enlistment, as announced by Captain Roberts, would not be made until June 1, 1875, and I reached Menardville early in March. I had intended going on to join Mr. Franks's outfit, but, as I have already explained, I hired out to Mr. Ellis until I could enlist in Captain Roberts' company.

About the middle of May, 1875, Joe Franks had worked back into Menard County. I wished to see my old friends in his outfit, and so went over to meet them. While there I mentioned that I was going to join the rangers. A cowboy named Norman Rodgers, who was working for Mr. Franks, said he would also like to join, so we decided we would go over to Captain Roberts together and see if we couldn't get him to recruit us in his company.

Rodgers and I rode over to the ranger camp beyond Menardville. Neither of us had ever been in such a camp before nor did we know anyone in the company. Of the first ranger we met we inquired where we could find the captain. His tent was pointed out to us and we went toward it.

"Jim," said Norman as we approached the tent, "you will have to do the talking."

Captain Roberts met us as we came up and invited

us to be seated. I told him at once that we had come to enlist as rangers. He asked us our names, where we were working, and finally inquired if we had anyone that would recommend us. We had not thought of references, but told him that probably Mr. Franks or Mr. Ellis would stand for us, as they were well-known and prominent cattlemen for whom we had worked.

Captain Roberts looked straight at me and said, "Did you say your name was Gillett?"

"Yes, Jim Gillett," I replied.

He then asked me where I was born, and I told him at Austin, Texas.

"Are you a son of James S. Gillett who was adjutant general under Governor Sam Houston?"

I told him I was.

"I have often heard my father, Buck Roberts, speak of your father," he said in a friendly tone.

Captain Roberts then asked us what kind of horses we had, telling us that a ranger was required to have a good mount, for each man was allowed to have only one horse, which had to be a good one, that could be ridden every day for a month if necessary. I told him I had two good pony mares. He burst out laughing, and said a mare was not allowed in the service. He told us to go and see what kind of mounts we could get, and then come back and let him inspect the animals. He never once said he would accept us, but as the interview was now over and he had not refused us we went back to camp feeling very hopeful we would soon be rangers.

I secured a big black pony and Norman a gray one, not as large as mine but a much prettier horse. We returned to the ranger camp a few days later mounted on these ponies. The captain looked them over, said they were rather small but that he would accept them, and told us to be at his camp by May thirty-first to be sworn into the service. We left camp that evening all puffed up at the prospect of being Texas Rangers.

The last day of May arrived. Norman Rodgers and myself, with many other recruits we had never seen before, were at the ranger camp. On June 1, 1875, at ten o'clock we were formed in line, mounted, and the oath of allegiance to the state of Texas was read to us by Captain Roberts. When we had all signed this oath we were pronounced Texas Rangers. This was probably the happiest day of my life, for in joining the rangers I had realized one of my greatest ambitions.

Immediately after being sworn in the men were divided into messes, ten men to the mess, and issued ten days' rations by the orderly sergeant. These consisted of flour, bacon, coffee, sugar, beans, rice, pepper, salt, and soda. No potatoes, syrup, or lard was furnished, and each man had to supply his own cooking utensils. To shorten our bread we used bacon grease. Beef was sometimes supplied the men, but wild game was so plentiful that but little other meat was required. Furthermore, each recruit was furnished a Sharps carbine, .50 caliber, and one .45 Colt's pistol. These arms were charged to us, their cost to be deducted from our first pay. Our salary of $40 per month was paid in quarterly installments. The state also supplied provender for the horses.

Though a ranger was forced to supply his own mount, the state undertook to pay for the animal if it were killed or lost in an Indian fight. To establish impartially the value of our animals, Captain Roberts marched us into Menardville and asked three citizens of the town to place a value on each man's mount. This was done, and I was highly gratified when old Coley, my mount, was appraised at $125. This formality over, the company was moved from Little Saline to Camp Las Moras, five miles southwest of Menardville, Texas. We were now ready to begin scouting for Indians.

As is usual under similar circumstances, the new recruits came in for their share of pranks and mishaps. One raw rooky in my mess, fired with love of economy, undertook to cook ten days' rations for the whole mess at one time. He put a quantity of rice on the fire. Soon it began to boil and swell, and that surprised ranger found his rice increasing to unheard-of proportions. He filled every cooking vessel in the mess with half-cooked rice, and still the kettle continued to overflow. In desperation he finally began to pour it on the ground. Even then he had enough rice cooked to supply the entire company.

Another recruit, anxious to test his new weapons, obtained Captain Roberts' permission to go. hunting. He had not gone far from camp when he began firing at some squirrels. One of his bullets struck the limb of a tree and whizzed close to camp. This gave an old ranger an idea. He hastened after the hunter and gravely arrested him, declaring that the glancing bullet had struck a man in camp and that Captain Roberts had ordered the careless hunter's arrest. The veteran brought in a pale and badly-scared recruit.

One of the favorite diversions of the old rangers was to make a newcomer believe that the state furnished the rangers with socks and start him off to the captain's tent to demand his share of free hosiery. The captain

James B. Gillett. From a photograph taken early in his ranger's career.

took these pranks in good part and assured the crest-fallen applicant that the rangers were only playing a joke on him, while his tormentors enjoyed his discomfiture from a safe distance.

When they had run out of jokes the men settled down to the regular routine of camp. Each morning the orderly sergeant had roll call, at which time he always detailed six or eight men with a non-commissioned officer to take charge of the rangers' horses and the pack-mules until relieved the following morning by a new guard. The guard was mounted and armed and drove the loose stock out to graze. The horses were never taken far from camp for fear of being attacked by Indians, and also to keep them near at hand in case they were needed quickly.

The rangers not on guard spent their time as they wished when not on duty, but no man could leave the camp without the captain's permission. The boys played such games as appealed to them, horseshoe pitching and cards being the favorite diversions. As long as it did not interfere with a man's duty as a ranger, Captain Roberts permitted pony-racing, and some exciting contests took place between rival horse owners. Besides these diversions hunting and fishing were always available, for the woods and streams were stocked with game and fish.

I soon had cause to congratulate myself on my enlistment in Company D, for I found Captain D. W. Roberts the best of company commanders. At the time I joined his command he was thirty-five years of age, very slender, and perhaps a little over six feet tall. His beard and hair were dark auburn. He always dressed neatly and was kind and affable in manner, looking more like the dean of an eastern college than the great captain he was.

Captain Roberts was a fine horseman and a good shot with both pistol and rifle. He was also a fine violinist, and often played for the boys. He had been raised on the frontier and had won such a reputation as an Indian fighter that the state legislature presented him with a fine Winchester rifle for his gallantry in fighting the redskins. The captain had made a close study of the habits and actions of the Indians, and their life was an open book to him. This, of course, gave him a great advantage in following and fighting them, and under his able leadership Company D became famous. There was not a man in the company who did not consider it a compliment to be detailed on a scout with Captain Roberts.

In the latter part of the summer or early fall of 1875, Captain Roberts visited Colorado County, Texas, and returned with a bride, a Miss Lou Conway. Mrs. Roberts was a refined and elegant lady, and soon adapted herself to the customs of the camp. She was with her husband on the San Saba River during the winter of 1875-1876 and soon became as popular with the company as Captain Roberts himself.

Most people would consider the life of the Texas Ranger hard and dangerous, but I never found it so. In the first place, the ranger was always with a body of well-armed men, which was more than a match for any enemy that might be met. Then, there was an element of danger about it that appealed to any red-blooded American. All of western Texas was a real frontier then, and for one who loved nature and God's own creation, it was a paradise on earth. The hills and val-

I Join the Rangers

leys were teeming with deer and turkeys, thousands of buffalo and antelope were on the plains, and the streams all over Texas were full of fish. Bear caves and bee trees abounded. In the springtime one could travel for hundreds of miles on a bed of flowers. Oh, how I wish I had the power to describe the wonderful country as I saw it then! How happy I am now in my old age that I am a native Texan and saw the grand frontier before it was marred by the hand of man.

The Lipan, Kickapoo, Comanche, and Kiowa Indians used to time their raids so as to reach the Texas settlements during the light of the moon so they would have moonlight nights in which to steal horses and make their getaway before they could be discovered. By morning, when their thefts became known, they would have a long lead ahead and be well on their way into the plains and mountains. The captains of the ranger companies knew of this Indian habit, and accordingly kept scouts constantly in the field during the period of the raids. The redskins, coming in from the plains where water was scarce, generally took the near cut to the headwaters of the Colorado, Concho, San Saba, Llano, Guadalupe, and Nueces rivers. By maintaining scouts at or near the heads of these streams the rangers frequently caught parties of Indians going in or coming out from the settlements, and destroyed them or recaptured the stolen stock.

The first light moon in June Captain Roberts ordered a detail of fifteen men in command of Sergeant James B. Hawkins to make a ten days' scout toward the headwaters of the North Llano River. He was to select a secluded spot near old Fort Territ and make camp there. Each morning a scout of one or two men would be sent out ten or fifteen miles to the south and another party a like distance toward the north to hunt for Indian trails. The main body of rangers, keeping carefully concealed, was in readiness to take up an Indian trail at a moment's notice, should one be found by the scouts.

One morning Sergeant Hawkins ordered me to travel south from camp to the head draws of the South Llano and watch for pony tracks.

"Suppose the Indians get me?" I asked, laughingly, as I mounted my pony.

"It's your business to keep a sharp lookout and not let them catch you," he replied.

However, though I watched very carefully, I could find no pony tracks or Indian trails.

We had with us on this scout Mike Lynch, an Irishman. Though he was old and gray-headed, he was a good ranger, and had much native wit. One morning it was Uncle Mike's turn to go on scout duty, but in a few hours he was seen coming into camp with his horse, Possum, on the jump. He reported a fresh Indian trail about ten miles north of our camp. When asked how many pony tracks he had seen, Lynch declared he had counted seventeen and thought there were more. As the Indians usually came in on foot or with as few ponies as they could get along on until they could steal others, Sergeant Hawkins suspected the tracks Lynch had seen were those of mustangs. The excited scout declared vehemently that the tracks were not those of wild horses but of Indians. The sergeant was just as positive that no Indian party was responsible for the trail, and the two had quite a heated argument over the tracks.

I Join the Rangers

"But how do you know it is an Indian trail?" demanded Hawkins.

"Because I know," cried Lynch in a loud voice.

That settled it. Horses were saddled and mules packed as quickly as possible, and the rangers marched over to the suspicious trail. When Sergeant Hawkins examined it he soon perceived that the sign had been made by mustangs but he could not convince the hard-headed Irishman of this fact until he had followed the trail two or three miles and showed him the mustang herd quietly grazing under some shade trees. Uncle Mike did not mention Indian trail any more on that scout. Though we did not find any trails or Indians the scouting party killed two black bears, several deer, and about fifteen wild turkeys.

Early in September, 1875, Captain Roberts again ordered Sergeant Hawkins to take fifteen men and make a ten days' scout on the Brady Mountains. To my great joy I was detailed on this expedition. When near the head of Scalp Creek, Menard County, on our return trip, the sergeant told the boys to keep a sharp lookout for a deer, as we would reach the San Saba by noon and would camp on that stream for the night. We had not traveled far before Ed Seiker killed a nice little spiked buck. We strapped him on one of the pack mules, and when we arrived at the river we came upon a flock of half-grown wild turkeys. Bill Clements leaped from his horse and killed six of them.

We then camped, hobbled and side-lined our horses, and put a strong guard with them. While some of the boys were gathering wood for our fire they found an old elm stump ten to twelve feet high, with bees going in at the top. One of the rangers rode over to Rufe

Winn's ranch and borrowed an ax and a bucket. When he returned we cut the tree and got more honey than sixteen men could eat, besides filling the bucket with honey, which we gave to Mrs. Winn in return for the use of her ax. Then, after dinner, out came fishing tackle and, using venison for bait, we caught more catfish than the entire crowd could eat.

Hunting conditions in those days were ideal. I have known a single scout to kill three or four bears on a single trip. The companies to the north of us were never out of buffalo meat in season. Then, in the fall, one could gather enough pecans, as fine as ever grew, in half a day to last the company a month. I have seen hundreds of bushels of the nuts go to waste because there was no one to gather them—besides they sold on the market for fifty cents per bushel. No wonder that a boy who loved the woods and nature was charmed and fascinated with the life of the Texas Ranger. It was a picnic for me from start to finish, and the six years I was with the battalion were the happiest and most interesting of my life.

But hunting and fishing and vacation scouts were not the sole duties of a ranger. Pleasure was abundant, but there were times when all these things were laid aside. For the game guns and the fishing rod we exchanged our carbines and our six-shooters and engaged in hazardous expeditions after marauding redskins. I was soon to experience this aspect of ranger life, for in the latter part of August, 1875, I became a real ranger and entered upon the real work of our battalion—that of protecting the frontier against the roving Indians and engaging them in regular pitched battles.

CHAPTER IV

MY FIRST BRUSH WITH INDIANS

THE latter part of August, 1875, Private L. P. Seiker was sent on detached service to Fort Mason, about fifty miles due east of our camp. While there a runner came in from Honey Creek with the report that a band of fifteen Indians had raided the John Gamble ranch and stolen some horses within twenty-five steps of the ranch house. The redskins appeared on their raid late in the evening and the runner reached Mason just at dark.

Lam Seiker had just eaten his supper and was sitting in the lobby of the Frontier Hotel when the message came. He hurried to the livery stable, saddled his horse, old Pete, and started on an all-night ride for the company. The nights in August are short, but Seiker rode into our camp about eight o'clock the following morning and reported the presence of the Indians.

The company horses were out under herd for the day, but Captain Roberts sent out hurry orders for them. Sergeant Plunk Murray was ordered to detail fifteen men, issue them ten days' rations and one hundred rounds of ammunition each. Second Sergeant Jim Hawkins, Privates Paul Durham, Nick Donnelly, Tom Gillespie, Mike Lynch, Andy Wilson, Henry Maltimore, Jim Trout, William Kimbrough, Silas B. Crump, Ed Seiker, Jim Day, John Cupps, and myself, under command of Captain Roberts, were selected as the personnel of the scout. As can be imagined, I was delighted with my good fortune in getting on the party and looked forward with intense satisfaction to my first brush with Indians.

The mules were soon packed and by the time the horses reached camp the scout was ready. Sergeant Hawkins, as soon as the men had saddled their horses, walked over to the captain, saluted, and told him the scout was ready. Before leaving camp Captain Roberts called to Sergeant Murray and told him that he believed the Indians had about as many horses as they could well get away with, and that they would probably cross the San Saba River near the mouth of Scalp Creek and follow the high divide between the two streams on their westward march back into the plains. If the redskins did not travel that way the captain thought they would go up the Big Saline, follow the divide between the North Llano and San Saba rivers westward, and escape, but he was confident the band would travel up the divide north of Menardville. He determined to scout that way himself, and instructed Murray to send two rangers south over to the head-waters of Bear Creek to keep a sharp lookout for the trail. These two scouts were to repeat their operations the next day, and if they discovered the Indian trail Murray was to make up a second scout and follow the redskins vigorously.

His plan outlined, Captain Roberts gave the order to mount and we rode toward Menardville, making inquiry about the Indians. All was quiet at this little frontier village, so we crossed the San Saba River just below the town and after passing the ruins of the Spanish fort Captain Roberts halted his men and prepared to send out trailers. Two of the best trailers in the command were ordered to proceed about four hundred

My First Brush with Indians

yards ahead of the party and keep a close watch for pony tracks while they traveled due north at a good saddle-horse gait. The main body of men, under the captain himself, would follow directly behind the outposts.

Our party had traveled about eight or nine miles when Captain Roberts' keen eyes discovered a lone pony standing with his head down straight ahead of us. He sighted the animal before the trailers did, and remarked to us that there the trail was. The outposts halted when they saw the pony and waited for us to come up. Sure enough, here was the Indian trail, probably twenty yards wide. Captain Roberts dismounted and walked over the sign, scrutinizing every pony track, bunch of grass, and fallen leaf. He then examined the old pony. The animal was cut with a lance, with his back sore and his feet all worn out. It was then between twelve and one o'clock, and the captain thought the Indians had passed that way about sunrise, for the blood and sweat on the horse were now dry. The trail showed the raiders were driving rather fast and were probably thirty-five or forty miles ahead of us. The captain decided it would be a long chase and that we would have to walk them down if we caught them at all.

There was no water on this divide so we took the trail without stopping for dinner. Captain Roberts had a fine saddle horse, old Rock, and we followed the trail at a steady gait of five or six miles an hour. At sundown we reached the old government road that runs from Fort McKavett to Fort Concho. We were then about twelve or fifteen miles south of Kickapoo Springs, so we turned up the road, reaching the springs late at night. The horses had not had a drop of water since leaving the San Saba that morning, and, facing a hot August sun all day, the men were pretty well tired out when they reached camp, had supper and got to bed. We estimated we had ridden about sixty miles since leaving camp. During the day Captain Roberts' horse cast a shoe, so Tom Gillespie shod him by firelight, as it was the captain's intention to resume the trail at daylight.

The following morning Captain Roberts took a southwest course from Kickapoo Springs and paralleled the Indian trail we had left the evening before. It was late in the day before we picked the trail up again, and many of the boys were afraid we had lost it altogether, but the captain laughed at their fears and never doubted that we should find it again. The Indians, as their trail showed, were now traveling over a tolerably rough country, which made our progress slow. About noon we found some rain-water, and camped for dinner and to give the horses a short rest.

When the boys went out to catch their mounts we found that we had camped in a bed of rattlesnakes. Two of our horses had been bitten. Jim Day's Chico had a head as big as a barrel, while the captain's horse, old Rock, had been bitten on his front leg just above the ankle, and it had swollen up to his body. Neither of the animals was able to walk. Jim Day could not be left alone in that Indian country, so Captain Roberts detailed Private Cupps to stay with him until the horses died or were able to travel; in either case they were then to return to camp. The animals soon recovered and Day and Cupps beat us back to camp.

The pack loads were now doubled on one mule so

My First Brush with Indians

Captain Roberts could ride the other. Reduced to thirteen men, we followed the Indians until night. It was a hard day on both men and beasts, so we camped where we found a little water in a draw that drained into the South Concho River. Considering the way we had come the captain thought we had covered sixty miles during the day's ride. We had two rather old men on the scout, Mike Lynch and Andy Wilson, and they were nearly all in. I awoke Andy at two o'clock to go on guard. The poor fellow was so stiff he could hardly stand, and I tried to get him to go back to bed, telling him I would stand his guard, but he was game, and in a few minutes limped out to the horses and relieved me.

Early in the morning we were up and traveling. The mule Captain Roberts was riding did not step out as fast as old Rock had done, and the boys had an easier time keeping up. We camped at noon on just enough rain-water to do us and took up the trail again after dinner. The trailers stopped suddenly, and as we rode up Captain Roberts asked what was the matter. They said it seemed as though the Indians at this point had rounded up the horses and held them for some cause or other.

The captain dismounted and swept the country with his field glasses. He circled around where the horses had been standing and found where a lone Indian had walked straight away from the animals. He followed the tracks to an old live-oak tree that had been blown down. Then the reason for the stop became apparent. The Indians had sighted a herd of mustangs grazing just beyond this tree and the redskin had slipped up on them and killed a big brown mare. Captain Roberts picked up the cartridge shell the brave had used and found it to be from a .50 caliber buffalo gun. We also found the mustang, from which the Indians had cut both sides of ribs and one hind quarter.

Captain Roberts was much elated. "Boys," he said with a smile, "we now have ninety-five chances out of a hundred to catch those Indians. They will not carry this raw meat long before stopping to cook some. We have followed them now over one hundred and fifty miles, and they have never stopped to build a fire. They are tired and hungry and probably know where there is water not far away."

He spoke with such confidence that I marveled at his knowledge of the Indian habits.

We were now on the extreme western draw of the South Concho River, far above the point at which the water breaks out into a running stream. Finally, the trail led out on that level and vast tract of country between the head of South Concho and the Pecos on the west. Here the Indians had turned a little north from the general direction they had been traveling, and all of a sudden we came to some rock holes filled with rainwater.

Here the redskins had built three fires, cooked both sides of the mustang ribs, and picked them clean. From this high table-land they could look back over their trail for fifteen miles. The captain thought they had been there early in the morning, as the fires were out and the ashes cold. We did not lose any time at this camp, but hurried on, following the trail until late in the evening, when the trailers again halted. When we came up we found that the trail, which had been going west for nearly two hundred miles, had suddenly turned straight north.

My First Brush with Indians

Captain Roberts seemed to be puzzled for a time, and said he did not understand this move. About one mile north there was a small grove of mesquite timber. This he examined through his glasses, seeming to me to examine each tree separately. The trail led straight into these trees, and we followed it. In the mesquite timber we found the Indians had hacked some bushes partly down, bent them over, cut up the horse meat they had been carrying with them into tiny strips, strung it on the bushes and, building a fire beneath them, had barbecued their flesh. The redskins had made the prettiest scaffold for cooking meat I ever saw. We found plenty of fire here, and the captain was sure we would have an Indian fight on the morrow.

From the trees the trail swung west again. The redskins were traveling slowly now, as they evidently thought they were out of danger. Just before sundown the scout halted, and we were ordered not to let any smoke go up lest the band we were trailing should spot it and take alarm. As soon as we had cooked our supper Captain Roberts had the fires carefully extinguished. It had been a good season on the table-lands and there were many ponds filled with water, some of them one hundred yards wide. We camped on the edge of one of these big holes, and where the Indians had waded into it the water was still muddy. The boys were cautioned not to strike a match that night as we were certain the Indians were not far ahead of us. We had covered between forty and fifty miles that day.

Camp was called at daybreak. We dared not build a fire, so we had no breakfast. We saddled our horses and again took the trail. Old Jennie, the pack-mule, was packed for the last time on earth, for she was killed in the fight that shortly followed. As soon as it was light enough to see a pony track two of the boys traced it on foot and led their horses, the remainder of our party coming along slowly on horseback. By sunrise we were all riding and following the trail rapidly, eager to sight the marauding thieves. We had traveled some five or six miles when Paul Durham called Captain Roberts' attention to a dark object ahead that looked as if it were moving. The captain brought his field glasses to bear on the object specified and exclaimed it was the Indians.

He ordered the boys to dismount at once, tighten their cinches, leave their coats and slickers, and make ready to fight. As we carried out this order a distressing stillness came over the men. Captain Roberts and Sergeant Hawkins were the only ones of our party who had ever been in an Indian fight, and I suppose the hearts of all of us green, unseasoned warriors beat a little more rapidly than usual at the prospect of soon smelling powder. Captain Roberts called out to us in positive tones not to leave him until he told us to go, and not to draw a gun or pistol until ordered, declaring that he wanted no mistake made on the eve of battle. He ordered the pack-mule caught and led until we went into the fight, when she was to be turned loose.

The Indians were on an open prairie dotted here and there with small groves of mesquite timber. The captain thought our only chance was to ride double file straight at them in the hope they would not look back and discover us. We moved forward briskly and got within four or five hundred yards of the redskins before they sighted us.

At once there was a terrible commotion. It was the

My First Brush with Indians

custom of the plains Indians, when they had stolen a lot of horses, for each to select from the number the best pony he could pick out, and tying a rope around its neck, let the pony drag it along the ground. In case of discovery the braves would quickly leap from the pony they were riding, grab the rope of the fresh one, and mounting it bareback, escape from their pursuers. On catching sight of us they performed this maneuver almost in the twinkling of an eye; then, led by their old chief, they took positions on a little elevated ground some two hundred yards beyond the loose horses. They stationed themselves about fifteen or twenty feet apart, their battle line when formed being about one hundred yards long. As each warrior took his station he dismounted, stood behind his horse, and prepared to fire when given the signal.

The captain with a smile turned to us and said, "Boys, they are going to fight us. See how beautifully the old chief forms his line of battle." From a little boy I had longed to be a ranger and fight the Indians. At last I was up against the real thing and with not so much as an umbrella behind which to hide. I was nervous. I was awfully nervous.

We were now within one hundred steps of the redskins. Then came the order to dismount, shoot low, and kill as many horses as possible. The captain said as we came up that every time we got an Indian on foot in that country we were sure to kill him. With the first shot everybody, Indians and rangers, began firing and yelling.

In a minute we had killed two horses and one Indian was seen to be badly wounded. In another minute the redskins had mounted their horses and were fleeing in

41

every direction. Captain Roberts now ordered us to mount and follow them. The roar of the guns greatly excited my pony and he turned round and round. I lost a little time in mounting, but when I did get settled in the saddle I saw an Indian running on foot. He carried a Winchester in his hand and waved to another Indian who was riding. The latter turned and took the one on foot up behind him. As they started away for a race I thought to myself that no grass-fed pony on earth could carry two men and get away from me and old Coley. The Indians had a good animal, but I gradually closed on them. The redskin riding behind would point his gun back and fire at me, holding it in one hand. I retaliated by firing at him every time I could get a cartridge in my old Sharps carbine. I looked back and saw Ed Seiker coming to my aid as fast as old Dixie would run. He waved encouragement to me.

Finally, the old brave ceased shooting, and as I drew a little closer he held out his gun at arm's length and let it drop, probably thinking I would stop to get it. I gave it but a passing glance as I galloped by. He then held out what looked to be a fine rawhide rope and dropped that, but I never took the bait. I just kept closing in on him. He now strung his bow and began using his arrows pretty freely. Finally, he saw I was going to catch him, and turned quickly into a little grove of mesquite timber. I was considered a fairly good brush rider, and as we went in among the trees I drew up within twenty steps of the brave, jumped from my mount, and made a sort of random shot at the horse, Indian, and all. The big .50 caliber bullet struck the Indian pony just where its head coupled on its neck, passed through the head and came out over the left eye.

My First Brush with Indians

It killed the horse at once, which fell forward twenty feet.

The old warrior hit the ground running, but I jumped on my horse and ran after him. As I passed the dead horse I saw the front rider struggling to get from under it. To my surprise I saw he was a white boy between fifteen and sixteen years old with long, bright red hair.

By this time Ed Seiker had arrived and was dismounting. The fugitive warrior now peeped from behind a tree and I got a fine shot at his face but overshot him six inches, cutting off a limb just over his head. He broke to run again, and as he came into view Ed placed a bullet between his shoulders. He was dead in a minute. When Ed and I walked up to the dead Indian we found he had also been shot in one ankle and his bow had been partly shot in two. In his quiver he had only three arrows left.

We hurried back to the dead horse to help the white boy, but he had extricated himself and disappeared. We then returned to the dead warrior and Seiker scalped him. We took his bow, shield, and a fine pair of moccasins. I also found a fine lance near where the horse fell, and I presume it was carried by the white boy. We found the redskin had no Winchester cartridges, and this was why he dropped the gun—he could not carry it and use his bow. We went back over the trail, but were unable to find the gun the brave had dropped as a bait.

By noon that day the boys had all returned to where the fight had begun and the Indian horses had been left. Jim Hawkins and Paul Durham captured a Mexican boy about fifteen years old. He looked like an Indian, had long plaited hair down his back, was bare-headed, and wore moccasins and a breech-clout. Had he been in front of me I would surely have killed him for a red-skin. Captain Roberts spoke Spanish fluently, and from this boy he learned that the Indians were Apaches. He was taken back to our camp, and finally his uncle came and took him home. He had been captured while herding oxen near old Fort Clark, Texas, and an elder brother, who was with him at the time, had been killed.

The boys were then sent back by Captain Roberts to find the white lad who had been with the Indian Seiker had killed. Though we searched carefully we could find no trace of the mysterious youngster. Forty-nine years later I met this boy, now an old man, at a reunion of the Old Time Trail Drivers' Association in San Antonio, and learned that his name was F. H. Lehman. He had been captured by the Indians in Mason County some years before our encounter, and had now become one of them. He had hidden in the grass while the rangers were hunting him, and after they gave up the search and disappeared he had followed on the trail of the Indians until he rejoined them.

When the rangers had all gathered after the fight our pack-mule, Jennie, was missing. We supposed that in the run she had followed the Indians off. Six months later Ed Seiker was detailed to pilot a body of United States soldiers over that same country to pick out a road to the Pecos River. He visited our old battlefield and found Jennie's carcass. She had a bullet hole in the center of her forehead. The Indians in shooting back at their attackers probably hit her with a chance shot. The pack-saddle was still strapped to her body, but wolves had eaten all the supplies. Five hundred

My First Brush with Indians

rounds of ammunition were still with her, showing that no one had seen her since the day of her death.

Lacking Jennie's supplies, we had nothing to eat except the barbecued horse meat we had captured from the Indians. This had no salt on it, and I could not swallow it. In the fight we killed three horses and one Indian and captured the Mexican lad. At least two redskins were badly wounded, and as victors we captured fifty-eight head of horses and mules, several Indian saddles and bridles, and many native trinkets. Not a man or a horse of our party was hurt, the pack-mule being our only fatality. Captain Roberts said that but for the inability of our hard-ridden horses to overtake the fresh mounts of the Indians, not a soul of them would have escaped us.

We turned our faces homeward, hungry and tired but highly elated over our success. The second day after the fight we reached Wash Delong's ranch on the headwaters of the South Concho River. Mr. Delong, a fine frontiersman, killed a beef for us and furnished us with flour and coffee without cost. Three days later we were back at our camp at Las Moras. The stolen animals were returned to their owners, and thus ended my first campaign against the Indians.

CHAPTER V

THE MASON COUNTY WAR

SOON after our return from our first brush with Indians we were introduced to yet another phase of ranger activity—the quieting of feuds, for not only were the rangers employed in protecting the frontiers against the Indians, but they were also frequently called upon to preserve law and order within the towns and cities of the state. In those early days men's passions were high and easily aroused. In a country where all men went armed, recourse to firearms was frequent, and these feuds sometimes led to active warfare between the adherents of each party, to the great discomfort of the citizens among whom such a miniature war was staged.

Mason and the adjoining county, Gillespie, had been settled by Germans in the early history of the state. These settlers were quiet and peaceful and made most excellent citizens, loyal to their adopted country and government when undisturbed. Most of these Germans engaged in stock raising and were sorely tried by the rustlers and Indians, who committed many depredations upon their cattle.

In the latter part of September, 1875, Tim Williamson, a prominent cattleman living in Mason County, was arrested on a charge of cattle theft by John Worley, a deputy sheriff of that county. Previous to that time there had been a number of complaints about the loss of cattle, and the Germans charged that many of their cattle had been stolen and the brands burned. Much indignation had been aroused among the stockmen of the county, and threats of violence against the thieves were common.

As soon as the news of Williamson's arrest on a charge of cattle thieving became known a large mob formed and set out in pursuit of the deputy sheriff and his prisoner. On his way to Mason, Worley was overtaken by this posse. When he saw the pursuing men Williamson divined their purpose and begged the sheriff to let him run in an effort to save his life. Worley refused and, it is said, drew his pistol and deliberately shot Williamson's horse through the loin, causing it to fall. Unarmed and unmounted, Williamson was killed without a chance to protect himself and without any pretense of a trial. After the murder Worley and the mob disappeared.

Whether or not Williamson was guilty of the charge against him, he had friends who bitterly resented the deputy sheriff's refusal to allow the murdered man a chance for his life, and his death caused a great deal of excitement and bitter comment in the county. A man named Scott Cooley, an ex-ranger of Captain Perry's Company D, was a particular friend of Williamson and his family. At the time of his friend's murder Cooley had quit the ranger service and was cultivating a farm near Menardville. He had worked for the dead man and had made two trips up the trail to Kansas with him. While working with the murdered cattleman Cooley had contracted a bad case of typhoid fever and had been nursed back to health by Mrs. Williamson's own hands.

When the news of Tim Williamson's murder reached Scott Cooley he was much incensed, and vowed vengeance against the murderers of his friend. He left his farm at once and, saddling his pony, rode into the town of Mason heavily armed. He had worked out a careful plan of his own and proceeded to put it into execution immediately on his arrival. Stabling his horse in a livery barn, he registered at the hotel. As he was entirely unknown in Mason, Cooley remained in town several days without creating any suspicion. He proved himself a good detective, and soon discovered that the sheriff and his deputy were the leaders in the mob that had killed his friend. Biding his time and pursuing his investigations he soon learned the name of every man in the posse that had murdered Williamson.

His information complete, Cooley decided upon action. He mounted his pony and rode out to the home of John Worley, whom he found engaged in cleaning out a well. The avenger dismounted, asked for a drink of water, and entered into conversation with the unsuspecting man. Finally, as Worley was drawing his assistant out of the well, Cooley asked him if his name was John Worley. The deputy sheriff replied that it was. Cooley then declared his mission and shot Worley to death.

At the first crack of Cooley's pistol Worley let the windlass go, and the man he was drawing out of the well fell back about twenty-five feet into it. Cooley deliberately stooped down, cut off Worley's scalp, put it in his pocket, and galloped off. Victim number one was chalked up to Williamson's credit. Making a quick ride across Mason County to the western edge of Llano County, Cooley waylaid and killed Pete Border, the second on his list of mob members.

These two murders struck terror into the heart of nearly every citizen of Mason County. No one could

A Typical Ranger Encampment. Company D in camp at Fort Inge in 1884. Several of these men were subsequently killed in action.

The Mason County War

tell who would be the next victim of the unerring aim of Scott Cooley's rifle. The people of the whole county rose in arms to protect themselves. The sheriff, terrified lest he be the next victim of Cooley, promptly left Mason and never returned. Tim Williamson had other friends eager to avenge him, and the killing of Border was their rallying signal. John and Mose Beard, George Gladden, and John Ringgold immediately joined Cooley in his work of vengeance. The gang rode into the town of Mason, and in a fight with a posse of citizens killed another man.

Fearing the outbreak of a real feud war in Mason, the governor of Texas ordered Major Jones to the relief of the frightened citizens. The order reached Major Jones while he was on his way down the line near the head of the Guadalupe River. He at once turned his company back, and with a detachment of ten men from Company D marched to Mason. Company A, Major Jones's escort, was then commanded by Captain Ira Long, and the thirty men in that company and the ten boys of Company D gave the major forty men for his relief expedition.

Before the rangers could reach Mason, the sheriff's party had a fight with Cooley's gang down on the Llano River and killed Mose Beard. On his arrival in Mason, Major Jones sent scouts in every direction to hunt Cooley. He kept this up for nearly two weeks but without result. He finally learned that nearly the whole of his command, especially the Company D boys who had ranged with Cooley, was in sympathy with the outlaw and was making no serious attempt to locate or imperil him. It was even charged that some of the Company D rangers met Cooley at night on the outskirts

49

of Mason and told him they did not care if he killed every damned Dutchman in Mason County who formed part of the mob that had murdered Williamson.

Major Jones saw he would have to take drastic steps at once. He drew up his whole force of forty men and made them an eloquent speech. He said he had a special pride in the Frontier Battalion and was making it his life's study, and that he personally had a kindly feeling for every man in the service. He then reminded the men in the most feeling manner of the oath they had taken to protect the state of Texas against all her enemies whatsoever, an oath every true man was bound to honor. He declared he knew many of the command had a friendly feeling for Scott Cooley, especially those boys who had shared the life of a ranger with him, and that he, himself, felt keenly the position in which they were placed. While Tim Williamson had met a horrible death at the hands of a relentless mob, this did not justify Cooley in killing people in a private war of vengeance in defiance of the law and the rangers.

As the climax of his speech the major said: "Men, I now have a proposition to make to you. If every man here who is in sympathy with Scott Cooley and his gang and who does not wish to pursue him to the bitter end will step out of the ranks I will issue him an honorable discharge and let him quit the service clean."

The major paused and about fifteen men stepped to the front.

"Gentlemen," continued Major Jones, "those who do not avail themselves of this opportunity I shall expect to use all diligence and strength in helping me to break up or capture these violators of the law."

After the discharge of the Cooley sympathizers, the

A Later View of Company D. Captain Jones was killed in 1893. This picture shows his successor in command, Captain John R. Hughes (seated on chair in right foreground), a group of his men, and a captive bandit.

rangers went to work with a new vigor, and finally captured George Gladden and John Ringgold. Gladden was sent to the penitentiary for twenty-five years, while Ringgold received a life sentence. Probably Scott Cooley was informed of Major Jones's appeal to the rangers, for he became less active around Mason after this. John Beard, it was reported, skipped Texas and went to Arizona.

Soon after Cooley killed John Worley, Norman Rodgers got permission from Captain Roberts to ride over to Joe Franks's cow outfit to exchange his horse for a better one. When Rodgers rode into the cowboy camp he noticed a man resting under a tree near the fire. The stranger called one of the cowboys and asked him who Norman was. As Rodgers left camp this man followed him and asked if he was one of Roberts' rangers and if he knew Major Reynolds. Rodgers replied that he knew Reynolds very well.

The man then declared he was Scott Cooley and, reaching into his pocket, he pulled out John Worley's scalp.

"You take this to Major Reynolds with my compliments, but don't you tell anybody you saw me."

Rodgers duly delivered the scalp and Reynolds cautioned him to say nothing about it. Forty years afterward, at an old settlers' reunion in Sweetwater, Norman Rodgers mentioned this incident in a speech—he had kept his promise to Cooley and Reynolds all these years.

Having lost his friends and his sympathizers in the rangers, Cooley returned to Blanco County, where he had formerly lived. Here he was stricken with brain fever, and though tenderly nursed, shielded by his friends, he died without ever being brought to trial for his killings. This ended the Mason County War, but before the feud died some ten or twelve men were killed and a race war was narrowly averted.

CHAPTER VI

MAJOR JONES AND HIS ESCORT

DESPITE their usefulness in protecting the frontiers and in maintaining law and order, the Texas Rangers have always had to fight more or less strenuously to obtain from the state legislature the necessary appropriation for their annual maintenance. Whenever the appropriation is small there is but one remedy—reduce the personnel of each company to the lowest limits possible. In the fall of 1875 the adjutant general notified the captains all along the line to reduce their companies to twenty men each for the winter at the end of the current quarter. As the day for reduction arrived there were some anxious moments among the men of Company D as no one knew just who was to be retained in the service.

On December first Captain Roberts formed the command in line and explained it was his sad duty to reduce the company to twenty men, and announced that the orderly sergeant would read the names of those to be retained in the company. The sergeant then stepped forward and began to read. First Sergeant Plunk Murray, Second Sergeant James Hawkins, First Corporal Lam Seiker, Second Corporal Tom Griffin, and Privates Charles Nevill, Tom Gillespie, Nick Donley, Jim Trout, Henry Maltimore, Kit Maltimore, Jack Martin, W. T. Clements, Ed Seiker, Andy Wilson, J. W. Bell, Norman Rodgers, Dock Long, Tom Mead, Frank Hill, and Jim Gillett were the lucky ones to be retained in the command. The remainder of the company was thereupon discharged. My relief may be imagined when my name was read, for I had learned to love the ranger life and was loath to quit it.

After reduction we went into winter camp in a bend of the San Saba River about three miles east of Menardville. In the river bottom was plenty of good timber, so each mess of five men built a log cabin, sixteen to eighteen feet square, for their occupancy. These cabins, each with a chimney and a fireplace, formed the western side of our horse corral and made most comfortable winter abodes. During the winter the boys played many tricks on each other, for there were no Indian raids during the time we were in this winter camp. One of the favorite stunts was to extract the bullet from a cartridge, take out the powder and wrap it in a rag, and then, while the inmates of a given cabin would be quietly smoking or reading or talking around their fire, climb upon the roof and drop the rag down the chimney. When the powder exploded in the fire the surprised rangers would fall backward off their benches, to the huge glee of the prank player. At other times a couple of rangers would post themselves outside a neighbor's cabin and begin to yell, "Fire! Fire!!" at the top of their lungs. If the cabin owners did not stand in the doorway to protect it all the rangers in camp would rush up and throw bedding, cooking ustensils, saddles and bridles, guns and pistols outside as quickly as they could. In a jiffy the cabin would be cleaned out and the victims of the joke would have to lug all their belongings back in again.

But not all our time was spent in practical joking. Many of the rangers were of a studious mind, and during the long winter evenings they pored over their books. Several of our boys, by such study over a period of years, qualified themselves for doctors, lawyers, and other professional callings.

One of the rangers, Nick Donley, was a baker by trade, and he soon built a Dutch oven and made bread for the rangers. We pooled our flour and had fresh, warm bread every evening. This was so good and we ate so much of it that our allowance of flour would not last for the period issued, and Captain Roberts was compelled to order the bake-oven torn down. Thereafter the boys baked their own bread and the flour lasted.

Some of the rangers had captured bear cubs, and we had them in camp with us as pets. They grew rapidly and were soon big fellows and immensely popular with the boys. Sometimes a bear would break loose from its chain, and then all of us would turn out to hunt the escaped pet. Most often we would find him seated in a tree which he had climbed as soon as he had broken his shackles. I cannot here forbear mentioning the useful little pack-mules that served the rangers so long and so well. When the battalion was formed in 1874 a number of little bronco mules were secured for packing. They soon learned what was expected of them and followed the rangers like dogs. Carrying a weight of one hundred and fifty to two hundred pounds, they would follow a scout of rangers on the dead run right into the midst of the hottest fight with Indians or desperadoes. They seemed to take as much interest in such an engagement as the rangers themselves.

These little pack animals had as much curiosity as a child or a pet coon. In traveling they sometimes met a bunch of horses or several campers along the highway. Immediately they would run over for a brief visit with the strangers, and when the rangers had gone on a thousand yards or more would scamper up to us as fast as they could run. Later, when the rangers drew in from the frontier and scouted in a more thickly-settled country the mules with their packs would march up to strange horses and frighten them out of their wits. Once, in Austin, one of our mules calmly trotted up to a mule that was pulling a street car. As the pack-mule would not give right of way the street-car mule shied to one side and pulled its conveyance completely off the track, to the surprise of its driver. The tiny animals pulled off several stunts like this and caused so much complaint that Adjutant General Jones issued an order for all rangers to catch and lead their pack-mules when passing through a town.

As soon as we were located in the new camp Privates Nevill, Bell, and Seiker obtained permission from Captain Roberts to visit Austin to buy a case of ten Winchesters. Up to this time the company was armed with .50 caliber Sharps carbines. These guns would heat easily and thus were very inaccurate shooters. The state furnished this weapon to its rangers at a cost of $17.50, and at that time furnished no other class of gun. The new center-fire 1873-model Winchester had just appeared on the market and sold at $50 for the rifle and $40 for the carbine. A ranger who wanted a Winchester had to pay for it out of his own pocket and supply his own ammunition as well, for the state furnished cartridges only for the Sharps gun. However, ten men in Company D, myself included, were willing to pay the price to have a superior arm. I got carbine number 13401, and for the next six years of my ranger career I never used any other weapon. I have killed almost every kind of game that is found in Texas, from the biggest old bull buffalo to a fox squirrel with this little .44 Winchester. Today I still preserve it as a prized memento of the past.

The boys were all anxious to try their new guns, and as Christmas approached we decided to have a real Yule-tide dinner. Ed Seiker and myself visited a big turkey-roost on the head of Elm Creek and killed seven big wild turkeys, and on our return Seiker bagged a fine buck deer. J. W. Bell hunted on the San Saba and brought in six or eight wild geese and about a dozen mallard ducks. Donley, the baker, made the pies, while Mrs. Roberts furnished the fruit-cake. Some of the boys made eggnog, and altogether we had the finest Christmas dinner that ever graced the boards of a ranger camp. The village of Menardville was not far away, and most of the rangers visited it during Christmas week for the dancing. Jack Martin once remarked to Mrs. Roberts that there was very little society about a ranger camp. She told the joke on him and thereafter as long as he lived he was known as "Society Jack."

During the winter we laid out a race course and had much sport with our horses. But there was work as well as play that winter. Though Captain Roberts kept scouts in the field during the entire winter they never discovered any Indian trails. The rangers had not yet turned their attention to outlaws, so we were not burdened with chained prisoners as we were in after years. This winter camp on the San Saba was the pleasantest time in my service with the rangers.

The first week in April, 1876, we moved out of our winter quarters to a camp some six or seven miles above Menardville and located in a pecan grove on the banks of the San Saba. We were all glad to get into our tents again after four months spent in log cabins. I remember our first night at the new camp. The boys set out some hooks and caught four or five big yellow catfish weighing twenty-five or thirty pounds each—enough fish to last the twenty men several days.

As the spring opened, Captain Roberts began sending out scouts to look for Indian signs. I remember I was detailed on a scout that was commanded by a noncommissioned officer. We were ordered to scout as far north as the union of the Concho and Colorado rivers. After crossing the Brady Mountains we struck a trail of Indians going out. The redskins had probably been raiding in San Saba or McCulloch County. Their trail led west as straight to San Angelo as a bird could fly. Though the Indians were not numerous and had only a few horses, the trail was easily followed. As well as we could judge the redskins had passed on a few days before we discovered their sign. We found where they had stolen some horses, for we picked up several pairs of hobbles that had been cut in two and left behind. At that time there were several big cattle ranches in the Fort Concho country, and in going to and from water the cattle entirely obliterated the trail. We worked hard two days trying to find it and then gave up the hunt. We needed the genius of Captain Roberts to help us out that time.

On June 1, 1876, the company was increased to forty men. Some of the boys who had quit at Mason the fall before now reëntered the service. Especially do I remember that "Mage" Reynolds enlisted with Company D once more.

During the summer of 1876 Major Jones planned a

big scout out on the Pecos to strike the Lipans and Kickapoos a blow before they began raiding the white settlements. This scout started from Company D in July. The major drafted about twenty men from my company, his whole escort Company A of thirty men, and marched into Kerr County. Here he drafted part of Captain Coldwell's Company F, making his force total about seventy men with three wagons and about twenty pack-mules.

The column traveled down the Nueces, then by Fort Clark up the Devils River to Beaver Lake. Here Captain Ira Long with twenty men and the wagon train was sent up the San Antonio and El Paso road to old Fort Lancaster on the Pecos, where he was to await the arrival of Major Jones with the main force.

From Beaver Lake, the major with fifty men and the twenty pack-mules turned southwest and traveled down Johnston's Run to the Shafer Crossing on the Pecos. From this crossing we scouted up the Pecos to the mouth of Independence Creek. The country through this section was very rough but very beautiful. We saw several abandoned Indian camps, especially at the mouth of the creek. Here we found the pits and the scaffolds on which the redskins had dried their meat, also evidence that many deer hides had been dressed and made into buckskin. Bows and arrows had also been manufactured in these camps. From this section the Indians had been gone probably a month or more.

After ten days of scouting we joined Captain Long at Fort Lancaster and marched up Live Oak Creek to its head. Here we prepared to cross the big stretch of table-land between the Pecos and the headwaters of the South Concho. We filled what barrels we had with water, marched out from the creek, and traveled about ten miles into the plains by night and made a dry camp. We got an early start next day and traveled until night without finding water. The stock suffered greatly from thirst, and the men had only a little water in their canteens. All the land ponds had been dry two weeks or more, and I saw twelve head of buffalo that had bogged and died in one of them. Here we found an abandoned Indian camp, where the redskins had dressed many antelope hides. At one old bent mesquite tree the antelope hair was a foot deep, with thirty or forty skulls scattered about.

By the second morning both men and horses were suffering a great deal from thirst and Major Jones gave orders to begin the march at four o'clock. We got away on time and reached water on the South Concho at two p.m., the third day out from Live Oak Creek. As soon as we got near the water we found a number of straggling buffalo, and killed two, thus securing a supply of fresh meat. We camped two days at this water and then marched back to Company D by easy stages. Here Major Jones turned back up the line with his escort, after being out on this scout about a month.

On his return toward the Rio Grande, Major Jones reached Company D the last week in August and camped with us until September first, the end of the fiscal year for the rangers. On this date many men would quit the service to retire to private life, while some would join other companies, and new recruits would be sworn into the service. This reorganization usually required two or three days.

Nearly every ranger in the battalion was anxious to be at some time a member of Major Jones's escort com-

Major Jones and His Escort

pany. The escort company was not assigned a stationary post nor did it endeavor to cover a given strip of territory. Its most important duty was to escort the major on his periodic journeys of inspection to the other companies along the line. The escort always wintered in the south and made about four yearly tours of the frontier from company to company, taking part in such scouts as the major might select and being assigned to such extraordinary duty as might arise. In 1874, when the Frontier Battalion was first formed, Major Jones recruited his escort from a detail of five men from each of the other companies. However, in practice, this led to some confusion and envy in the commands and Major Jones found it expedient to have a regular escort company, so he selected Company A for this purpose. This remained his escort until he was promoted to adjutant general.

In September, 1876, there were several vacancies in Major Jones's escort, and several old Company D boys, among them "Mage" Reynolds, Charles Nevill, Jack Martin, Bill Clements, and Tom Gillespie, wished to enlist in Company A. They wanted me to go with them, but I hesitated to leave Captain Roberts. My friends then explained that we could see a lot more country on the escort than we could in a stationary company; and that we would probably be stationed down on the Rio Grande that winter, and going up the line in the spring would see thousands of buffalo. This buffalo proposition caught me, and I went with the boys. After fifteen months' ranging with Captain Roberts I now joined Company A.

Early in September Major Jones marched his escort down to within five or six miles of San Antonio and camped us on the Salado while he went in to Austin. By the first of October he was back in camp, and started up the line on his last visit to the different companies before winter set in.

Major John B. Jones was a small man, probably not more than five feet seven inches tall, and weighed about one hundred and twenty-five pounds. He had very dark hair and eyes and a heavy dark moustache. He was quick in action, though small in stature, and was an excellent horseman, riding very erect in the saddle.

The major was born in Fairfield District, South Carolina, in 1834, but emigrated to Texas with his father when he was only four years old. He was prominent in Texas state affairs from a very early age and served gallantly with the Confederate army during the Civil War. On the accession of Governor Coke in 1874 he was appointed to command the Frontier Battalion of six companies of Texas Rangers. From his appointment until his death in Austin in 1881, Major Jones was constantly engaged in repulsing bloody raids of Indians, rounding up outlaws, and making Texas secure and safe for the industrious and peaceful citizen. In this work his wonderful tact, judgment, coolness, and courage found ample scope.

From the organization of the battalion in 1874 until Major Jones was made adjutant general, Dr. Nicholson was always with him. The doctor was a quaint old bachelor who loved his toddy. The boys would sometimes get him as full as a goose, and the major would give the doctor some vicious looks at such times. Dr. Nicholson was a great favorite with all the men, and it is said he knew every good place for butter, milk, and eggs from Rio Grande City to Red River, a trifling dis-

General John B. Jones.

Major Jones and His Escort

tance of eight hundred miles. The doctor always messed with Major Jones, and, mounted on a fine horse, traveled by his side. I don't think Dr. Nicholson ever issued a handful of pills to the boys during the year—he was just with us in case he was needed. When the escort was disbanded he retired to private life at Del Rio, Texas, and finally died there.

This inspection tour was a wonderful experience for me. The weather was cool and bracing, and the horses had had a month's rest. We had with us a quartet of musicians, and after the day's march they would often gather around the camp-fire and give us a concert. Vernon Wilson played the guitar, Columbus Callaway the banjo, and W. T. Clements the violin. The major would frequently walk down and listen to the music. Nor was music our only amusement. Major Jones had provided his escort with a fish seine, and when we were camped on a big creek or river the boys would unroll the net, make a haul, and sometimes catch enough fish to supply the thirty men several days.

When recruited to its full strength, Company A consisted of a captain, orderly sergeant, second sergeant, first and second corporals, and twenty-six privates. Two four-mule wagons hauled the camp equipage, rations for the men, and grain for the horses. One light wagon drawn by two mules and driven by George, the negro cook, carried the mess outfit, bedding, tent, etc., of Major Jones and Dr. Nicholson.

Each morning at roll call the orderly sergeant detailed a guard of nine men and one non-commissioned officer to guard for twenty-four hours. When ready to begin our day's journey, the company was formed in line and the men counted off by fours. On the march

Six Years with the Texas Rangers

Major Jones and Dr. Nicholson rode in front, followed by the captain of the company, the orderly sergeant, and the men in double file. Following these came the wagons. An advance guard of two men preceded the column about one-half mile. Four men, known as flankers, two on each side of the company, paralleled the column at a distance of one-half to one mile, depending on the nature of the country. In a rough, wooded section the flankers traveled close in, but in an open country they sometimes spread out quite a distance. The non-commissioned officer with the remaining guard covered the rear and brought up the pack-mules. Thus protected, it was almost impossible for the command to be surprised by Indians.

Major Jones paid no attention to roads unless they happened to coincide with his line of march. In clear weather he made use of landmarks, and in cloudy or foggy weather traveled by compass. At one time he had with him two Tonkawa Indians as guides. For protection this tribe lived near Fort Griffin, a large military post. One of these old braves, known as Jim, had been given an old army coat with the shoulder straps of a general on it. Jim wore this coat tightly buttoned up and marched at the head of the column with as much dignity and importance as a general-in-chief. His companion wore a high-crowned beaver stovepipe hat with the top gone, and carried an old umbrella that someone had given him. Fitted out in this ridiculous and unique manner he marched for days with the umbrella over him. Think of an Indian shading himself from the sun!

Major Jones never paid much attention to these Indians unless he wished to inquire the lay of the country or the distance to some water hole. They did pretty

Major Jones and His Escort

much as they pleased, sometimes riding in front with the major, sometimes with the guard, and at others with the men. These redskins were a constant source of amusement to the boys. Jim and his pal were good hunters but as lazy as could be. They got into the habit of killing a buffalo late in the evening when they knew it was almost time to pitch camp, cutting out just enough meat for themselves and letting the remainder go to waste. The major told them that when they killed a buffalo he wanted to know of it so he could secure the meat for the company. The Tonks paid no attention to this request, and late one evening came into camp with five or six pounds of buffalo meat.

The orderly sergeant spied them, so he walked over to Major Jones and said, "Major, those two old Ton kawas are back in camp with just enough meat for themselves."

"Sergeant, you get a pack-mule, take a file of men with you, and make those Indians saddle their horses and go with you to get that buffalo," the major commanded, determined that his order should be obeyed by the Indians.

The sergeant went to the Indians, who were busy about the fire roasting their meat, and told them what the major had said. Jim declared that he was tired and did not wish to go. The non-commissioned officer replied that that made no difference and commanded him and his pal to get their ponies and lead the way to the dead buffalo.

"Maybe so ten miles to buffalo," protested Jim, trying to avoid going.

The sergeant knew they were lying, for of all the Indians that ever inhabited Texas the Tonkawas were the biggest cowards. Just mention the Comanches or Kiowas to them and they would have a chill. It was well known that the Tonks would not venture very far away from the protection of the rangers for fear of being killed by their enemies. As soon as they knew they had to do as ordered, they mounted their ponies and led the sergeant over a little hill, and in a valley not more than half a mile from camp was the fat buffalo the Indians had killed. The animal was soon skinned and brought into camp, where all had plenty of fresh meat.

These Tonks were as simple as children and as superstitious as negroes. The weather had been hot and dry for several days. Old Jim thereupon killed some hawks with his bow and arrows, plaited the long tail and wing feathers into his pony's mane and tail, and said it would make "heap rain." Sure enough, in three or four days a hard thunder-shower came up and thoroughly wet everybody on the march. Jim, with only his old officer's coat for protection, was drenched to the skin, and his pony looked like a drowned rat. The wood, grass, everything was wet. Jim stood by, shivering with the cold, and watched the boys use up almost their last match trying to make a fire. Suddenly, with a look of disgust, he ran to his horse, which was standing near, and plucked every hawk feather out of the animal's tail and mane and, throwing them on the ground, stamped upon them violently as if that would stop the rain.

After the escort had crossed the Colorado River on its way northward we found an advance guard of buffalo on its way south, and it was an easy matter to keep the company in fresh meat. We spent about one week with Company B on the upper Brazos, then turned south again to make our winter camp near old Frio Town in

Major Jones and His Escort

Frio County. It was November now and freezing hard every night.

The last guard would call the camp early, so we generally had breakfast and were ready to move southward by daylight. We did not stop a single time for dinner on this return trip, just traveled at a steady gait all day long. After traveling in this way without dinner for a week or so, the boys began making at breakfast what they called "bacon pies,"—strips of broiled bacon placed between slices of bread—which they ate for lunch as we marched along. It was not until many years afterward, when I became a Mason, that I learned the reason for our forced marches. Major Jones was in line to be made Most Worshipful Grand Master of Masons in Texas and he had to be in Houston on the first Tuesday in December for the annual meeting of the Most Worshipful Grand Lodge. If there were other Masons in the company besides Major Jones I never knew it.

At this time we had for commander of the escort, Lieutenant Benton. He was in bad health and rode most of the way back in one of the wagons. On arriving at the end of the line he tendered his resignation and was succeeded by Captain Neal Coldwell. The company camped for the winter on Elm Creek, three miles southwest of old Frio Town.

Captain Neal Coldwell was born in Dade County, Missouri, in May, 1844, and served gallantly throughout the Civil War in the Thirty-second Regiment, Texas cavalry, commanded by Col. W. P. Woods. At the organization of the Frontier Battalion in 1874, he was commissioned captain of Company F.

It is difficult, in a single sketch, to do Captain Coldwell justice or convey any correct idea of what he accomplished as a Texas Ranger. The station of Company F, the southernmost company of the line, was the most unfavorable that could well be given him. His scouting grounds were the heads of the Guadalupe, Nueces, Llano, and Devils rivers, the roughest and most difficult part of southern Texas in which to pursue Indians, yet he held them in check and finally drove them out of that part of the state.

CHAPTER VII

THE HORRELL-HIGGINS FEUD

BY the end of the year 1876 the Indians had been pretty well pushed back off the frontier, so that there were very few fights with them after 1877. From the spring of 1877 onward the rangers were transformed into what might properly be called mounted state police, and accordingly turned their attention to ridding the frontier of the outlaws that infested nearly every part of Texas. During the winter of 1876-1877, Captain Neal Coldwell broke up a band of thieves which was operating in the northwestern part of Atascosa County. I remember helping him capture a man named Wolf. He was wanted for murder, and we made several scouts after him before we succeeded in landing him safely in irons.

In April, 1877, Major Jones reached Coldwell's company and at once made arrangements to march up the line on a visit of inspection. When the major reached the headwaters of the South Llano River he halted his escort and detailed several small scouting parties of five or six men, each with orders to arrest every man who could not give a good account of himself. One scout was sent down the South Llano, a second down Johnson's Fork, while a third was ordered over the divide with instructions to hit the head of the North Llano and sweep down that river—all three parties to rejoin Major Jones and the main escort near where Junction City now stands. In these outlaw raids some fifty or sixty men were arrested and brought in. Many of the suspects were released upon examination, but I remem-

69

ber one scout brought in two escaped convicts who had been captured up on Copperas Creek. We bagged several men wanted for murder and some horse and cattle thieves. Old Kimble County had never had such a clean-up of bandits in her history.

While these prisoners were being held in camp, other scouts were sent out in the northern part of the county with orders to sweep Bear Creek, Gentry, Red Creek, Big and Little Saline, cross the San Saba River in Menard County, and sweep up that stream from old Peg Leg Station to Menard. Many more suspects were caught in this haul.

With a party of scouts I was detailed on a mission to Fort McKavett, at that time one of the big military posts on the frontier. Many hard characters and gamblers gathered about these posts to fleece the soldiers out of their easy-made money. We made several arrests here, and camped for noon one mile below the government post on the San Saba River. During the dinner hour my horse, a gray, in lying down to wallow, rolled on some broken beer bottles and cut his back so badly that he was unfit for use for some time. When the escort moved north I was left with old Company D until the arrival of Company A on its return march some six weeks later. I thereby missed some of the exciting scouts that took place on the march north.

When Major Jones reached Coleman City he found orders from Governor Coke to send a scout of rangers to Lampasas County to help the civil authorities suppress a war known as the Horrell-Higgins feud. Second Sergeant N. O. Reynolds was detached from Company A and with ten men ordered to proceed to Lampasas and report to the sheriff of that county.

The Horrell-Higgins Feud

After leaving Coleman, Major Jones visited the northernmost ranger company and began his return march. This was to be his last trip with his escort, for immediately upon his return to Austin he was commissioned adjutant general of Texas. As there was no longer a major of the battalion, there was no need of an escort, so old Company A took its place on the line as a stationary company. Captain Neal Coldwell was ultimately made quartermaster of the battalion, and I believe ranked as major.

I was picked up at Company D by the escort on its return march and was with Company A when it was made a stationary command and located in Frio County.

During the late summer of 1877, a party of filibusterers under command of a Mexican general named Winkler assembled in Maverick County, near Eagle Pass, and prepared to invade Mexico. Captain Coldwell, then commanding Company A, was ordered to the Rio Grande to break up the expedition. This he did by arresting more than fifty participants. I was with him on this expedition and saw much border service during this summer.

I remember a scout I was called on to make with Captain Coldwell over in Bandera County. The captain took with him John Parker, Hawk Roberts, and myself. In one week's time we caught some ten or twelve fugitives from justice and literally filled the little jail at Bandera. Captain Coldwell detailed Hawk Roberts and myself to capture an especially bad man wanted in Burnet County for murder. The captain warned us to take no chances with this man—this meant to kill him if he hesitated about surrendering. I can't remember this murderer's name at this late date, but I recall per-

71

fectly the details of his capture. Sheriff Jack Hamilton of Bandera County sent a guide to show us where the fugitive lived. The guide led us some fifteen miles northwest of Bandera and finally pointed out the house in which the murderer was supposed to be. He then refused to go any farther, saying he did not want any of this man's game, for the fellow had just stood off a deputy sheriff and made him hike it back to Bandera.

It was almost night when we reached the house, so Roberts and I decided to wait until morning before attempting the arrest. We staked our horses, lay down on our saddle-blankets without supper, and slept soundly till dawn. As soon as it was daylight we rode over near the house, dismounted, slipped up, and, unannounced, stepped inside the room. The man we wanted was sleeping on a pallet with a big white-handled .45 near his head. Hawk Roberts kicked the pistol out of his reach. The noise awakened the sleeper and he opened his eyes to find himself looking into the business ends of two Winchesters held within a foot of his head. Of course he surrendered without fight. His wife, who was sleeping in a bed in the same room, jumped out of it and heaped all kinds of abuse on us for entering her home without ceremony. She was especially bitter against Sheriff Hamilton, who, she said, had promised to notify her husband when he was wanted so he could come in and give himself up. She indignantly advised her husband to give old Sheriff Hamilton a damned good whipping the first chance he had.

While Company A was rounding up outlaws along the border, Sergeant Reynolds was covering himself with glory in the north. On reaching Lampasas and reporting to the sheriff, as ordered by Major Jones, the sergeant was told that the Horrell boys were living on the Sulphur Fork of the Lampasas River and were defying the authorities to arrest them.

The Horrells were native Texans and had been raised on the frontier. These brothers, five of whom were involved in the feud (the sixth, John Horrell, had been killed at Las Cruces, New Mexico, previously), were expert riders, and, having grown up with firearms in their hands, were as quick as lightning with either Winchester or pistol. Sam Horrell, the eldest, was married and had a large family of children. He was a farmer, and lived a quiet life over on the Lampasas River. The other four boys, Mart, Tom, Merritt, and Ben, were all cattlemen. They stood well in the community, but were considered dangerous when aroused.

At this time Lampasas was a frontier town and wide open as far as saloons and gambling were concerned. The Horrells, like most cattlemen of the period, loved to congregate in town, go to the saloons and have a good time, perhaps drink too much, and sometimes at night shoot up the town for fun, as they termed it. Some of the more pious and more settled citizens of the town, who did not approve of these night brawls, called upon Governor Edmund J. Davis to give them protection. Governor Davis had formed in Texas a state police force. Naturally its members were rank Republicans, and many of them were termed carpet-baggers. This body was never popular in Texas, especially as many of the force were negroes.

In answer to the call of the citizens, Governor Davis dispatched Captain Williams with three white men and one negro to Lampasas. On the way up Captain Williams met several freighters going to Austin and stopped one of them, John Means, to ask the distance to Lampasas. The captain had been drinking, and he told Mr. Means he was going to town to clean up those damned Horrell boys.

The little squad of police reached Lampasas about three p.m., hitched their horses to some live-oak trees on the public plaza, left the negro to guard them, and then made a bee line to Jerry Scott's saloon on the west side of the square. Mart, Tom, and Merritt Horrell, with some ten or fifteen cowmen, were in the saloon drinking, playing billiards, and having a good time generally. One man was picking a banjo and another playing a fiddle. Captain Williams, an exceedingly brave but unwise man, took in the situation at a glance as he walked up to the bar and called for drinks.

He turned to Bill Bowen, a brother-in-law to Merritt Horrell, and said, "I believe you have a six-shooter. I arrest you."

"Bill, you have done nothing and need not be arrested if you don't want to," interrupted Mart Horrell.

Like a flash of lightning Captain Williams pulled his pistol and fired on Mart Horrell, wounding him badly. The Horrell boys drew their guns and began to fight. Captain Williams and one of his men, Dr. Daniels, were shot down in the saloon. William Cherry was killed just outside the door, and Andrew Melville was fatally wounded as he was trying to escape. He reached the old Huling Hotel, where he died later. At the first crack of a pistol the negro policeman mounted his horse and made a John Gilpin ride for Austin. Thus, within the twinkling of an eye, four state police were killed and only one of the Horrells wounded.

The Horrell-Higgins Feud

Tom and Merritt Horrell carried the wounded Mart to their mother's home, some two hundred yards from Scott's saloon, then mounted their horses and rode away. Great excitement prevailed in the town. The state militia was called out, and Governor Davis hurried other state police to Lampasas. They scoured the country for the Horrell boys, but to no avail.

Mart Horrell and Jerry Scott were arrested and carried to Georgetown, Williamson County, and placed in jail. Mart Horrell's wife went to the jail to nurse her husband and, of course, kept her brothers-in-law informed as to Mart's condition. As soon as he was well the Horrell boys made up a party and rode to Williamson County and assaulted the jail at night. The citizens and officers of Georgetown, taken unawares, put up a stiff fight, but the Horrells had ten or fifteen well-organized and armed men with them. They took stations at all approaches to the jail and kept up a steady fire with their Winchesters at anyone who showed up to oppose them. Mr. A. S. Fisher, a prominent lawyer of the town, took an active hand in the fight and was badly wounded. Bill Bowen was slightly wounded while battering in the jail door with a sledge hammer. Mart Horrell and Jerry Scott were liberated and rode off with their rescuers.

By the next evening the Horrells were back in Lampasas County. They at once made arrangements to leave the country and go to New Mexico. They had gathered about them Bill and Tom Bowen, John Dixon, Ben Turner, and six or eight other men as desperate and dangerous as themselves. They were so formidable that they no longer attempted to hide, but openly and without hindrance gathered their cattle and sold the remnant to Cooksey and Clayton, to be delivered to them in Coleman County. They even notified the sheriff of Lampasas County just what day they would pass with their herd through Russell Gap, but they were not molested.

As a cowboy I had worked for Cooksey and Clayton, and was with them when they delivered cattle to the Horrell boys on Home Creek, Coleman County. I had dinner in camp with the outlaws, who made no effort to hide from the authorities. I remember they sat about the camp with Winchesters across their laps.

When all was ready, the Horrells moved slowly out of the country with their families and cattle and finally reached New Mexico, settling on the head of the Hondo River in Lincoln County. They had not been at their new home many months before Ben Horrell was shot and killed at a fandango near old Fort Stanton. Ben's brothers at once repaired to the dance hall and killed eight Mexicans and one woman.

This brought on a war between the Horrell boys and the Mexican population along the Hondo River, and it is said that in the fights that followed many Mexicans were killed between Fort Stanton and Roswell. In one of these pitched battles Ben Turner was killed. Turner was prominent in all of the fights staged by the Horrells, was with them when Captain Williams was killed, and was one of the party that made the assault on the Georgetown jail. His death was keenly felt by his companions.

Having now outlawed themselves in New Mexico, the Horrells could no longer stay in that country. They turned back to Texas, and next year showed up at their old haunts in Lampasas County. The shock of the Civil

The Horrell-Higgins Feud

War was beginning to subside and the state was now under civil government with a Democratic governor in office. The friends of the Horrells advised them to surrender to the authorities to be tried for the killing of Captain Williams and his men. They were assured a fair trial by the best citizens of Lampasas County. Accordingly, they gave themselves up, and on the trial were acquitted of the charges against them.

They had not long been at ease before Merritt, the youngest of the brothers, was accused by Pink Higgins of unlawfully handling his cattle. Shortly afterward, while Merritt was seated unarmed in a chair in the old Jerry Scott saloon, Pink Higgins stepped to the back door of the place and shot him. Thus Merritt met his death in the same saloon where four years before he had been a party to the killing of Captain Williams. At this time Mart and Tom Horrell were living on Sulphur Fork of Lampasas River, where the news of their brother's death was quickly carried to them. They armed themselves and started on a run for Lampasas.

This move had been anticipated by the Pink Higgins party. They waylaid the Horrell boys outside the town and at their first fire killed Tom Horrell's horse and badly wounded Mart. Tom advanced single-handed on the attackers and put them to flight. He then partly supported and partly carried his brother to the home of Mr. Tinnins, a neighbor, where a doctor was hurried to the wounded man.

Thus Lampasas County was again the scene of war with Mart, Tom, and Sam Horrell, Bill and Tom Bowen, John Dixon, and Bill Crabtree on one side and Pink Higgins, Bob Mitchell, and their friends on the other. These two factions met in the town of Lampasas and a furious battle followed. A man was killed on each side and the population greatly endangered. Hence the governor's order to Major Jones to send rangers to the aid of the officers at Lampasas.

When Sergeant N. O. Reynolds reported to the sheriff, he was informed that the Horrell boys were living ten miles east of Lampasas and had ten or twelve desperate men with them, so that it meant certain death to anyone who should attempt to capture them.

"But, Mr. Sheriff, I am sent here to effect the capture of all offenders against the law, and it is my duty at least to make the attempt," replied the brave Reynolds.

"These men have never been arrested," declared Sheriff Sweet, "and it is my honest opinion they cannot be."

Reynolds then asked if the sheriff would send a guide to show him where the Horrells lived. The rangers left Lampasas late in the night and finally the guide pointed at a flickering light about a mile off.

"There is where the Horrell boys live. I am going back to town," he said.

When asked if he would not accompany the rangers to the house, the guide replied, "No, not for a million dollars!" With this he turned his horse and rode away.

Reynolds thought it would be best to wait until daylight before attempting the arrest. He planned to surprise the outlaws, if possible, but if the rangers should be discovered and an engagement come on they were to fight to the last man. As soon as dawn broke they proceeded on foot to the Horrell brothers' ranch. It was a moment of great anxiety as they approached the house, but not a sound was heard, not a dog barked.

The Horrell-Higgins Feud

Sergeant Reynolds and his men tiptoed right into the room in which the Horrells were sleeping. Some of the men were on pallets on the floor, while others slept in beds in the one big room. Each ranger pointed a cocked Winchester at the head of a sleeper. Reynolds then spoke to Mart Horrell. At the sound of his voice every man sat up in bed and found himself looking into the muzzle of a gun. The sergeant quickly explained that he was a ranger and had come to arrest them. Mart replied they could not surrender, and Tom Horrell said it would be better to die fighting than to be mobbed.

This gave Reynolds his cue. He warned the outlaws that if anything was started there would be a dozen dead men in that house in one minute and advised them to listen to what he had to say. He then guaranteed the Horrells upon his honor that he would not turn them over to the sheriff to be put in jail and mobbed, but promised he would guard them in his camp until they could secure a preliminary examination and give bond.

"Boys, this seems reasonable," said Mart Horrell, rising to his feet. "I believe these rangers can be relied on to protect us. Besides, this fight has been thrust upon us. If we can get a hearing we can give bond."

They all agreed, finally, to this proposition of Sergeant Reynolds and mounting their horses were marched into the town of Lampasas under guard of the rangers.

The news of the capture of the Horrells spread like wildfire through the town and county. Hundreds of people flocked to Lampasas to see Sergeant Reynolds, the man who had accomplished the impossible in rounding up the desperate band. The news was rushed to Austin, and General Jones himself hurried to the scene.

79

This exploit of Sergeant Reynolds brought him great credit, and he was at once commissioned first lieutenant, and given command of a company.

The Horrells were admitted to bond, after a preliminary hearing. After their release Mart Horrell came to Lieutenant Reynolds and feelingly thanked him for carrying out his promise. With tears streaming down his face he grasped the lieutenant's hand and said, "You are undoubtedly the bravest man in the world today." About six months after this a country merchant of Bosque County was found murdered and his store robbed, and Mart and Tom Horrell, Bill Crabtree, John Dixon, and Tom Bowen were accused of the crime. The two Horrells were arrested and thrown into the Bosque County jail at Meridian. While they were confined here a mob stormed the jail and shot them to death. The Higgins and Mitchell factions finally surrendered to the authorities. Pink Higgins was tried, and acquitted of the murder of Merritt Horrell. This ended the feud, but it started Lieutenant Reynolds on a new and important phase of his career as a ranger.

CHAPTER VIII

SERVICE WITH REYNOLDS, THE INTREPID

AS soon as Sergeant Reynolds was commissioned first lieutenant he was placed in command of Company E, then stationed in Coleman County, but immediately ordered to Lampasas. At this time Captain Sparks resigned the command of Company C, and this company was also ordered to report to Lieutenant Reynolds at the same town. Late in August the two commands went into camp at Hancock Springs. Major Jones then authorized Lieutenant Reynolds to pick such men as he desired from these two companies for his own company, after which the major either discharged the remainder or transferred them to other commands. No other officer in the battalion, I believe, was ever accorded this privilege.

Lieutenant Reynolds had a week or ten days in which to make his selection, so he studied the muster rolls of the companies carefully. He had ranged under such great captains as Perry, D. W. Roberts, Neal Coldwell, and with Major Jones himself. He knew what qualities were needed in a good ranger and made his selections accordingly. From old Company A Reynolds selected C. L. Nevill, Tom Gillespie, Shape Rodgers, Jack Martin, W. T. Clements, and four others whose names I do not now remember. These were the scouts who had helped him capture the Horrells and naturally were his first choice. From Company E came Dick Ware, who one year later killed the noted train robber, Sam Bass, then served Mitchell County as its first sheriff for many years, and was finally appointed United States marshal for the western district of Texas by President Cleveland. Henry Thomas, Millard Mourland, George Arnett, and other Company E boys were selected. Henry Maltimore, Ben and Dock Carter, Bill Derrick, Chris Connor, Henry McGee, Abe Anglin, J. W. Warren, Dave Ligon, Lowe Hughes, George (Hog) Hughes, and others were picked from Company C.

When he had exhausted the two companies, Reynolds turned to General Jones and said, "There is a ranger down on the Rio Grande in Neal Coldwell's company that I want."

"Who is it?" asked the general.

"Private Jim Gillett."

"You shall have him," promised General Jones. "I will send an order to Captain Coldwell tonight to have Gillett report to you here."

It was late in the evening when Company A's mail came in from Frio Town, but Captain Coldwell sent for me as soon as General Jones's order arrived, and told me that I must leave the company next morning and report to the adjutant general at Austin. I was nonplussed, for I did not know what the order meant. Out on the frontier where we then were operating we seldom read newspapers or heard what the other companies were doing, so I did not even know that Reynolds had captured the Horrell boys and had been commissioned to command Company E. The following morning I bade Captain Coldwell and the Company A boys good-bye and started on my long ride to Austin.

As I jogged along I asked myself many times why I was ordered to report at Austin, and, boylike, it made me nervous and uneasy. It took me two days to reach San Antonio and three more to ride to Austin. I arrived in the latter town just at nightfall, but I was at the adjutant general's office as soon as it was opened next morning.

Presently General Jones entered with some officers of the state militia. He shook hands with me and invited me to be seated, saying he had some business to attend to for the moment. It was probably an hour before the officers left and the general could turn to me. He very kindly inquired as to my trip and asked about Captain Coldwell and the company. He then told me about the arrest of the Horrell boys and Sergeant Reynolds' commission as first lieutenant commanding Company E, vice Lieutenant Foster resigned. He explained Reynolds had requested that I be attached to his command, and ordered me to report to my new commander in Lampasas without delay.

I excused myself at once and lost no time in getting my horse out of the livery stable and resuming my way. A great load was lifted from my mind, and I was about as happy as a boy could be. I sang and whistled all the way to Liberty Hill, thirty miles from Austin. The following day about two p.m. I rode into Reynolds' camp at Hancock Springs.

I attracted some attention as I rode in, for I wore a big Mexican hat mounted with silver, and a buckskin jacket fringed from shoulder to elbow, with a bunch of flowers braided in highly colored silk on its back. On my heels were enormous Mexican spurs. I never saw a ranger sent to the Rio Grande for the first time who did not rig himself out in some such outlandish attire, only to discard it a few weeks later, never to wear it again. I was no exception, and I think every man in camp tried on my hat.

Lieutenant Reynolds selected C. L. Nevill for first sergeant, Henry W. McGee as second sergeant, and J. W. Warren and L. W. Conner, first and second corporals, respectively. On September 1, 1877, the company was sworn in. The new command was the most formidable body of men I had ever seen. Our commander, Lieutenant Reynolds, was over six feet tall and weighed probably one hundred and seventy-five pounds. He was a very handsome man, a perfect blond, with steel-blue eyes and a long, light moustache. At that time he was about thirty years of age, vigorous in mind and body, and had a massive determination to succeed as a ranger. His mind was original, bold, profound, and quick, with a will that no obstacle could daunt. He was the best ranger in the world—there was never another like him. The lieutenant was a native of Missouri, and was always known as Major or "Mage" Reynolds. It was said that Reynolds, though a mere boy, had served with the Confederates in the latter part of the Civil War. He was one of a party that captured a troop of Federal cavalry, the major of which was well supplied with clothing. The captors, however, were very scantily clad and Reynolds appropriated the major's uniform, hence his nickname "Mage." In later years, when I had grown more intimate with him and was probably closer to him than any other, I mentioned this story. He neither affirmed nor denied it, declaring he was a Missourian by birth, a bootmaker by trade, and that his early history could interest no one.

First Sergeant Nevill was six feet and one inch in height and weighed one hundred and eighty-five pounds.

Service with Reynolds, the Intrepid

All the non-commissioned officers were at least six feet tall and built in proportion, and many of the privates were from five feet eleven inches to six feet in height. I was probably the lightest man in the company, being only five feet nine inches and weighing but one hundred and forty pounds.

When the company's roster was complete Lieutenant Reynolds had but twenty-eight men,—lacking two of his full complement of thirty. The company was then ordered to Austin, but before being assigned to its position on the frontier the lieutenant enlisted John and Will Banister, two celebrated frontiersmen. They were old cowboys, splendid riders, good shots, and well acquainted with every part of Kimble, Menard, Mason, and Kerr counties, in which Company E was destined to operate. In appearance and ability this company compared favorably with any thirty rangers ever sent to the Texas frontier. Nearly every member of the company had had more or less experience as an officer, and all were exceedingly fine marksmen. Sergeant Henry McGee had been marshal of Waco and had figured in several pistol duels in that city. Dave Ligon, the oldest man in the command, had been a Confederate soldier and had served with General Forrest's cavalry.

In the summer of 1877 Lieutenant Armstrong of Captain Hall's company, assisted by Detective Jack Duncan of Dallas, Texas, captured the notorious John Wesley Hardin. It has been said by some wag that Texas, the largest state in the Union, has never produced a real world's champion at anything. Surely this critic overlooked Hardin, the champion desperado of the world. His life is too well known in Texas for me to go into detail, but, according to his own story, which

Six Years with the Texas Rangers

I have before me, he killed no fewer than twenty-seven men, the last being Charley Webb, deputy sheriff of Brown County, Texas. So notorious had Hardin become that the state of Texas offered $4,000 reward for his capture. Hardin had left Texas and at the time of his capture was in Florida. His captors arrested and overpowered him while he was sitting in a passenger coach.

In September, 1877, Sheriff Wilson of Comanche County, in whose jurisdiction Hardin had killed Webb, came to Austin to convey the prisoner to Comanche for trial. Wilson requested the governor for an escort of rangers. Lieutenant Reynolds' company, being in Austin at the time, was ordered to accompany Wilson and protect Hardin from mob violence. This was the first work assigned Company E under its new commander.

The day we left Austin between one and two thousand people gathered about the Travis County jail to see this notorious desperado. The rangers were drawn up just outside the jail, and Henry Thomas and myself were ordered to enter the prison and escort Hardin out. Heavily shackled and handcuffed, the prisoner walked very slowly between us. The boy who had sold fish and game on the streets of Austin was now guarding the most desperate criminal in Texas; it was glory enough for me.

At his trial Hardin was convicted, and sentenced to twenty-five years in the penitentiary. He appealed his case and was returned to Travis County for safekeeping. The verdict of the trial court was sustained, and one year later, in September, 1878, Lieutenant Reynolds' company was ordered to take Hardin back to Comanche County for sentence. There was no railroad at Comanche at that time, so a detachment of rangers, myself among them, escorted Hardin to the penitentiary. There were ten or twelve indictments still pending against him for murder in various counties, but they were never prosecuted.

Hardin served seventeen years of his sentence, and while in prison studied law. Governor Hogg pardoned him in 1894 and restored him to full citizenship.

Despite all the kind advice given him by eminent lawyers and citizens, Hardin was unequal to the task of becoming a useful man. He practiced law for a time in Gonzales, then drifted away to El Paso, where he began drinking and gambling. On August 19, 1895, he was standing at a bar shaking dice when John Selman, constable of Precinct No. 1, approached him from behind and with a pistol blew his brains out. Though posing as an officer, Selman was himself an outlaw and a murderer of the worst kind. He killed Hardin for the notoriety it would bring him and nothing more.

After delivering Hardin to the sheriff of Travis County in 1877, Lieutenant Reynolds was ordered to Kimble County for duty. Of all the counties in Texas at that time Kimble was the most popular with outlaws and criminals, for it was situated south of Menard County on the North and South Llano rivers, with cedar, pecan, and mesquite timber in which to hide, while the streams and mountains furnished fish, game, and wild cattle in abundance for subsistence.

On the South Llano lived old Jimmie Dublin. He had a large family of children, most of them grown. The eldest of his boys, Dick, or Richard, as he was known, and a friend, Ace Lankford, killed two men at a country store in Lankford's Cove, Coryell County,

Six Years with the Texas Rangers

Texas. The state offered $500 for the arrest of Dublin and the county of Coryell an additional $200. To escape capture Dick and his companion fled west into Kimble County. While I was working as cowboy with Joe Franks in the fall of 1873 I became acquainted with the two murderers, for they attached themselves to our outfit. They were always armed and constantly on the watch for fear of arrest. Dublin was a large man, stout and of dark complexion, who looked more like the bully of a prize ring than the cowman he was. I often heard him say he would never surrender. While cow-hunting with us he discovered that the brushy and tangled region of Kimble County offered shelter for such as he, and persuaded his father to move out into that county.

Dublin had not lived long in Kimble County before another son, Dell Dublin, killed Jim Williams, a neighbor. Thus two of the Dublin boys were fugitives charged with murder. They were supposed to be hiding near their father's home. Bill Allison, Starke Reynolds, and a number of bandits, horse and cattle thieves, and murderers were known to be in Kimble County, so Lieutenant Reynolds was sent with his company to clean them up.

It was late in October, 1877, when the company reached its destination and camped on the North Llano River below the mouth of Bear Creek. As soon as our horses were rested and camp was fully established for the winter we began scouting. Several men wanted on minor charges were captured. We then raided Luke Stone's ranch, which was about ten miles from our camp, and captured Dell Dublin. He was fearfully angry when he found escape impossible. He tore his shirt

bosom open and dared the rangers to shoot him. While
he was being disarmed his elder brother, Dick, rode out
of the brush and came within gunshot of the ranch before he discovered the presence of the rangers. He
turned his horse quickly and made his escape, though
the rangers pursued him some distance and fired many
shots at him. When Dick learned that the Banister boys
and myself were with Lieutenant Reynolds' company
and hot on his trail, remembering us as beardless boys
with the Joe Franks's cow outfit, he declared he would
whip us with a quirt as a man would whip a dog if he
ever came upon us. However, he never attempted to
make good his threat, but took very good care to keep
out of our way until the fatal January 18, 1878.

There was no jail in Kimble County, so with a detachment of rangers I took Dell Dublin and our other
prisoners to the Llano County lockup.

Shortly afterward Reynolds selected Sergeant Mc-
Gee, Tom Gillespie, Dick Harrison, and Tim McCarthy
and made a scout into Menard County. He also had
with him his negro cook, George, to drive his light
wagon. On the return toward Bear Creek the scout
camped for the night at Fort McKavett. At that time
each frontier post had its chihuahua or scab town, a little
settlement with gambling halls, saloons, etc., to catch
the soldiers' dollars. At Fort McKavett were many
discharged soldiers, some of them negroes from the
Tenth Cavalry. These blacks had associated with white
gamblers and lewd women until they thought themselves the equals of white men, and became mean and
overbearing.

On this particular night these negro ex-soldiers gave a
dance in scab town, and our negro, George, wanted to go.

Six Years with the Texas Rangers

He was a light mulatto, almost white, but well thought of by all the boys in the company. He obtained Lieutenant Reynolds' permission to attend the dance, and borrowed Tim McCarthy's pistol to carry to it. When George arrived at the dance hall the ex-soldiers did not like his appearance, as he was allied with the rangers, whom they despised. They jumped on George, took his pistol, and kicked him out of the place. The boys were all in bed when George returned and told McCarthy that the negroes at the dance hall had taken his pistol from him.

Lieutenant Reynolds was sleeping near by and heard what George said. He raised up on his elbow and ordered Sergeant McGee to go with McCarthy and George and get the pistol. The negroes saw McGee coming and, closing the door, defied him to enter the dance hall.

McGee was cool and careful. He advised the negroes to return the pistol, but they refused, saying they would kill the first white-livered —— who attempted to enter the house. The sergeant then stationed himself at the front door, ordered McCarthy to guard the back entrance of the place, and sent George for the lieutenant. Reynolds hurried to the scene, taking with him Tom Gillespie and Dick Harrison. He knocked on the door and told the blacks he was the commander of the rangers and demanded their surrender. They replied with an oath that they would not do so. Reynolds then ordered the house cleared of women and gave the negroes five minutes in which to surrender.

Up to this time the women had been quiet, but they now began to scream. This probably demoralized the

Service with Reynolds, the Intrepid

men. One of them poked McCarthy's pistol, muzzle foremost, out of a window.

"Here, come get your damned pistol," he said.

McCarthy, a new man in the service, stepped up and grasped it. The instant the negro felt the touch of McCarthy's hand on the weapon he pulled the trigger. The ball pierced McCarthy's body just above the heart, giving him a mortal wound.

At the crack of the pistol the rangers opened fire through the doors and windows on the negroes within the house. Reynolds and his men then charged the place, and when the smoke of battle cleared they found four dead men and a little girl who had been killed by accident. Only one black escaped. He was hidden under a bed, and as the rangers came in, made a dash to safety under cover of darkness. McCarthy died the following day and was buried near old Fort McKavett. Negro George fought like a tiger and won the boys' praise.

A few days afterward the sheriff of Tom Green County, following the trail of a bunch of stolen cattle from San Angelo, came into our camp. Lieutenant Reynolds sent Sergeant Nevill and a scout of rangers with the sheriff. The trail led over to the South Llano, where the cattle were recovered. While scouting around the herd, Sergeant Nevill discovered a man riding down the trail toward him. He and his men secreted themselves and awaited the stranger's approach. It was getting quite dark, and when the newcomer had ridden almost over the concealed rangers without noticing their presence they rose up, presented their guns, and ordered him to halt.

"Yes—like hell!" he exclaimed, and, turning his horse, dived into a cedar brake. A shower of bullets followed, but failed to strike the fugitive. It was the notorious Dick Dublin with a $700 reward on his head.

Sergeant Nevill returned to camp with about fifty head of cattle on which the brand had been defaced with a hot iron, but he had let the most notorious criminal in the county escape. Lieutenant Reynolds was disappointed at this, and said he did not understand how four crack rangers could let a man ride right over them and then get away. He declared his negro cook could have killed Dublin had he been in their place. This mortified the boys a great deal.

The latter part of December, 1877, Lieutenant Reynolds sent a scout out on Little Saline, Menard County. On Christmas Day this detail had a running fight with four men. John Collins, the man who stole a yoke of oxen at Fredericksburg and drove them up to within two miles of our camp, was captured, as was also John Gray, wanted for murder in one of the eastern counties. Jim Pope Mason, charged with the murder of Rance Moore, was in this skirmish, but escaped.

One cold morning about the middle of January Corporal Gillett, with Privates John and Will Banister, Tom Gillespie, Dave Ligon, and Ben Carter, was ordered on a five days' scout. We saddled our horses and packed two mules. When all was ready I walked over to Lieutenant Reynolds. He was sitting on a camp stool before his tent and seemed in deep study. I saluted and asked for orders.

"Well, Corporal," he said, after a moment's hesitation, "it is a scout after Dick Dublin again. That man seems to be a regular Jonah to this company. He lives only ten miles from here and I have been awfully disappointed at not being able to effect his capture. It is a

Mounted Rangers in Readiness for a Scout. From a photograph of Captain Hughes's Company taken in the middle nineties. Three of these men were later killed in action.

Service with Reynolds, the Intrepid

reflection on all of Company E. There is one thing sure, if I can't capture him I will make life miserable for him. I will keep a scout in the field after him constantly."

I then asked if he had any instructions as to the route I should travel.

"No, no," he replied. "I rely too much on your judgment to hamper you with orders. After you are once out of sight of camp you know these mountains and trails better than I do. Just go and do your best. If you come in contact with him don't let him get away."

After riding half a mile from camp the boys began inquiring where we were going and who we were after. I told them Dick Dublin. We quit the road and traveled south from our camp over to the head of Pack Saddle Creek. Here we turned down the creek and rounded up the Potter ranch, but no one was at home, so we passed on into the cedar brake without having been seen.

On the extreme headwaters of South Llano River some cattlemen had built a large stock pen and were using it to confine wild cattle. This was far out beyond any settlement and probably fifty or sixty miles from our camp. I thought it possible that Dick Dublin might be hanging around the place, so we traveled through the woods most of the way to it. Here I found that the cattlemen had moved.

The scout had now been out two days, so we began our return journey. We traveled probably twenty-five miles on the third day. On the fourth day I timed myself to reach the Potter ranch about night. Old man Potter, a friend and neighbor of Dublin's, lived here with two grown sons. It was known that Dublin frequented the place, and I hoped to catch him here unawares. About sundown we were within a mile of the ranch. Here we unsaddled our horses and prepared to round up the house. If we met with no success we were to camp there for the night. I left John Banister and Ligon to guard camp while Gillespie, Will Banister, and Ben Carter, with myself, approached the ranch on foot. If I found no one there I intended to return to our camp unseen and round up the ranch again the following morning.

We had not traveled far before we discovered a man riding slowly down the trail to the Potter ranch. We remained hidden and were able to approach within fifty yards of the house without being seen. We now halted in the bed of a creek, squatting down in the shallow water, for a short consultation. The one-room cabin had only a single door, and before it was a small wagon. The Potters cooked out-of-doors between the house and the wagon. We could see a horse tied to the south side of the vehicle, but could not see the camp-fire for the wagon and the horse. To our right, and about twenty-five steps away, old man Potter and one of his sons were unloading some hogs from a wagon into a pen.

We knew the moment we left the creek bed we would be in full view of the Potters and the ranch house. We decided, then, that we would advance on the house as fast as we could run and so be in good position to capture the man who had ridden into the camp. We rose from the creek running. Old man Potter discovered us as we came into view and yelled, "Run, Dick, run! Here come the rangers!"

We then knew the man we wanted was at the camp. We were so close upon Dublin that he had no time to mount his horse or get his gun, so he made a run for the brush. I was within twenty-five yards of him when he came from behind the wagon, running as fast as a big man could. I ordered him to halt and surrender, but he had heard that call too many times and kept going. Holding my Winchester carbine in my right hand I fired a shot directly at him as I ran. In a moment he was out of sight.

I hurried to the place where he was last seen and spied him running up a little ravine. I stopped, drew a bead on him, and again ordered him to halt. As he ran, Dublin threw his hand back under his coat as though he were attempting to draw a pistol. I fired. My bullet struck the fugitive in the small of the back just over the right hip bone and passed out near his left collar bone. It killed him instantly. He was bending over as he ran, and this caused the unusual course of my ball.

The boys, whom I had outrun, now joined me, and Carter fired two shots at Dublin after he was down. I ordered him to desist as the man was dead. I examined the body to make sure it was Dublin, for I knew him intimately, as I had cow-hunted with him before I became a ranger. We found him unarmed, but he had a belt of cartridges around his waist. He was so completely surprised by our sudden appearance he could do nothing but run. The $700 reward on him could never be collected, as it was offered for his arrest and conviction. Dublin's brothers, Role and Dell, swore vengeance against me and the Banister boys, but nothing ever came of the oath.

In the month of February, 1878, Lieutenant Reynolds started to Austin with five prisoners we had captured in Kimble and Menard counties. They were chained together in pairs, John Stephens, the odd man, being shackled by himself. As guard for these prisoners

Reynolds had detailed Will and John Banister, Dave Ligon, Ben Carter, Dick Ware, and myself.

On the Junction City and Mason road, some ten miles east of our camp, was the small ranch of Starke Reynolds, a fugitive from justice, charged with horse-stealing and assault to kill. Company E had scouted for him in Kimble County and had rounded up his ranch many times. We knew he was in the county, but he always managed to escape us. As we passed this ranch, Lieutenant Reynolds and Privates Ware, Carter, Ligon, and myself were marching in front, with a four-mule wagon following us, in which were the chained prisoners. Behind it came the Banisters, who were on guard that day and detailed to keep a constant watch on the captive outlaws.

We passed the Starke Reynolds home about ten o'clock in the morning, and Lieutenant Reynolds remarked that it was hardly worth while to round up the house as he had done so many times in the past without result, but that he would surely like to capture the fellow. We had not ridden more than half a mile beyond the ranch when we came face to face with Starke himself. He was a small man and riding an exceedingly good brown pony. We were about four hundred yards apart and discovered each other at the same instant. The outlaw was carrying a small sack of flour in front of him. He immediately threw this down, turned his horse quickly, and made a lightning dash for the Llano bottoms, some three miles away.

At that point the Junction City and Mason road winds along a range of high mountains with the country sloping downward to the Llano River. This grade was studded with scrubby live oak and mesquite brush

Service with Reynolds, the Intrepid

not thick enough to hide a man but sufficiently dense to
retard somewhat his flight through it. We gave chase
at once and for a mile and a half it was the fastest race
I ever saw the rangers run. We were closely bunched
the entire distance, with Lieutenant Reynolds, who was
riding a fast race horse, always slightly in the lead. He
finally got close enough to the fugitive to demand his
surrender. Starke only waved his gun defiantly and re-
doubled his speed. Lieutenant Reynolds then drew his
six-shooter and began firing at the outlaw. After empty-
ing this he began using his Winchester.

The Llano bottoms were now looming up in front of
us. The race had been fast enough to run every horse
into a big limber, and Carter, Ware, and Ligon now
dropped out. Up to this time I had contented myself
with trying to keep up with Lieutenant Reynolds, for
it is always easier to follow a man through the brush
than to run in the lead. I had a good grip on my bridle
reins and was trying to steady my pony as best I could.
I now saw that the outlaw was beginning to gain on us.
I ran up beside the lieutenant and said: "He is getting
away from us. May I go after him?"

Lieutenant Reynolds turned to me with the wildest
look on his face I have ever seen. His hat was gone, his
face was badly scratched by the brush, and the blood was
running down over his white shirt bosom.

"Yes, God damn him! Stop him or kill him!"

I changed the bridle reins to my left hand, drew my
gun with my right and, digging my spurs deep into my
pony's side, I was out of sight of the lieutenant in three
hundred yards. The fugitive saw that I was alone and
that I was going to overhaul him. He suddenly brought

his pony to a standstill, jumped down, took shelter behind the animal, and drew a bead on me with his gun.

"God damn you, stop, or I'll kill you!" he cried.

I tried to obey his order, but my pony was running down hill and ran straight at him for twenty-five yards more before I could stop. I jumped down from my horse and made ready to fight, but Starke broke for a thicket on foot. As soon as he ran out from behind his pony I fired at him. The bullet must have come rather close to him, for he turned quickly and took shelter behind his mount again. As he peeped over his saddle at me I attempted to draw a bead on his head, but I was tired, nervous, and unsteady. Before I could shoot, Dave Ligon galloped up to the outlaw and ordered him to surrender and drop his gun, which Starke did at once. The boys had heard me shoot and in five minutes were all on the scene.

The captive was searched and ordered to remount his pony. With one of the boys leading it, we started back to the wagon, nearly three miles away. As soon as the outlaw was a prisoner and knew he would not be harmed no matter what he said, he began a tirade against the rangers. He declared the whole battalion was a set of damned murderers, especially Company E, and said it was curbstone talk in Menard, Mason, and Kimble counties that Lieutenant Reynolds' men would kill a man and then yell for him to throw up his hands. He kept up this running talk until he exhausted Lieutenant Reynolds' patience. The latter then ordered Starke to shut up, and declared the speaker was a damned liar, for Company E never killed a man without first giving him a chance to surrender. Lieutenant Reynolds then said that with the last old brier-breaker captured he had accomplished the task set him and was now ready to go elsewhere.

As we rode along, one of the boys remarked that my pony was limping badly.

"I wish his leg would come right off up to his shoulder," declared Starke in disgust. "If it hadn't been for him I would have made it to the bottoms and escaped."

On approaching the wagon the prisoner Stephens, a man of some intelligence and humor, stood up and called out to Starke, "By God, old man, they got you! They rode too many corn-fed horses and carried too many guns for you. I don't know who you are, but I'm sorry for you. While they were chasing you I got down on my knees here in this wagon and with my face turned up to the skies I prayed to the Almighty God that you might get away."

Starke was chained to this good-natured liar, and now, for the first time, seemed to realize his condition. He asked Lieutenant Reynolds to send word to his family that he had been captured. The lieutenant thereupon sent one of the boys to Starke's home to tell Mrs. Reynolds that the rangers would camp on Red Creek for dinner, and if she wished to see her husband we would be there probably two hours.

Presently Starke's old gray-haired father came to our midday camp. When he saw his son chained, he burst out crying, saying: "My son, it is not my fault that you are in this condition. I did my best to give you good advice and tried to raise you right."

After dinner we resumed our march toward Austin. Starke Reynolds was finally turned over to the sheriff of Tarrant County. He was admitted to bail and gave bond, but before he came to trial he was waylaid and killed, supposedly by relatives of the man he had previously attempted to murder.

Early in the spring of 1878 a ranchman living five miles above our camp saw a bunch of Indians on Bear Creek, Kimble County, and at once reported to Lieutenant Reynolds. The redskins had been seen late in the evening, and by the time a scout could be started after them it was almost night. The lieutenant, however, followed the trail until it entered a cedar brake. It was then too dark to work farther, so the scout returned to camp to make arrangements to resume the trail the following morning. On the march back to camp the rangers picked up a paint pony with an arrow sticking in its hip. The Indians had probably tried to catch the horse and, failing to do so, had shot it, as was their custom.

Just after dark a runner from Junction City came in and reported that a bunch of redskins had been seen near the town stealing horses. It was a beautiful moonlight night and a close watch was kept on our horses. At midnight John Banister, an alert man on guard, noticed that one of our pack-mules hitched at the end of our picket line was pulling back on its rope and looking over a brush fence that enclosed the camp. With Winchester in hand Banister passed through a gate and walked slowly down the fence and into some small underbrush near the mule.

Suddenly a man rose to his feet and fired on Banister at a distance of not more than ten steps, then broke and ran. Banister at once opened fire on the Indian. The very first report of a gun brought every man in camp out of his bed. We could see the flashes of Banister's gun and went to his aid in our night clothes and bare-

Captain D. W. Roberts.

Lieutenant N. O. Reynolds.

Captain Neal Coldwell.

Captain George W. Baylor.

Four Great Ranger Leaders

footed. I ran down by the picket line of horses and jumped the fence where the mule had seen the redskin. By moonlight I could glimpse the Indian running down the river bank. I shot at him several times as he ran, but without effect. Some two hundred yards below our camp was a ford on the Llano and the fugitive was making for it.

By the time he reached the crossing and plunged into the river, eight or nine of the rangers, who had followed Banister on the high ground, were in a position to shell the swimmer as he crossed. Probably a hundred shots were fired at him, but he finally disappeared in the brush on the south side of the river. A later inspection of the place where he had crossed showed the timber cut all to pieces but, strange to say, not a shot hit him, as far as we ever knew. We found a blanket where the savage had risen and shot at Banister and, measuring the ground, found that the ranger was but twelve short steps from the Indian when fired upon. It was a miracle that he was not killed; the bullet, a .45 caliber, buried itself in some sacks of corn in a tent just back of him.

The next morning we found where ten or twelve Indians had waited under some large pecan trees while this scout slipped up to our camp to investigate and steal a horse. The trees were about four hundred yards from camp and on the opposite side of the river. Some of the rangers jokingly said those old braves must have thought their scout had stirred up hell at the ranger camp.

On account of the range cattle and horses along the Llano River, Lieutenant Reynolds lost some eight or ten hours the next morning before picking up the Indian trail. This gave the redskins ten or twelve hours' start, as they were at our camp just at midnight. The trail passed west between the North and South Llano rivers and followed a rough mountain country, which made pursuit difficult and slow. We followed the savages five or six days and finally abandoned the trail near the head of Devils River after a heavy rain.

While we had been active in rounding up the numerous outlaws and cattle thieves who infested Kimble County, we had not been able to clear up the mystery of the Peg Leg stage robbers, which had long baffled the best detectives, sheriffs, and rangers. Peg Leg was a small stage station on the San Saba in the midst of a rough and very mountainous country. Here the stage was repeatedly held up, and as repeatedly the robbers escaped. The scene of the holdup was many times examined and parties made determined efforts to trail the bandits, but always without success, for the trail was quickly lost in the rough mountains. One of the features that proved particularly puzzling was the constant recurrence of an exceedingly small footprint at each robbery. These marks were so small as to convince many observers that a woman from Fort McKavett or Fort Concho was operating with the bandit gang. Naturally, the rangers were anxious to round up this group of outlaws and put a stop to their depredations.

In May, 1878, Sergeant Nevill made a scout on the South Llano and captured Bill Allison, a son-in-law of old Jimmie Dublin, father of the bandit, Dick Dublin. Allison was wanted on several charges of cattle theft, and was taken to Austin for safekeeping. After remaining in the Travis County jail for nearly a year without being able to give bond, he became discouraged. He believed his brothers-in-law, the Dublins, were not

Service with Reynolds, the Intrepid

aiding him to get bond, and became bitter and resentful toward them. This antagonism finally led to the unveiling of the Peg Leg mystery.

In the spring of 1879 Dick Ware and I took some prisoners to the Austin jail. Allison saw us and called to me. He and I had been cowboys together long before I became a ranger.

"Jim," said Allison, "you know I have been cooped up here in this jail for nearly a year. People who ought to be my friends have evidently abandoned me and I am not going to stand it any longer. I can put the Peg Leg stage robbers behind the bars, and I am going to do it."

Ware, who was something of a diplomat, said: "Hold on, Bill. If you have anything to confess we will get an order from the sheriff to take you to see General Jones so you can talk to him."

The general at once wrote a note to Dennis Corwin, sheriff of Travis County, asking that he let Allison accompany us to his office. The sheriff turned his prisoner over to us and we took him to General Jones, who had a private interview with him for over an hour. What Allison confessed we did not know, but we returned him to the jail.

General Jones moved quickly. He at once sent orders to Captain D. W. Roberts of Company D, who was then stationed in Menard County, which joins Kimble County on the north, to send a scout of rangers into Kimble County and try to capture the Dublins, Mack Potter, and Rube Boyce.

Arriving in Kimble County, the detail arrested Role and Dell Dublin, Mack Potter, and Rube Boyce. In the running fight that resulted in their capture Role re-

103

ceived a bad wound in the hip. The two Dublin brothers and Mack Potter when arraigned in federal court pleaded guilty to stage robbery and were sentenced to fifteen years at hard labor. During their trial the mystery of the Peg Leg robberies was finally cleared up. The Dublin boys were the guiding spirits in the holdups and worked with great cleverness. Old man Jimmie Dublin's ranch on the South Llano was their headquarters. From the ranch to Peg Leg Station on the San Saba it was about sixty miles across a rough, mountainous country. As there were no wire fences in those days the robbers would ride over to the station, rob the stage, and in one night's ride regain their home. Traveling at night, they were never observed. Dick Dublin, whose death while resisting capture has already been described, was the leader of the bandit gang. Even the mystery of the tiny footprints was disclosed: they were made by Mack Potter, who had an unusually small foot for a man.

While Rube Boyce was confined in the Travis County jail he made one of the most sensational escapes in the criminal annals of Texas. Mrs. Boyce called at the prison with a suit of clean underclothes for her husband. The basket in which she carried them was examined and she was admitted into the cell of her husband. However, she had hidden a big .45 Colt's revolver about her person and smuggled it in. Rube changed his underwear, put the soiled garments in the basket, and hid the pistol under them.

At the end of her visit Mrs. Boyce started out and Rube accompanied her down the corridor to the door. Albert Nichols, the jailer, opened the door with his left hand to let the woman pass out, at the same time holding his pistol in his right hand. As the door swung open, Rube reached into the basket he was carrying for his wife, whipped out the hidden pistol, thrust it into the jailer's face, and ordered him to drop his .45 and step within the jail. Realizing that a second's hesitation would mean his death, Nichols complied and was locked in by the outlaw.

Boyce then ran out of the back yard of the jail, mounted a pony that had been hitched there for him, and galloped out of Austin, firing his pistol as he ran. He made a complete get-away. Three or four years later he was arrested at Socorro, New Mexico, and returned to Austin. At his trial for participation in the Peg Leg stage robberies he was acquitted, and perhaps justly so, for Bill Allison declared to me that Dick Dublin with his brothers, Dell and Role, and Mack Potter were the real robbers.

The arrest and conviction of the Dublins, together with the other men Lieutenant Reynolds had captured or killed, completely cleaned out the stage robbers, cattle and horse thieves, and murderers who had made Kimble County their rendezvous. Today, this is one of the most prosperous and picturesque counties in the state. Its citizens are law-abiding and energetic. Junction City, the county seat, is a fine town of probably twenty-five hundred inhabitants.

Forty years ago, the time of which I write, there were no courthouses in Kimble County. The first district courts were held under the spreading boughs of a large oak tree. The rangers guarded the prisoners under another tree at a convenient distance from the judge and his attendants.

Late in the spring or early summer of 1878 at a

session of the County Court of San Saba County, Billy Brown was being prosecuted by County Attorney Brooks for a violation of the prohibition laws. Brown took offense at a remark of the prosecuting attorney and attempted to draw his six-shooter on him. T. J. T. Kendall, a law partner of Brooks, saw Brown's move and quickly whipping out his own pistol, killed Brown in the courtroom. Then, fearing a mob if captured, Kendall fortified himself in a second story of the courthouse and refused to surrender. He held the whole town at bay while his wife administered to his wants. Meantime, he sent a hurry call to the nearest rangers asking for protection against mob violence. Captain Arrington received the message and sent a detachment from Coleman to San Saba to preserve order.

General Jones was notified and ordered Lieutenant Reynolds at Junction City to march to San Saba with his company, take charge of Kendall, and relieve Captain Arrington's men. It was probably two weeks after the killing before Company E reached San Saba, but Mr. Kendall was still holding the fort in the upper story of the courthouse.

On the arrival of Reynolds' company, Kendall asked the court for a preliminary examination. When court convened, the prisoner waived examination and asked for transference to the Travis County jail at Austin. The court, realizing the feeling against him, ordered his removal thither.

When the time came to remove him a hack was driven up to the courthouse door, where a great crowd had assembled to see the prisoner. Jim Brown, sheriff of Lee County, and brother of Bill Brown, had taken his station, heavily armed, within ten feet of the door. Just be-

Service with Reynolds, the Intrepid

fore Mr. Kendall descended the courthouse steps Lieutenant Reynolds ordered the crowd to fall back fifty feet from the hack. All immediately obeyed with the exception of Jim Brown, who sat perfectly still on his horse. The lieutenant looked at Brown for a minute, then turned to his rangers and ordered them to draw their guns and move everyone fifty yards from the courthouse. Like a flash every ranger drew his gun, dismounted, and waved the crowd back.

Brown turned to Reynolds and said, "I am going to Austin with you."

"If you do, you will go in irons. Move back!"

Brown, who had killed several men, slowly turned his horse and rode away. He did not know the man with whom he was dealing. Lawyer Kendall was thereupon carried to Austin without incident. At his trial on the charge of murdering Brown he was acquitted.

When we reached Austin, Jim Brown met Lieutenant Reynolds on the street and apologized for the way he had acted at San Saba. He said he had fully intended to kill Kendall as he approached the hack, but the presence of so many rangers caused him to change his mind. Lieutenant Reynolds declared he was anticipating just such a move and had instructed his men to shoot Brown into doll rags at his first move.

Soon after this Lieutenant Reynolds moved Company E down on the San Saba to a beautiful pecan grove, an ideal summer camp, about two miles from the town of San Saba. From this point we scouted all over Llano, Lampasas, Burnet, and San Saba counties at our favorite pursuit of rounding up bad men. It was from this camp that we made our sensational ride to Round Rock after Sam Bass, the notorious train robber.

CHAPTER IX

SAM BASS AND HIS TRAIN ROBBER
GANG

SAM BASS was born in Indiana, on a farm near Mitchell, Lawrence County, July 21, 1851. He came to Texas while a youth and worked for W. F. (Dad) Egan, sheriff of Denton County, until he reached manhood. While still an exemplary and honest young man Bass came into possession of a race pony, a little sorrel mare. On Saturday evenings, when most of the neighborhood boys met in Denton, Bass raced his pony with much success. Mr. Egan soon noticed that Sam was beginning to neglect his work because of his pony and, knowing only too well what this would lead to, he advised Sam to sell his mare. Bass hesitated, for he loved the animal. Finally matters came to such a point that Mr. Egan told Sam he would have to get rid of the horse or give up his job. Thereupon Bass promptly quit, and this was probably the turning point in his life.

Bass left Denton County in the spring of 1877 and traveled to San Antonio. Here many cattlemen were gathered to arrange for the spring cattle-drive to the north. Joel Collins, who was planning to drive a herd from Uvalde County to Deadwood, Dakota, hired Bass as a cowboy. After six months on the trail the herd reached Deadwood and was sold and all the cowboys paid off by Mr. Collins.

At that period Deadwood was a great, wide-open mining town. Adventurers, gamblers, miners, and cattle-men all mingled together. Though Joel Collins had

bought his cattle on credit and owed the greater part of
the money he had received for them to his friends in
Texas, he gambled it all away. When he sobered up and
realized the money was gone he did not have the moral
courage to face his friends and creditors at home. He
became desperate, and with a band of his cowboys held
up and robbed several stagecoaches in the Black Hills.
These robberies brought Collins very little booty, but
they started Sam Bass on his criminal career.

In the fall of 1877 Collins, accompanied by Bass,
Jack Davis, Jim Berry, Bill Heffridge, and John
Underwood, better known as Old Dad, left Deadwood
and drifted down to Ogallala, Nebraska. Here he conceived, planned, and carried into execution one of the
boldest train robberies that had ever occurred in the
United States. When all was ready these six men,
heavily armed and masked, held up the Union Pacific
train at Big Springs, a small station a few miles beyond
Ogallala. The bandits entered the express car and
ordered the messenger to open the safe. The latter explained that the through safe had a time lock and could
only be opened at the end of the route. One of the robbers then began to beat the messenger over the head
with a six-shooter, declaring he would kill him if the
safe were not opened. Bass, always of a kindly nature,
pleaded with the man to desist, declaring he believed the
messenger was telling the truth. Just as the robbers were
preparing to leave the car without a cent, one of them
noticed three stout little boxes piled near the big safe.
The curious bandit seized a coal pick and knocked off
the lid of the top box. To his great joy and delight he
exposed $20,000 in shining gold coin! The three boxes

each held a similar amount, all in $20 gold pieces of the mintage of 1877.

After looting these boxes the robbers went through the train, and in a systematic manner robbed the passengers of about $5,000. Before daylight the bandits had hidden their booty and returned to Ogallala. They hung around town several days while railroad officials, United States marshals, and sheriffs' parties were scouring the country for the train robbers.

While in Ogallala, before and after the robbery, Collins and his men frequented a large general-merchandise store. In this store was a clerk by the name of Leech who had once been an express messenger on the Union Pacific and who was well acquainted with the officials of that company. Of course the great train robbery was the talk of the town. Leech conversed with Collins and his gang about the holdup, and the bandits declared they would help hunt the robbers if there was enough money in it.

The suspicions of Leech were aroused and he became convinced that Collins and his band were the real holdup men. However, he said nothing to anyone about this belief, but carefully watched them. Finally, Collins came to the store and, after buying clothing and provisions, told Leech that he and his companions were going back to Texas and would be up the trail the following spring with another herd of cattle. When Collins had been gone a day's travel, Leech hired a horse and followed him. He soon found the route the suspects were traveling, and on the second day he came upon them suddenly while they were stopping at a roadside farmhouse to have some bread cooked. Leech passed by without being noticed and secreted himself near the highway. In a short time Collins and his men passed on and Leech trailed them until they went into camp. When it was dark the amateur detective crept up to the bandits, but they had gone to sleep and he learned nothing.

The next day Leech resumed the trail. He watched the gang make their camp for the night and again crept up to within a few yards of them. The bandits had built a big fire and were laughing and talking. Soon they spread out a blanket, and to the onlooker's great astonishment brought out some money bags and emptied upon the blanket sixty thousand dollars in gold. From his concealed position Leech heard the robbers discuss the holdup. They declared they did not believe anyone had recognized or suspected them and decided it was now best for them to divide the money, separate in pairs, and go their way. The coin was stacked in six piles, and each man received $10,000 in $20 gold pieces. It was further decided that Collins and Bill Heffridge would travel back to San Antonio together; Sam Bass and Jack Davis were to go to Denton County, while Jim Berry and Old Dad were to return to the Berry home in Mexico, Missouri.

As soon as Leech had seen the money and heard the robbers' plans he slipped back to his horse, mounted, and rode day and night to reach Ogallala. He notified the railroad officials of what he had seen, and gave the names and descriptions of the bandits and their destinations. This information was sent broadcast over southern Nebraska, Kansas, Indian Territory, and Texas. In the fugitive list sent to each of the companies of rangers Sam Bass was thus described: "Twenty-five to twenty-six years old, 5 feet 7 inches high, black hair, dark brown eyes, brown moustache, large white teeth, shows them when talking; has very little to say."

A few days after the separation of the robbers, Joel Collins and Bill Heffridge rode into a small place in Kansas called Buffalo Station. They led a pack pony. Dismounting from their tired horses and leaving them standing in the shade of the store building, the two men entered the store and made several purchases. The railroad agent at the place noticed the strangers ride up. He had, of course, been advised to be on the lookout for the train robbers. He entered the store and in a little while engaged Collins in conversation. While talking, the robber pulled his handkerchief out of his coat pocket and exposed a letter with his name thereon. The agent was a shrewd man. He asked Collins if he had not driven a herd of cattle up the trail in the spring. Collins declared he had, and finally, in answer to a direct question, admitted that his name was Joel Collins.

Five or six hundred yards from Buffalo Station a lieutenant of the United States army had camped a troop of ten men that was scouting for the train robbers. As soon as Collins and Heffridge remounted and resumed their way the agent ran to the soldiers' camp, pointed out the bandits to the lieutenant, and declared, "There go two of the Union Pacific train robbers!"

The army officer mounted his men and pursued Collins and Heffridge. When he overtook the two men he told them their descriptions tallied with those of some train robbers he was scouting for, and declared they would have to go back to the station and be identified. Collins laughed at the idea, and said that he and his companion were cattlemen returning to their homes in Texas. They reluctantly turned and started back with the soldiers. After riding a few hundred yards the two robbers held a whispered conversation. Suddenly they pulled their pistols and attempted to stand off the lieutenant and his troop. The desperadoes were promptly shot and killed. On examining their pack the soldiers found tied up in the legs of a pair of overalls $20,000 in gold, 1877 mintage. Not a dollar of the stolen money had been used, and there was no doubt about the identity of the men.

Not long after the separation of the robbers in Nebraska, Jim Berry appeared at his home in Mexico, Missouri. At once he deposited quite a lot of money in the local bank and exchanged $3,000 in gold for currency, explaining his possession of the gold by saying he had sold a mine in the Black Hills. Three or four days later the sheriff of the county learned of Berry's deposits and called at the bank to see the new depositor's gold. His suspicion became a certainty when he found that Berry had deposited $20 gold pieces of 1877.

That night the sheriff with a posse rounded up Berry's house, but the suspect was not there. The home was well provisioned, and the posse found many articles of newly purchased clothing. Just after daylight, while searching about the place the sheriff heard a horse whinny in some timber near by. Upon investigating this he suddenly came upon Jim Berry sitting on a pallet. Berry discovered the officer at about the same time and attempted to escape by running. He was fired upon, one bullet striking him in the knee and badly shattering it. He was taken to his home and given the best of medical attention, but gangrene set in and he died in a few days. Most of his $10,000 was recovered. Old Dad evidently quit Berry somewhere en route, for he made good his escape with his ill-gotten gain and was never apprehended.

Sam Bass and Jack Davis, after the separation in Nebraska, sold their ponies and bought a light spring wagon and a pair of work horses. They placed their gold pieces in the bottom of the wagon, threw their bedding and clothes over it, and in this disguise traveled through Kansas and the Indian Territory to Denton County, Texas. During their trip through the Territory, Bass afterward said, they camped within one hundred yards of a detachment of cavalry. After supper they visited the soldiers' camp and chatted with them until bedtime. The soldiers said they were on the lookout for some train robbers who had held up the Union Pacific in Nebraska, never dreaming for a moment that they were conversing with two of them. The men also mentioned that two of the robbers had been reported killed in Kansas.

This rumor put Bass and Davis on their guard, and on reaching Denton County they hid in the elm bottoms until Bass could interview some of his friends. On meeting them he learned that the name and description of every one of the train robbers was in the possession of the law officers; that Collins, Heffridge, and Berry had been killed; and that every sheriff in northern Texas was on the watch for Davis and himself. Davis at once begged Bass to go with him to South America, but Bass refused, so Davis bade Sam good-bye and set out alone. He was never captured. On his deathbed Bass declared he had once received a letter from Jack Davis written from New Orleans, asking Bass to come there and go into the business of buying hides.

Bass had left Denton County early in the spring an

honest, sincere, and clean young man. By falling in with evil associates he had become within a few months one of the most daring outlaws and train robbers of his time. Before he had committed any crime in the state the officers of northern Texas made repeated efforts to capture him for the big reward offered by the Union Pacific and the express company, but owing to the nature of the country around Denton and the friends Bass had as long as his gold lasted, they met with no success.

Bass's money soon attracted several desperate and daring men to him. Henry Underwood, a younger brother of Old Dad, Arkansas Johnson, Jim Murphy, Frank Jackson, Pipes, Herndon, Bill Collins, the last named a cousin of Joel Collins, and two or three others joined him in the elm bottoms. Naturally Bass was selected as leader of the gang. It was not long before the outlaw chief planned and executed his first train robbery in Texas, at Eagle Ford, a small station on the Texas Pacific Railroad, a few miles out of Dallas. In quick succession the bandits held up two or three other trains, the last being at Mesquite Station, ten or twelve miles east of Dallas. From this robbery they secured about $3,000. They met with opposition here, for the conductor, though armed with only a small pistol, bravely fought the robbers and seriously wounded one of them.

The whole state was now aroused by the repeated train holdups. General Jones hurried to Dallas and Denton to look over the situation and, strange to say, he arranged to organize a company of rangers at Dallas. Captain June Peak, a very able officer, was given the command. No matter how brave a company of recruits may be, it takes time and training to get results from

them, and when this raw company was thrown into the
field against Bass and his gang the bandit leader played
with it as a child plays with toys. Counting the thirty
rangers and the different sheriffs' parties, there were
probably one hundred men in pursuit of the Bass gang.

Sam played hide-and-seek with them all and, it is said,
never ranged any farther west than Stephens County
or farther north than Wise. He was generally in Dallas,
Denton, or Tarrant County. He would frequently visit
Fort Worth or Dallas at night, ride up with his men
to some outside saloon, get drinks all around, and then
vamoose. Finally, in a fight at Salt Creek, Wise County,
Captain June Peak and his rangers killed Arkansas
Johnson, Bass's most trusted lieutenant. About the
same time as this battle the rangers captured Pipes,
Herndon, and Jim Murphy and drove Bass and his
two remaining companions out of northern Texas.

After the fight on Salt Creek only Sam Bass, Sebe
Barnes, and Frank Jackson were left of the once formidable gang. These men had gained nothing from their
three train robberies in northern Texas, and were so hard
pressed by the officers of the law on all sides that Bass
reluctantly decided to leave the country and try to make
his way to Mexico. Through some pretended friends
of Bass General Jones learned of the contemplated
move. He, with Captain Peak and other officers, approached Jim Murphy, one of Bass's gang captured
about the time of the Salt Creek fight, who was awaiting trial by the federal authorities for train robbery,
and promised they would secure his release if he would
betray Bass. Murphy hesitated and said his former
chief had been kind to his family, had given them money
and provisions, and that it would be ungrateful to be-

tray his friend. The general declared he understood
Murphy's position fully, but Bass was an outlaw, a pest
to the country, who was preparing to leave the state and
so could no longer help him. General Jones warned
Murphy that the evidence against him was overwhelm-
ing and was certain to send him to federal prison—
probably for life—and exhorted him to remember his
wife and children. Murphy finally yielded and agreed
to betray Bass and his gang at the first opportunity.

According to the plan agreed upon, Murphy was to
give bond and when the federal court convened at
Tyler, Texas, a few weeks later he was not to show up.
It would then be published all over the country that
Murphy had skipped bond and rejoined Bass. This was
carried out to the letter. Murphy joined Bass in the elm
bottoms of Denton County and agreed to rob a train or
bank and get out of the country. Some of Bass's friends,
suspicious of Murphy's actions, wrote Sam that he was
playing a double game and advised him to kill the traitor at once. Bass immediately confronted Murphy with
these reports and reminded him how freely he had
handed out his gold to Murphy's family. Bass declared
he had never advised or solicited Jim to join him, and
said it was a low-down, mean, and ungrateful trick to
betray him. He told Murphy plainly if he had anything
to say to say it quickly. Barnes agreed with his chief
and urged Murphy's death.

The plotter denied any intention of betraying Bass
and offered to take the lead in any robbery he should
plan and be the first to enter the express car or climb
over the bank railing. Bass was mad and so was Barnes.
They determined to kill the liar at once. Frank Jackson
had taken no part in the conversation, but he now de-

clared he had known Murphy since he was a little boy (they were, in fact, cousins), and he was sure Murphy was sincere and meant to stand by them through thick and thin. Bass was not satisfied, and insisted that Murphy be killed then and there. Jackson finally told Bass and Barnes that they could not kill Murphy without first killing him. Although the youngest of the party—he was only twenty-two years old—Jackson had great influence over his chief. He was brave and daring, and Bass at that time could not very well get along without him, so his counsel prevailed and Murphy was spared. The bandits then determined to quit the country. Their plan was to rob a small bank somewhere en route to Mexico and thus secure the funds needed to facilitate their escape, for they were all broke.

Bass, Sebe Barnes, Frank Jackson, and Jim Murphy left Denton County early in July, 1878. With his usual boldness, Bass, after he had passed Dallas County, made no attempt at concealment, but traveled the public highway in broad daylight. Bass and Barnes were still suspicious of Murphy, and never let him out of their sight, though they refused to talk to him or to associate with him in any way. When Bass reached Waco the party camped on the outskirts of the town and remained there two or three days. They visited the town each day, looked over the situation, and in one bank saw much gold and currency. Jackson was enthusiastic and wanted to rob it at once. Bass, being more careful and experienced, thought it too hazardous an undertaking, for the run through crowded streets to the outskirts of the city was too far, and so vetoed the attempt.

While in Waco the gang stepped into a saloon to get a drink. Bass laid a $20 gold piece on the bar and re-

Sam Bass and His Train Robber Gang

marked, "There goes the last twenty of the Union Pacific money, and damned little good it has done me." On leaving Waco the robbers stole a fine mare from a farmer named Billy Mounds and traveled the main road to Belton. They were now out of money and planned to rob the bank at Round Rock, Williamson County.

General Jones was now getting anxious over the gang. Not a word had been heard from Jim Murphy since he had rejoined the band, for he had been so closely watched that he had had no opportunity to communicate with the authorities, and it seemed as if he would be forced to participate in the next robbery in spite of himself.

At Belton, Sam sold an extra pony his party had after stealing the mare at Waco. The purchaser demanded a bill of sale, as the vendors were strangers in the country. While Bass and Barnes were in a store writing out the required document, Murphy seized the opportunity to write a short note to General Jones, saying, "We are on our way to Round Rock to rob the bank. For God's sake be there to prevent it." As the postoffice adjoined the store, the traitor succeeded in mailing his letter of betrayal a moment before Bass came out on the street again. The gang continued their way to Round Rock and camped near the old town, which is situated about one mile north of new Round Rock. The bandits concluded to rest and feed their horses for three or four days before attempting their robbery. This delay was providential, for it gave General Jones time to assemble his rangers to repel the attack.

After Major Jones was made adjutant general of Texas he caused a small detachment of four or five rangers to camp on the Capitol grounds at Austin. He drew his units from different companies along the line. Each unit would be detailed to camp in Austin, and about every six weeks or two months the detail would be relieved by a squad from another company. It will readily be seen that this was a wise policy, as the detail was always on hand and could be sent in any direction by rail or on horseback at short notice. Besides, General Jones was devoted to his rangers and liked to have them around where he could see them daily. At the time of which I write four men from Company E—Corporal Vernon Wilson and Privates Dick Ware, Chris Connor, and Geo. Harold—were camped at Austin. The corporal, who was a nephew of Governor Coke and a well-educated man, helped General Jones as a clerk in his office, but was in charge of the squad on the Capitol grounds, slept in camp, and had his meals with them.

When General Jones received Murphy's letter he was astonished at Bass's audacity in approaching within fifteen or twenty miles of the state capital, the very headquarters of the Frontier Battalion, to rob a bank. The letter was written at Belton, Texas, and received at the adjutant general's office on the last mail in the afternoon. The company of rangers nearest Round Rock was Lieutenant Reynolds' Company E, stationed at San Saba, one hundred and fifteen miles distant. There was no telegraph to San Saba then. General Jones reflected a few minutes after receipt of the letter and then arranged his plan rapidly.

He turned to Corporal Wilson and told him that Sam Bass and his gang were, or soon would be, at Round Rock, to rob the bank there.

"I want you to leave at once to carry an order to

Sam Bass and His Train Robber Gang

Lieutenant Reynolds. It is sixty-five miles to Lampasas and you can make that place early enough in the morning to catch the Lampasas and San Saba stage. You must make that stage at all hazards. Save neither yourself nor your horse, but get these orders to Lieutenant Reynolds as quickly as possible," he ordered.

Corporal Wilson hurried to the livery stable, saddled his horse, and got away from Austin on his wild ride just at nightfall. His horse was fresh and fat and in no condition to make such a run. However, Wilson reached Lampasas at daylight next morning and made the outgoing stage to San Saba, but killed his gallant little gray horse in doing it. From Lampasas to San Saba was fifty miles, and it took the stage, which was a small, two-horse outfit, all day to make the trip. As soon as he landed in town Wilson hired a horse and galloped three miles down to Lieutenant Reynolds' camp and delivered his orders.

After dispatching Corporal Wilson to Lieutenant Reynolds, General Jones hurried over to the ranger camp on the Capitol grounds and ordered the three rangers, Ware, Connor, and Harold, to proceed to Round Rock, put their horses in Highsmith's livery stable, and keep themselves concealed until he himself could reach them by train next morning. The following morning General Jones went to Round Rock, accompanied by Morris Moore, an ex-ranger now serving as deputy sheriff of Travis County. On reaching his destination the general called on Deputy Sheriff Grimes of Williamson County and told him Bass was expected in town to rob the bank, and that a scout of rangers would be in town as soon as possible. Jones advised Grimes to keep a sharp lookout for strangers, but on no account to attempt an arrest until the rangers could arrive.

I well remember the hot July evening when Corporal Wilson arrived in our camp with his orders. The company had just had supper, and the horses had been fed and tied up for the night. We knew the sudden appearance of the corporal meant something of unusual importance. Soon Sergeant Nevill came hurrying to us with orders to detail a party for an immediate scout. Lieutenant Reynolds' orders had been brief, but to the point: "Bass is at Round Rock. We must be there as early as possible tomorrow. Make a detail of eight men and select those that have the horses best able to make a fast run. And you, with them, report to me here at my tent ready to ride in thirty minutes."

First Sergeant C. L. Nevill, Second Sergeant Henry McGee, Second Corporal J. B. Gillett, Privates Abe Anglin, Dave Ligon, Bill Derrick, and John R. and W. L. Banister were selected for the detail. Lieutenant Reynolds ordered two of our best little pack-mules hitched to a light spring hack, for he had been sick and was not in condition to make the journey horseback. In thirty minutes from the time Corporal Wilson reached camp we were mounted, armed, and ready to go. Lieutenant Reynolds took his seat in the hack, threw some blankets in, and Corporal Wilson, who had not had a minute's sleep for over thirty-six hours, lay down to get a little rest as we moved along. We left our camp on the San Saba River just at sunset and traveled in a fast trot and sometimes in a lope the entire night.

Our old friend and comrade, Jack Martin, then in the mercantile business at the little town of Senterfitt, heard us pass by in the night, and next morning said to

Sam Bass and His Train Robber Gang

some of his customers that hell was to pay somewhere as the rangers had passed his store during the night on a dead run.

The first rays of the rising sun shone on us at the crossing of North Gabriel, fifteen miles south of Lampasas. We had ridden sixty-five miles that short summer night—we had forty-five miles yet to go before reaching Round Rock. We halted on the Gabriel for a breakfast of bread, broiled bacon, and black coffee. The horses had a bundle of oats each. Lieutenant Reynolds held his watch on us and it took us just thirty minutes to breakfast and be off again. We were now facing a hot July sun and our horses were beginning to show the effects of the hard ride of the night before and slowed down perceptibly. We did not halt again until we reached the vicinity of old Round Rock between one and two o'clock in the afternoon of Friday, July nineteenth. The lieutenant camped us on the banks of Brushy Creek and drove into new Round Rock to report his arrival to General Jones.

Bass had decided to rob the bank on Saturday, the twentieth. After his gang had eaten dinner in camp Friday evening they saddled their ponies and started over to town to take a last look at the bank and select a route to follow in leaving the place after the robbery. As they left camp Jim Murphy, knowing that the bandits might be set upon at any time, suggested that he stop at May's store in old Round Rock and get a bushel of corn, as they were out of feed for their horses. Bass, Barnes, and Jackson rode on into town, hitched their horses in an alley just back of the bank, passed that building, and made a mental note of its situation. They then went up the main street of the town and entered

Copprel's store to buy some tobacco. As the three bandits passed into the store, Deputy Sheriff Moore, who was standing on the sidewalk with Deputy Sheriff Grimes, said he thought one of the newcomers had a pistol.

"I will go in and see," replied Grimes.

"I believe you have a pistol," remarked Grimes, approaching Bass and trying to search him.

"Yes, of course I have a pistol," said Bass. At the words the robbers pulled their guns and killed Grimes as he backed away to the door. He fell dead on the sidewalk. They then turned on Moore and shot him through the lungs as he attempted to draw his weapon.

At the crack of the first pistol Dick Ware, who was seated in a barber shop only a few steps away waiting his turn for a shave, rushed into the street and encountered the three bandits just as they were leaving the store. Seeing Ware rapidly advancing on them, Bass and his men fired on him at close range, one of their bullets striking a hitching post within six inches of his head and knocking splinters into his face. This assault never halted Ware for an instant. He was as brave as courage itself and never hesitated to take the most desperate chance when the occasion demanded it. For a few minutes he fought the robbers single-handed. General Jones, returning from the telegraph office, ran into the fight. He was armed with only a small Colt's double-action pistol, but threw himself into the fray. Connor and Harold had now come up and joined in the fusillade. The general, seeing the robbers on foot and almost within his grasp, drew in close and urged his men to strain every nerve to capture or exterminate them. By

Sam Bass and His Train Robber Gang

this time every man in the town who could secure a gun had joined in the fight.

The bandits had now reached their horses, and realizing their situation was critical they fought with the energy of despair. If ever a train robber could be called a hero, Frank Jackson proved himself one. Barnes was shot down and killed at his feet and Bass was mortally wounded and unable to defend himself or even mount his horse, while the bullets continued to pour in like hail from every quarter. With heroic courage, Jackson held the rangers back with his pistol in his right hand while with his left he unhitched Bass's horse and assisted him into the saddle. Then, mounting his own horse, Jackson and his chief galloped out of the very jaws of hell itself. In their flight they passed through old Round Rock, and Jim Murphy, standing in the door of May's store, saw them go by on the dead run. The betrayer noticed that Jackson was holding Bass, pale and bleeding, in the saddle.

Lieutenant Reynolds, entering Round Rock, came within five minutes of meeting Bass and Jackson in the road. Before he reached town he met posses of citizens and rangers in pursuit of the robbers. When the fugitives reached the cemetery they halted long enough for Jackson to secure a Winchester they had hidden in the grass there; then they left the road and were lost for a time. The battle was now over and the play spoiled by two overzealous deputies bringing on a premature fight, after they had been warned to be careful. Naturally, Moore and Grimes should have known that the three strangers were the Sam Bass gang.

Lieutenant Reynolds started Sergeant Nevill and his rangers early next morning in search of the flying bandits. After traveling some distance in the direction the robbers had last been seen we came upon a man lying under a large oak tree. Seeing we were armed, as we advanced upon him he called out to us not to shoot, saying he was Sam Bass, the man we were hunting.

After entering the woods the evening before, Bass had become so sick and faint from loss of blood that he could go no farther. Jackson had dismounted and wanted to stay with his chief, declaring he was a match for all their pursuers.

"No, Frank," replied Bass. "I am done for."

The wounded leader told his companion to tie his horse near at hand so he could get away if he should feel better during the night. Jackson was finally prevailed upon to leave Bass and make his own escape.

When daylight came Saturday morning Bass got up and walked to a near-by house. As he approached the place a lady, seeing him approaching covered with blood, left the house and started to run off, as she was alone with a small servant girl. Bass saw she was frightened and called to her to stop, saying he was perishing for a drink of water and would return to a tree not far away and lie down if she would only send him a drink. She sent him a quart cup of water, but the poor fellow was too far gone to drink it. We found him under this tree an hour later. He had a wound through the center of his left hand, the bullet having pierced the middle finger.

Bass's death wound was given him by Dick Ware, who used a .45 caliber Colt's long-barreled six-shooter. The ball from Ware's pistol struck Bass's belt, cutting two cartridges in pieces and entering his back just above the right hip bone. The bullet mushroomed badly, and

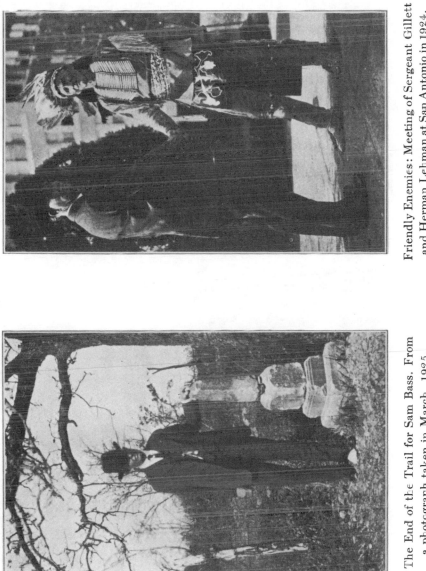

The End of the Trail for Sam Bass. From a photograph taken in March, 1925.

Friendly Enemies: Meeting of Sergeant Gillett and Herman Lehman at San Antonio in 1924.

made a fearful wound that tore the victim's right kidney all to pieces. From the moment he was shot until his death three days later Bass suffered untold agonies. As he lay on the ground Friday night where Jackson had left him the wounded man tore his undershirt into more than a hundred pieces and wiped the blood from his body.

Bass was taken to Round Rock and given the best of medical attention, but died the following day. While he was yet able to talk, General Jones appealed to him to reveal to the authorities the names of the confederates he had had that they might be apprehended.

"Sam, you have done much evil in this world and have only a few hours to live. Now, while you have a chance to do the state some good, please tell me who your associates were in those violations of the laws of your country."

Sam replied that he could not betray his friends, and that he might as well die with what he knew in him.

He was buried in the cemetery at old Round Rock, where a small monument was erected over his grave by a sister. Its simple inscription, defaced in recent years by relic-seekers, read:

SAMUEL BASS
Born July 21st, 1851
Died July 21st, 1878

A brave man reposes in death here. Why was he not true?

Frank Jackson made his way back to Denton County and hung around some time hoping to get an opportunity to murder the betrayer of his chief, an ingrate whose cause he himself had so ably championed. Jackson declared that if he could meet Jim Murphy he would kill him, cut off his head, and carry it away in a gunny sack.

Murphy returned to Denton, but learned that Jackson was hiding in the elm bottoms awaiting a chance to slay him. He thereupon asked permission of the sheriff to remain about the jail for protection. While skulking about the prison one of his eyes became infected. A physician gave him some medicine to drop into the diseased eye, at the same time cautioning him to be careful as the fluid was deadly poison. Murphy drank the entire contents of the bottle and was dead in a few hours. Remorse, no doubt, caused him to end his life.

Of the four men who fought the Round Rock battle with Sam Bass and his gang all are dead. Of the ten men who made the long ride from San Saba to Round Rock, I, alone, am still among the living.

CHAPTER X

A WINTER OF QUIET AND A TRANSFER

IN the fall of 1878 a stockman named Dowdy moved from southern Texas and settled on the headwaters of the Johnson Fork of the Guadalupe River in Kerr County. His family consisted of his wife, three grown daughters, a grown son, and a young son twelve or fourteen years old. Mr. Dowdy owned two or three thousand sheep and was grazing them on some fine upland pasture just above his home. He contracted for his winter supply of corn, and when the first load of grain arrived at the ranch the three girls walked out half a mile to where the sheep were grazing to stay with their younger brother while the elder returned to the ranch to measure and receive the corn. When young Dowdy returned to the sheep an hour later he was horrified to find that his three sisters and his little brother had been massacred by a band of roving Indians. From the signs on a high bluff near by, the sheep and their herders had been under observation by the redskins for some time; on seeing the only man leave, they descended upon the defenseless girls and boy and killed them. As there was no ranger company within one hundred miles of Kerr County at the time, a party of frontiersmen quickly gathered and followed the murderers, but after pursuing them for nearly two hundred miles the posse lost the trail in the rough Devils River country.

Kerr County then called for rangers, and General Jones ordered Lieutenant Reynolds to proceed thither and go into camp for the winter at the Dowdy ranch.

Six Years with the Texas Rangers

This descent upon the Dowdy family was the last raid ever made by Indians in Kerr County, and was perhaps the most heart-rending. We herded our horses that winter on the very ground where the unfortunate Dowdy girls and their brother were killed. At the time they were murdered the ground was soft and muddy from a recent rain, and for months afterward could be seen the marks where the poor girls had run on foot while the Indians charged on horseback. One of the young women had run nearly four hundred yards before she was overtaken and shot full of arrows. The murderers were probably Kickapoos and Lipans from the Santa Rosa Mountains of Mexico. They frequently raided southwestern Texas, stole hundreds of horses, and killed many people. While guarding their horses on the ground where the Dowdy family was killed, the rangers built a rock monument eight or ten feet high to mark the spot where the victims fell.

Lieutenant Reynolds kept scouting parties in the field at intervals throughout the winter but Indians never strike twice in the same place and the winter of 1878-1879 was the quietest one I ever spent as a ranger. Kerr County was pretty well cleared of outlaws and we made fewer arrests that season than ever before.

The rangers encountered but one real bad man in Kerr County. His name was Eli Wixon, and he was wanted for murder in eastern Texas. It was known that he would be at the polls to vote on election day, in November, so Lieutenant Reynolds sent Corporal Warren and Privates Will Banister, Abe Anglin, and Charles Ware to arrest him. Corporal Warren found his man at the polls and lost no time in telling Wixon what he was there for, ordering him to unbuckle his belt and drop his

A Winter of Quiet and a Transfer

pistol. Wixon hesitated, and finally called on his friends to protect him from the rangers.

The crowd came to his relief, and for a time it looked as if there would be trouble. Wixon abused the rangers, called them a set of dirty dogs, and dared them to shoot him. Corporal Warren was brave and resolute. He told Wixon his abuse did not amount to anything; the rangers were there to arrest him, and were going to do it. The corporal warned the citizens to be careful how they broke the law and said that if they started anything Wixon would be the first man killed.

Then, while Banister, Anglin, and Ware held the crowd back with their Winchesters, Warren disarmed Wixon, grasped his bridle reins, and led him away without further trouble. Lieutenant Reynolds took no chances with men of this sort, and as soon as Wixon was in camp he was promptly handcuffed and shackled. This measure usually took the nerve out of all so-called bad men, and it worked like a charm with our new prisoner.

As the winter wore on Lieutenant Reynolds, with but little to do, became restless. He once said of himself that he never had the patience to sit down in camp and wait for a band of Indians to raid the county so he might get a race. Action was what he wanted all the time, and when compelled to sit idly in camp he chafed like a chained bear.

When the legislature met early in 1879 it became known that it would be difficult to get an appropriation for frontier defense. From time immemorial there has been an element in the legislature from eastern Texas which has fought the ranger appropriation, and in this instance that element fought the ranger bill harder than ever. The fund appropriated for frontier defense two years before was now running short, and in order to make it last until it could be ascertained what the legislature would do, it became necessary for General Jones to order the various captains to discharge three men out of each company. A week later a similar order was promulgated, and this process was kept up until the battalion was reduced to almost one-half its former strength. Lieutenant Reynolds was compelled to sit idly by and see his experienced rangers dwindle away before his eyes, and what he said about those shortsighted lawmakers would not look well in print.

In March, 1879, Captain Pat Dolan, commander of Company F, then stationed on the Nueces River, seventy-five miles southwest of Reynolds' company, wrote the latter that a big band of horse and cattle thieves were reported operating in the vicinity of the head of Devils River and along the Pecos. He wished to take a month's scout out in that country, but since the ranger companies had been so reduced he did not feel strong enough alone to operate against them and leave a reserve in his own camp. He asked Lieutenant Reynolds, therefore, to send a detachment to coöperate with him. I was now a second sergeant, and with five men I was ordered to report to Captain Dolan for a three weeks' scout on Devils River and the Pecos. I reported to the commander of Company F and we scouted up the Nueces River, then turned west to Beaver Lake on the head of Devils River. From the lake we went over on Johnson's Run and covered the country thoroughly, but without finding the reported outlaws.

One morning, after starting out on our day's scout, Captain Dolan halted the command, and taking with him Private Robb, went in search of water. A heavy

A Winter of Quiet and a Transfer

fog came up after he left us and hung over the country the greater part of the day. The captain did not return to us, and Sergeant G. K. Chinn ordered his men to fire their guns to give the lost ones our position. We remained in the vicinity until night, and then returned to Howard's Well, a watering place on Johnson's Run. The following morning we scouted out to the point from which the captain had left us the day before. It was now clear, with the sun shining brightly, but the lost men could not be found. Dolan was an experienced frontiersman, and we concluded that, after finding himself lost in the fog, he would return to his headquarters on the Nueces, one hundred and twenty-five miles away. Sergeant Chinn, therefore, headed the command for this camp, and when we reached it we found Captain Dolan and Private Robb had preceded us. They had traveled through a bad Indian country with nothing to eat but what venison they had killed.

From Dolan's company I marched my detail back to Company E by easy stages and reached our camp at Dowdy's ranch the last week in March with our horses ridden down. We had covered something like five hundred miles without accomplishing anything.

As soon as I arrived I walked up to the lieutenant's tent to make my report. There I was met by First Sergeant C. L. Nevill, who told me that Lieutenant Reynolds had resigned and left the company. At first I thought the sergeant was only joking, but when I was convinced that the lieutenant had really gone I was shocked beyond measure. The blow was too strong and sudden for me, and I am not ashamed now at sixty-eight years of age to admit that I slipped out of camp, sat down on the bank of the Guadalupe River, and cried

133

like a baby. It seemed as if my best friend on earth had gone forever. Reynolds had had me transferred from Coldwell's company to his own when I was just a stripling. As soon as I was old enough to be trusted with a scout of men and the vacancies occurred I was made second corporal, first corporal, and then second sergeant. I was given the best men in the company and sent against the most noted outlaws and hardened criminals in the state. Lieutenant Reynolds had given me every chance in the world to make a name for myself, and now he was gone. I felt the loss keenly. I feel sure the records now on file in Austin will bear me out when I say Reynolds was the greatest captain of his time; the state lost a matchless officer when "Mage" Reynolds retired to private life. After leaving the ranger service he made Lampasas his home and served that county as its sheriff for several terms.

The legislature finally made a small appropriation for frontier defense. Sergeant Nevill was ordered to report at Austin with Company E for the reorganization of the command. Reynolds' resignation practically broke up the company, and though Sergeant Nevill was made lieutenant of Company E and afterward raised to a captaincy and left behind him an enviable record, yet he was not a "Mage" Reynolds by a long shot.

On reaching Austin, R. C. Ware and the Banister boys secured their transfers to Captain Marsh's Company B, while the Carter boys, Ben and Dock, C. R. Connor, and Bill Derrick resigned the service and retired to private life. Abe Anglin became a policeman at Austin. Henry Maltimore and myself, at our request, were transferred to Lieutenant Baylor's Company C for duty in El Paso County. With my transfer to this

A Winter of Quiet and a Transfer

command the winter of inaction was over, and I was soon to see some exciting times along the upper Rio Grande.

CHAPTER XI

THE SALT LAKE WAR AND A LONG TREK

AT the foot of the Guadalupe Mountains, one hundred miles east of El Paso, Texas, are situated several large salt deposits known as the Salt Lakes. These deposits were on public land. For a hundred years or more the residents along the Rio Grande in El Paso County and in northern Mexico had hauled salt from the lakes free of charge, for there was no one to pay, as the deposits were not claimed by any owner. All one had to do was to back a wagon to the edge of the lake, shovel it full of salt, and drive off.

From San Elizario to the Salt Lakes was a distance of ninety miles, and there was not a drop of water on the route. The road, which had long been traveled by big wagon trains, was almost as straight as an arrow and in fine condition. The salt-haulers would carry water in barrels to what was known as the Half-way Station, about forty-five miles from San Elizario. Here they would rest and water their horses and leave half their water for the return trip. They would then push on to the lakes, load their wagons, and rest the teams a day or two; on their return trip they would stop at the Half-way Station to water their animals and throw the empty barrels on top of the salt, and then continue without further halt to San Elizario on the Rio Grande.

Charley Howard, after his election as judge of the El Paso District, made his home at the old town of Franklin, now known as El Paso. He saw the possibilities of these salt lakes as a money-making proposi-

The Salt Lake War and a Long Trek

tion and, knowing they were on public land, wrote his father-in-law, George B. Zimpleman, at Austin, to buy some land certificates and send them to him so he could locate the land covering the salt deposits. As soon as the land was located Judge Howard forbade anyone to haul salt from the lakes without first securing his permission. The Mexicans along both sides of the Rio Grande adjacent to El Paso became highly indignant at this order. A sub-contractor on the overland mail route between El Paso and Fort Davis named Luis Cardis supported the Mexicans, and told them Howard had no right to stop them from hauling salt. Cardis was an Italian by birth, who had come to El Paso County in 1860, married a Mexican wife, identified himself with the county, and become prominent as a political leader. He was a Republican, while Judge Howard was a Democrat. Cardis and Howard soon became bitter enemies, and in September, 1878, the conflict between them became so acute that Howard killed his opponent with a double-barrel shotgun in S. Shultz and Brothers' store in Franklin. This at once precipitated the contest known as the Salt Lake War, for grave threats were made against Howard by the Mexicans.

After killing Cardis, Judge Howard fled to New Mexico, and from his seclusion in that state he called on the governor of Texas to send rangers to El Paso to protect him and the courts over which he presided. At that time not a company of the Frontier Battalion was within five hundred miles of the town. El Paso was seven hundred and fifty miles by stage from San Antonio or Austin and the journey required about seven days and nights of travel over a dangerous route—an unusually hard trip for any passenger attempting it.

Six Years with the Texas Rangers

The governor of Texas, therefore, sent Major John B. Jones from Austin to Topeka, Kansas, by rail and thence as far west into New Mexico as the Santa Fé Railroad ran at that time, and thence by stage down to El Paso. Major Jones dropped into the old town of Franklin unheralded and unknown. He sat about the hotel and gained the information he needed, then made himself known to the authorities and proceeded at once to organize and equip a company of twenty rangers. John B. Tays, brother to the Episcopal minister of that district, was made lieutenant of the new command, which was known as a detachment of Company C and stationed in the old town of San Elizario, twenty-five miles southeast of El Paso.

Soon after this detachment of rangers had been authorized, Judge Howard appeared at San Elizario and sought protection with it. No sooner had it become known that Judge Howard was back in Texas than the ranger company was surrounded by a band of armed Mexicans, two or three hundred in number, who demanded the body of the jurist. Lieutenant Tays refused to surrender Howard, and the fighting began, and was kept up at intervals for two or three days. Sergeant Mattimore, in passing through the courtyard of the buildings in which the rangers were quartered was shot down and killed by Mexican snipers located on top of some adobe buildings within range of the quarters. Then an American citizen, a Mr. Ellis, was killed near Company C's camp.

After several days of desultory fighting the leaders of the mob, under flag of truce, sought an interview with Lieutenant Tays. The lieutenant finally agreed to meet two of them, and while the parley was in progress

The Salt Lake War and a Long Trek

armed Mexicans approached the peace party one at a time until forty or fifty had quietly surrounded Lieutenant Tays and put him at their mercy. The mob then boldly demanded the surrender of the rangers, Judge Howard, and two other Americans, Atkinson and McBride, friends of the judge, who had sought protection with them.

There is no doubt that the Mexicans intimidated Lieutenant Tays after he was in their hands, probably threatening him with death unless their demands were granted. The lieutenant returned to the ranger camp with the mob and said, "Boys, it is all settled. You are to give up your arms and horses and you will be allowed to go free."

The rangers were furious at this surrender, but were powerless to help themselves, for the mob had swarmed in upon them from all sides. Billy Marsh, one of the youngest men in the company, was so indignant that he cried out to his commander, "The only difference between you and a skunk is that the skunk has a white streak down his back!"

Judge Howard, seeing the handwriting on the wall, began shaking hands and bidding his ranger friends good-bye. As soon as the Mexicans had gotten possession of the rangers' arms, Judge Howard, McBride, and Atkinson were lined up against an adobe wall and shot. Then some Mexicans placed a rope around Judge Howard's neck and, mounted on fast ponies, dragged the body about the streets of San Elizario, and finally threw it into a shallow well. The Mexicans then scattered, most of them crossing the Rio Grande into Mexico.

Lieutenant Tays at once resigned as commander of

the rangers, and Private Charles Ludwick was made first sergeant and placed in charge of the company until the governor of Texas could send a commissioned officer to take command of it. Had Lieutenant Tays held out twenty-four hours longer, a thing which he could easily have done, he would have escaped the disgrace and mortification of surrendering himself and his company to a mob of Mexicans, for within that time John Ford swept into the Rio Grande Valley with a band of New Mexico cowboys to relieve the besieged rangers. On learning the fate of Howard, McBride, Atkinson, Ellis, and Sergeant Mattimore, the rescue party raided up and down the valley from San Elizario to El Paso and killed several armed Mexicans who were accused of being members of the mob that had murdered the Americans. The present battalion of Texas Rangers was organized May 1, 1874, and in all their half century of service this surrender of Lieutenant Tays is the only black mark ever chalked up against them.

Afterward, when I arrived in El Paso with Lieutenant Baylor I had many talks with Privates George Lloyd, Doc Shivers, Bill Rutherford, and Santiago Cooper—all members of Tays's company. Most of them believed Lieutenant Tays had a streak of yellow in him, while a few thought he made a mistake in agreeing to an interview with the mob, thereby allowing himself to be caught napping and forced to surrender.

Conditions in El Paso County were now so bad that Lieutenant Baylor was ordered into the country to take command of the ranger company. Before leaving to assume his command, Lieutenant Baylor was called to Austin from his home in San Antonio and had a lengthy interview with Governor Roberts. Baylor was instructed

The Salt Lake War and a Long Trek

to use all the diplomacy possible to reconcile the two factions and settle the Salt Lake War peaceably. The governor held that both sides to the controversy were more or less to blame; what had been done could not be undone, and the restoration of order was now the prime requisite, rather than a punitive expedition against the members of the mob.

On July 28, 1879, Private Henry Maltimore and myself reached San Antonio from Austin and presented our credentials to Lieutenant Baylor, who advised us that he had selected August second as the day to begin his march from San Antonio to El Paso County. In his camp on the San Antonio River in the southern part of the city the lieutenant had mustered myself as sergeant, and Privates Henry Maltimore, Dick Head, Gus Small, Gus Krimpkau, and George Harold.

Early on the morning of August 2, 1879, our tiny detachment left San Antonio on our long journey. One wagon carried a heavy, old-fashioned square piano, and on top of this was loaded the lieutenant's household goods. At the rear of the wagon was a coop of game chickens, four hens and a cock, for Lieutenant Baylor was fond of game chickens as a table delicacy, though he never fought them. His family consisted of Mrs. Baylor, two daughters,—Helen, aged fourteen, and Mary, a child of four or five years,—and Miss Kate Sydnor, sister of Mrs. Baylor. The children and ladies traveled in a large hack drawn by a pair of mules. Rations for men and horses were hauled in a two-mule wagon, while the rangers rode on horseback in advance of the hack and wagons. Two men traveling to New Mexico in a two-wheeled cart asked permission to travel with us for protection. Naturally, we made slow progress with this unique combination. As well as I can remember, 1879 was a rather dry year, for not a drop of rain fell during this seven-hundred-mile journey. When we passed Fort Clark, in Kinney County, and reached Devils River we were on the real frontier and liable to attack by Indians at any time. It was necessary, therefore, to keep a strong guard posted at all times.

Around our camp-fires at night Lieutenant Baylor entertained us with accounts of early days on the frontier. He was born August 24, 1832, at old Fort Gibson in the Cherokee nation, now the state of Oklahoma. His father, John Walker Baylor, was a surgeon in the United States army. Lieutenant Baylor was a soldier by training and by inheritance. In 1879 he was in his forty-seventh year and stood six feet two inches tall, a perfect specimen of a hardy frontiersman. He was highly educated, wrote much for papers and magazines, was a fluent speaker, and a very interesting talker and story-teller. He was less reserved than any other captain under whom I ever served. He had taken part in many Indian fights on the frontier of Texas, and his descriptions of some of his experiences were thrilling. Lieutenant Baylor was a high-minded Christian gentleman and had been a member of the Episcopal Church from childhood. In all the months I served with him I never heard him utter an oath or tell a smutty yarn. He neither drank whiskey nor used tobacco. Had he written a history of his operations on the frontier and a biography of himself it would have been one of the strangest and most interesting books ever written.

I have not the power of language to describe Lieutenant Baylor's bravery, because he was as brave as it is possible for man to be. He thought everyone else should be the same, and did not see how a white man could be a coward. He was as tender-hearted as a child and would listen to any tale of woe. He frequently took men into the service and stood good for their equipment, and often he had to pay the bill out of his own pocket. All men looked alike to him, and he would enlist anyone when there was a vacancy in the company. The result was that some of the worst San Simon Valley rustlers got into the command and gave us no end of trouble, nearly causing one or two killings in our camp.

Baylor cared nothing for discipline in the company. A scout of ten or fifteen men would sometimes be strung out a mile or more on the march. To one who had commanded a regiment during the Civil War a detachment of Texas Rangers, doubtless, looked small and insignificant, so he let his men have pretty much their own way. To a man like myself, who had been schooled under such captains as Major Jones, Captain Coldwell, Captain Roberts, and Lieutenant Reynolds, commanders who were always careful of the disposition and conduct of their men, this method of Baylor's seemed suicidal. It seemed inevitable that we would some time be taken by surprise and shot to pieces.

Another peculiarity of this wonderful man was his indifference to time. He would strike an Indian trail, take his time, and follow it to the jumping-off place. He would say. "There is no use to hurry, boys. We will catch them after a while." For instance, the stage-driver and passenger killed in Quitman Canyon in January, 1880, had been dead two weeks before the lieutenant returned from a scout out in the Guadalupe Mountains. He at once directed me to make a detail of all except three men in camp, issue ten days' rations, and have the men ready to move early next morning. An orderly or first sergeant is hardly ever called upon to scout unless he so desires, but the lieutenant said: "You had better come along, Sergeant. You may get another chance to kill an Indian." It seemed unreasonable to think he could start two weeks behind a bunch of Indians and follow up and annihilate the whole band, but he did. Give Comanches or Kiowas two weeks' start and they would have been in Canada, but the Apaches were slow, and a different proposition with which to deal.

Baylor was one of the best shots with firearms I ever saw. He killed more game than almost the entire company put together. When we first went out to El Paso he used a Winchester rifle, but after the first Indian fight he concluded it was too light and discarded it for a .45-70 Springfield sporting rifle. He always used what he called rest sticks; that is, two sticks about three feet long the size of one's little finger. These were tied together about four or five inches from one end with a buckskin thong. In shooting he would squat down, extend the sticks an arm's length out in front of him with the longer ends spread out tripod-fashion on the ground. With his gun resting in the fork he had a perfect rest and could make close shots at long range. He always carried these sticks in his hand and used them on his horse as a quirt. In those days I used to pride myself on my shooting with a Winchester, but I soon found that Lieutenant Baylor had me skinned a mile when it came to killing game at long distance. I never could use rest sticks, for I always forgot them and shot offhand.

I cannot close this description of Lieutenant Baylor without mentioning his excellent wife, who made the long, tedious journey from San Antonio to El Paso

The Salt Lake War and a Long Trek

County with us. She was Sallie Garland Sydnor, born February 11, 1842. Her father was a wholesale merchant at Galveston, and at one time mayor of that city. Mrs. Baylor was a very refined woman, highly educated, and a skillful performer on the piano. Her bright, sunny disposition and kind heart won her friends among the rangers at once.

When we had passed Pecan Springs on Devils River there was not another cattle, sheep, or goat ranch until we reached Fort Stockton, two hundred miles to the west. It was just one vast uninhabited country. Today it is all fenced and thousands of fine cattle, sheep, and goats roam the hills. The Old Spanish Trail traverses most of this section, and in traveling over it today one will meet hundreds of people in high-powered automobiles where forty years ago it was dangerous for a small party of well-armed men to journey. While ascending Devils River I learned that Lieutenant Baylor was not only a good hunter, but a first-class fisherman as well, for he kept the entire camp supplied with fine bass and perch, some of the latter being as large as saucers.

Forty miles west of Beaver Lake we reached Howard's Well, situated in Howard's Draw, a tributary of the Pecos River. Here we saw the ruins of a wagon train that had been attacked by Indians a few months before. All the mules had been captured, the teamsters killed, and the train of sixteen big wagons burned. Had the same Indians encountered our little party of ten men, two women, and two children we would all have been massacred.

Finally, we reached old Fort Lancaster, an abandoned government post, situated on the east bank of

Live Oak Creek, just above the point where this beautiful stream empties into the Pecos. We camped here and rested under the shade of the big live-oak trees for several days. From this camp we turned north up the Pecos, one of the most curious rivers in Texas. At that time, before its waters were much used for irrigation in New Mexico, the Pecos ran bank full of muddy, brackish water almost the year round. Not more than thirty or forty feet wide, it is the crookedest stream in the world, and though only from three to ten feet deep, was so swift and treacherous that it was most difficult to ford. However, it had one real virtue; it was the best stream in Texas for both blue and yellow catfish that ranged in weight from five to forty pounds. We were several days traveling up this river to the pontoon crossing and we feasted on fish.

At Pontoon Crossing on the Pecos we intercepted the overland mail route leading from San Antonio to El Paso by way of Fredericksburg, Fort Mason, Menard, Fort McKavett, Fort Concho, Fort Stockton, and Fort Davis, thence west by Eagle Springs through Quitman Canyon, where more tragedies and foul murders have been committed by Indians than at any other point on the route. Ben Fricklin was the mail contractor. The stage stands were built of adobe and on the same unchanging plan. On each side of the entrance was a large room. The gateway opened into a passageway, which was roofed, and extended from one room to the other. In the rear of the rooms was the corral, the walls of which were six to eight feet high and two feet thick, also of sun-dried brick. One room was used for cooking and eating and the other for sleeping-quarters and storage. The stage company furnished the stage

The Salt Lake War and a Long Trek

tender with supplies and he cooked for the passengers, when there were such, charging them fifty cents per meal, which he was allowed to retain for his compensation.

When the stage rolled into the station the tender swung open the gates and the teams, small Spanish mules, dashed into the corral. The animals were gentle enough when once in the enclosure, but mean and as wild as deer when on the road. The stage company would buy these little mules in lots of fifty to a hundred in Mexico and distribute them along the route. The tiny animals were unbroken bronchos right off the range. They were tied up, or tied down, as the case might be and harnessed by force. When they had been hitched to the stagecoach or buckboard the gates to the corral were opened and the team left on the run. The intelligent mules soon learned that all they had to do was to run from one station to the next, and they could not be stopped between posts no matter what happened. Whenever they saw a wagon or a man on horseback approaching along the road they would shy around the stranger, and the harder the driver held them the faster they ran.

On our way out, our teams were pretty well fagged out, and often Lieutenant Baylor would camp within a few yards of the road. The Spanish stage mules would see our camp and go around us on the run, while their drivers would curse and call us all the vile names they could lay their tongues to for camping in the road.

When we camped at a station it was amusing to me to watch the stage attendants harness these wary little animals. The stage or buckboard was always turned round in the corral and headed toward the next station,

147

and the passengers seated themselves before the mules were hitched. When all was ready and the team harnessed the driver gave the word, the station keeper threw open the gates, and the stage was off on a dead run.

There should be a monument erected to the memory of those old stage-drivers somewhere along this overland route, for they were certainly the bravest of the brave. It took a man with lots of nerve and strength to be a stage-driver in the Indian days, and many of them were killed. The very last year the stage line was kept up (1880), several drivers were killed between Fort Davis and El Paso. Several quit the stage company and joined Lieutenant Baylor's company, and all of them made excellent rangers.

From Pontoon Crossing we turned due west and traveled the stage route the remainder of the way to El Paso County. At Fort Stockton we secured supplies for ourselves and feed for our horses, the first place at which rations could be secured since leaving Fort Clark. Fort Stockton was a large military post and was quite lively, especially at night, when the saloons and gambling halls were crowded with soldiers and citizen contractors. At Leon Holes, ten miles west of Fort Stockton, we were delayed a week because of Mrs. Baylor's becoming suddenly ill. Passing through Wild Rose Pass and up Limpia Canyon we suffered very much from the cold, though it was only the last of August. Coming from a lower to a higher altitude we felt the change at night keenly. That was the first cold weather I had experienced in the summer.

Finally, on September 12, 1879, we landed safe and sound in the old town of Ysleta, El Paso County, after forty-two days of travel from San Antonio. Here we

The Salt Lake War and a Long Trek

met nine men, the remnant of Lieutenant Tays's company of rangers. The first few days after our arrival were spent in securing quarters for Lieutenant Baylor's family and in reorganizing the company. Sergeant Ludwick was discharged at his own request, and I was made first sergeant, Tom Swilling second sergeant, John Seaborn first corporal, and George Lloyd second corporal. The company was now recruited up to its limit of twenty men. Before winter Lieutenant Baylor bought a fine home and fifteen or twenty acres of land from a Mr. Blanchard. The rangers were quartered comfortably in some adobe buildings with fine corrals near by and within easy distance of the lieutenant's residence. We were now ready for adventure on the border.

When we arrived at Ysleta the Salt Lake War had quieted down and order had been restored. Although nearly a hundred Mexicans were indicted by the El Paso County grand jury, no one was ever punished for the murder of Judge Howard and his companions. In going over the papers of Sergeant Ludwick I found warrants for the arrest of fifty or more of the mob members. Though most of the murderers had fled to Mexico immediately after the killing of the Americans, many of them had returned to the United States and their homes along the Rio Grande. I reported these warrants to Lieutenant Baylor and informed him that with the assistance of a strong body of rangers I could probably capture most of the offenders in a swift raid down the valley. The lieutenant declared that he had received instructions from Governor Roberts to exercise extreme care not to precipitate more trouble over Howard's death, and, above all things, not to incite a race war between the Mexican offenders and the white people of the country. He decided, therefore, that we had better not make any move at all in the now dead Salt Lake War. Of course I never again mentioned the matter to him.

Though the Salt Lake War was over, new and adventurous action was in store for us, and within less than a month after our arrival in Ysleta we had our first brush with the Apaches, a tribe of Indians I had never before met in battle.

CHAPTER XII

OUR FIRST FIGHT WITH APACHES

ON October 5, 1879, at midnight, Pablo Mejia brought Lieutenant Baylor a note from Captain Gregorio Garcia of San Elizario, stating that a band of Apaches had charged a camp of five Mexicans who were engaged in cutting hay for the stage company fourteen miles north of La Quadra stage station and had killed them. As first sergeant I was ordered to make a detail of ten men and issue them five days' rations. I detailed Second Sergeant Tom Swilling, Privates Gus Small, George Lloyd, John Thomas, George Harold, Doc Shivers, Richard Head, Bill Rutherford, and Juan Garcia for the scout, and myself made the tenth man. It required an hour to arouse the men, issue the rations and ammunition, and pack the two mules, so it was one o'clock in the morning when we finally left Ysleta.

By daylight we reached Hawkins Station, near where Fabin's Station now is. Here we were told we would find the survivor of the terrible massacre. Riding up to the door of the stage house, we had to thump some time before we had evidence that anyone was alive on the premises. Finally, the door was opened very cautiously about an inch and a Mexican peeped out. Lieutenant Baylor asked him if he had been one of the *grameros,* or hay cutters.

"*Si, senor,*" replied the sleepy Mexican.

Asked for an account of the massacre, the native said it was nearly dark when the Indians, numbering from twenty-five to fifty, charged the camp uttering such horrible yells that everyone took to his heels and was soon in the chaparral. The speaker saw his *pobrecito papa* (poor papa) running, with the Indians about to lance him, and knew that he and the remainder of the party were killed. Only he himself escaped. As he mentioned the tragic death of his beloved parent the tears rolled down his cheeks. Lieutenant Baylor comforted the weeper as best he could and asked him if he would not guide the rangers to the raided camp; he declined with thanks, saying he must stay to help the station keeper take care of the stage mules, but he directed us to the ranch where some of the dead men's families lived and where a guide could be obtained.

When we arrived at the ranch below Hawkins Station it was sunrise and we halted for breakfast after a night ride of forty miles. The people at the ranch were very uneasy when we rode up, but were rejoiced when they realized that we were rangers. On learning our mission they showed us every attention. Among the first to come out to us was an old Mexican who had been in the hay camp when it was attacked. He gave a lurid account of the onset. His son had been one of the *grameros,* and when he mentioned him the tears began to flow.

"Ah, hijo de mi cara Juan. I shall never see him again," he lamented. "All were killed and I alone escaped!"

Lieutenant Baylor then explained to the weeping father that his son was very much alive and that we had seen him that very night bewailing the death of the father he thought killed. It now developed that all the dead men were alive. When the camp was attacked all the Mexicans had scattered, and the Apaches had been

Our First Fight with Apaches

too busy looting the stores to follow the fugitives. More-over, those ranchers would fight and the Indians did not care to follow them into the brush.

A bright young Mexican went with us to the hay camp, which was about six miles toward Comales, where Don Juan Armendaris now has a cow ranch. The Apaches had made a mess of things in camp sure enough. They had broken all the cups and plates, poured salt into the sugar, this combination into the flour and beans, and the conglomeration of the whole upon the ground, as the sacks were all they wanted. They had smashed the coffee pot, the frying pan, the skillet, and the water barrels with an ax. Then, taking all the blankets, they had started eastward as though they intended to go to the Sierra Prieta, but after going a mile the trail turned south. We found the redskins had come from the north by way of Las Cornudas and were probably from Fort Stanton, New Mexico, on a raid into Mexico. They were in dry country and making for the Rio Grande, fourteen miles to the south. When they discovered the hay camp on their route they charged it and fired on the hay cutters. The Mexicans scattered and made their escape in the darkness, each thinking himself the sole survivor and so reporting on reaching his home, though as a matter of fact not a single life was lost.

Our guide went back to give the alarm to the ranches below and we followed the trail down the mesa until opposite the Mexican town of Guadalupe. There we crossed the overland stage route near the present Rio Grande station and found our guide waiting for us. He had discovered the trail, and fearing the Indians might ambush the road below, he had awaited our arrival. The trail made straight for the Rio Grande, crossing about one mile west of Guadalupe. From the pony and mule tracks Lieutenant Baylor judged there were fifteen to twenty Indians in the band. We had some trouble following the trail after we got to the river bottom, where loose horses and cattle ran, but a few of us dismounted and worked the trail out, crossed the river, and struck camp for dinner.

Lieutenant Baylor sent Pablo Mejia into town to inform the president of Guadalupe that we had followed a fresh Apache trail to the Rio Grande going south into Mexico, and to ask permission to follow the Indians into his country. The scout soon returned and reported that the president was not only pleased that we had pursued the redskins, but would willingly join us himself with all the men he could muster. Just after we crossed the river we came across a Mexican herder with a flock of goats. As soon as he heard we were trailing the Apaches he began yelling at the top of his voice and soon had the goats on the jump for town, though the Indians had passed the night before. We were quickly in the saddle again, and as we rode into the pueblo we were kindly received by the people. We found a mare the Apaches had killed just on the edge of town and from which they had taken some of the choice steaks.

After leaving Guadalupe the trail went south, following closely the stage road from Juarez to Chihuahua. Not long after leaving town we met a courier coming to Guadalupe from Don Ramon Arranda's ranch, San Marcos de Cantarica, twenty-one miles distant, who informed us that the Apaches had killed a herder on that ranch and had taken four horses and sixteen mules belonging to the stage company. We hurried onward and

Our First Fight with Apaches

reached Cantarica at sunset, having traveled seventy-eight miles since one o'clock that morning. Both men and horses were rather tired.

All was confusion at the ranch. The Mexican herder had been shrouded and laid out with a cross at his head and several little lighted candles near the body. Many women were sitting around the room with black shawls pulled up over their heads. The Apaches, numbering sixteen well-armed and well-mounted warriors, had slain their victim and captured the stock near the ranch about noon. Mexican volunteers from Guadalupe and San Ignacio began to ride in until our combined force numbered twenty-five or twenty-six men. Everyone was excited at the thought of a brush with the redskins responsible for the murder.

Accompanied by our volunteer allies we left the ranch at daylight next morning and picked up the trail at once. It led off south along the base of the Armagora or Sierra Bentano Mountains. As the Mexicans were familiar with the country they took the lead and followed the trail rapidly. About eleven o'clock the trailers halted at the mouth of the Canyon del Marranos, an ugly black hole cut in the mountains, looking grim and defiant enough without the aid of Apache warriors. When we had joined the Mexicans—we were traveling some half a mile behind them— Lieutenant Baylor and Captain Garcia held a short conference. The lieutenant turned to me and said that Captain Garcia declared the Indians were in the canyon among the rocks, and ordered me to detail two men to guard our horses while we scaled the mountain on foot and investigated it. I could not bring myself to believe that a band of Indians that had killed a man and driven off all the stage stock the day before had gone only thirty miles and was now lying in wait for us.

"You don't know the Apaches," Lieutenant Baylor declared, when I voiced my thoughts. "They are very different from the plains Indians, the kind you have been used to following. These Apaches delight to get into the rocks and lay for their enemies."

At the conference the Mexicans suggested that Lieutenant Baylor should take nine of his men and ten of their volunteers and follow the trail up the canyon, but the lieutenant declared that this would never do, as the Apaches had no doubt anticipated such a move and hidden themselves in the cliffs where they could kill their attackers without exposing themselves in the least. He proposed scaling the mountains and following them down on top of the ridge in the Indians' rear, and this was the strategy finally adopted.

The Mexicans dismounted and started up the mountain-side about one hundred yards to our left. Lieutenant Baylor and his eight rangers marched straight forward from our horses and began the ascent. As we went along, the lieutenant pulled some bunch grass and stuck it all around under his hatband so his head would look like a clump of grass and conceal his head and body if he should have to flatten himself on the ground. He counseled us to follow his example. I had taken some Mexican cheese out of my saddle pockets and was eating it as we marched carelessly up the mountain. Honestly, I did not believe there was an Indian within a hundred miles of us, but it was not long before I changed my mind. Suddenly there came a loud report of a gun and then another. I looked up to where the Mexicans had taken position behind a ledge of rocks and saw where a bullet had struck the stones a foot above their heads. I did not want any more cheese. I threw down what I had in my hand and spat out what I had in my mouth.

The Apache warriors, high in the cliffs above us, then turned their attention to our little band of rangers and fired twenty-five or thirty shots right into our midst. One of these big caliber bullets whizzed so close to my head that it made a noise like a wild duck flying down stream at the rate of fifty to sixty miles an hour. Lieutenant Baylor ordered us to charge at once.

In running up the mountain I was somewhat in advance of the boys. We came to a rock ledge three or four feet high. I quickly scaled this, but before I could straighten up an Indian rose from behind a rock about fifteen to twenty yards ahead and fired point-blank at me. The bullet struck a small soap-weed three feet in front of me and knocked the leaves into my mouth and face. I felt as if I had been hit, but it was leaves and not blood that I wiped out of my mouth with my left hand. I turned my head and called to the boys to look out, but the warning was unnecessary—they had already taken shelter under the ledge of rock.

Just as I turned my head a second shot from the Apache carried away the entire front part of my hat brim. I saw the warrior throw another cartridge into his gun and brought my Winchester quickly to bear upon him. When he saw that I was about to shoot he shifted his position and turned sideways to me. We both fired at the same instant. My bullet hit the redskin just above his hip and, passing straight through his body, broke the small of his back and killed him almost instantly. He was a big man, probably six feet tall, with his face painted in red and blue paint. He used an old octagon-barrel Winchester rifle and he had with him an old shirtsleeve, tied at one end, in which were two hundred and fifty Winchester cartridges.

Some Indians fifty yards up the mountain now began to shell our position, so I took shelter behind the ledge of rock. Fifteen or twenty feet to our left and a little higher up the mountain, Lieutenant Baylor was sheltered behind some boulders. He raised his head slightly above his parapet for a peep at the Indians and those keen-sighted warriors saw him; a well-directed shot cut part of the grass out of his hat. Had the bullet been six inches lower it would have struck him full in the face.

"Darn that old Indian," exclaimed Baylor, ducking his head. "If I had a shotgun I would run up and jump right on top of him."

The lieutenant was mad now, and ordered a charge. The boys hesitated, and George Harold, an old scout, said, "Lieutenant, if we leave this shelter and start up the mountain the Indians hidden behind those rocks seventy-five yards above will kill us all."

"Yes, I suppose you are right; they would be hard to dislodge," replied Baylor.

The Apaches evidently had plenty of ammunition, for they kept up a desultory fire all day. Seeing we were not going to fall into their trap, they turned their attention to our horses. Although the animals were four or five hundred yards from the foot of the mountain they killed Sergeant Swilling's horse, the bullet passing entirely through the body just behind the shoulders. When it staggered and tumbled over, Swilling began to mourn, for he had the horror of walking all western men have. John Thomas, however, got the laugh on him

Our First Fight with Apaches

by saying, "Sergeant, you had better wait and see if you are going back to camp." We could see the Indians' bullets knocking up dust all around the horses and the guard replying to the fire. Lieutenant Baylor now sent a man to the guard with an order to move the horses out of range.

During the afternoon the Apaches moved up higher toward the crest of the mountain, and in doing so one of the Indians exposed himself. The Mexicans to our left spotted him and killed him with a well-directed shot. The warrior fell in open ground where he was literally shot to pieces.

We had been without water all day, and when night came Lieutenant Baylor and Captain Garcia decided it was useless to continue the fight any longer, so we withdrew toward our horses. After reaching the animals we could still hear the Indians firing on our positions. We might have captured their horses by a charge, but we would have had to go down the side of the mountain and across a deep canyon where we would have been compelled to pick our way slowly under a constant cross fire from the concealed riflemen, and neither Baylor nor Garcia thought the horses worth the sacrifice required to capture them.

As the nearest water was thirty miles away and our men and horses were weary and thirsty, we rode back to the ranch of our hospitable friend, Don Ramon Arranda, where our horses were fed and we ourselves supplied with fresh milk and cheese. On our return to Guadalupe we were most kindly entertained by Mr. Maximo Arranda, custom-house officer at San Elizario, and brother to Don Ramon. We reached our headquarters at Ysleta after being out five days and traveling two hundred and twenty-two miles, sustaining no other damage than a few bruises from scaling the mountain and the loss of Sergeant Swilling's horse. This first brush with Apaches, however, was but a prelude to other expeditions after this tribe, and we were soon hot on the trail of Victorio, the Apache Napoleon.

CHAPTER XIII

SCOUTING IN MEXICO

ABOUT a month after our first brush with
Apaches, during November, 1879, Chief Victorio quit the Mescalero Reservation and with
a party of one hundred and twenty-five warriors and
a hundred women and children traveled south into
Mexico on a raid. This old chief was probably the best
general ever produced by the Apache tribe. He was a far
better captain than old Geronimo ever was, and ca-
pable of commanding a much larger force of men. His
second in command was Nana, also a very able officer.

Victorio knew every foot of the country and just
where to find wood, water, grass, and abundance of
game, so he took his time, and coming from New
Mexico down into the state of Chihuahua, stopped first
at the Santa Maria. The country about this stream is
very mountainous, especially to the south, and here he
could find refuge in case of an attack from Mexican
soldiers. Of this, however, there was not much danger
at that time, for the country was thinly settled, farming
and stock raising being confined to the neighborhood of
the small towns. Gradually Chief Victorio moved down
into the Candelaria Mountains, approaching them from
the northwest. Here he could get fresh range for his
large band of horses and be near the settlement of San
José, owned by Don Mariano Saminiego. Here, also,
he could watch the public road between Chihuahua and
El Paso del Norte, the present Juarez.

A sad and most heartrending tragedy resulted from
this move. Victorio was camped at the large tanks on the

north side and almost on top of the Candelaria Mountains, where he had fine range for his stock and plenty of game and wood. From these almost inaccessible peaks he could see for twenty or thirty miles in every direction and watch every move of travelers or hostile forces. The old chief now sent a small band of Indians, some six or seven in number, on a raid against the little settlement of San José. Here the Indians stole a bunch of Mexican ponies and hurried back to their camp. The townsmen discovered the loss of their ponies, and on examining the trail, found there was only a small band of Indians in the raiding party. A company of the principal citizens of San José, under the command of Don José Rodriguez, and augmented by volunteers from the little town of Carbajal, set out to locate the Indians and recover the stolen horses. The little band of men, fifteen in number, went to the northern side of the mountains and struck the trail of Victorio's band on an old beaten route used by the Indians, which passed from the Santa Maria River to the Candelaria Mountains. This road wound between two rocky peaks and then down the side of the hills to the plain between them and the Candelarias, ending at last at the big tank.

From his position on the tall peaks Victorio had seen the little body of Mexicans long before they struck his trail and, knowing they would never come upon the Candelarias after seeing the size of his trail, he sent forty or fifty of his warriors to form an ambuscade where the trail crosses the crest between the two peaks. He must have been with the braves himself, for the thing was skillfully planned and executed. On the north side of the trail there were only a few boulders, but on the south side the hills were very broken, rising in rough tiers of

Scouting in Mexico

stones. The Apaches hid in these rocks and awaited their victims. On November seventh, the Mexicans entered the narrow defile and as soon as they were between the two parties of Indians concealed on each side of the pass the Apaches on the north side of the trail fired a volley at them. The Mexicans thereupon made for the rocks on the south side, when the redskins in the cliffs above opened fire on them. Caught in this death trap, the entire force was massacred. When I walked over the ground some time afterward I saw where one Mexican had got into a crevice from which he could shoot anyone coming at him from the east or west. He was hidden also from the Indians in the cliffs above him, but his legs were exposed to the warriors on the north side and they had literally shot them off up to his knees. I also found seven dead Mexicans in a small gulley, and on a little peak above them I discovered the lair of one old Indian who had fired twenty-seven shots at the tiny group until he had killed them all, for I found that number of .45-70 cartridge shells in one pile. Practically all the horses of the Mexicans were killed. Some of the animals had been tied to Spanish dagger plants and when shot ran the length of their rope before falling. Some of the bodies rolled down the deep canyon until they reached the bottom of what we called the *Canaoa de la Muerte* (Canyon of Death), and the Indians removed none of the saddles or ropes from the dead horses.

When the company of Mexicans failed to return there was great sorrow and alarm in the little town of Carbajal. As it was supposed that only a small band of Apaches bent on horse stealing was in the Candelarias, another small band of fourteen men volunteered to go and see what had become of their friends and kindred. Don José Mario Rodriguez was appointed commander, and the little party took the trail of their comrades with sad forebodings. Old Victorio, from his watch towers in the Candelarias, saw this rescue party and prepared for its destruction. The signs indicated that the second party had walked into the same death trap as the first, but its members had scattered more in fighting and many of them were killed on the southern slope of the hills. Two had attempted to escape on horseback, but were followed and killed. I found one of these unfortunates in an open plain some six hundred yards from the hills. He had been surrounded, and, seeing escape was impossible, had dismounted, tied his horse to a Spanish dagger plant, and put up a good fight. I found thirty or forty cartridge shells near where he had fallen. His pony had been killed and the dagger plant shot to pieces. The Apaches had cut off his right hand and had carried away his gun, six-shooter, saddle, and bridle.

When neither party came back, then, indeed, was there sorrow in the town of Carbajal, for twenty-nine of her principal citizens had left never to return. Wives, mothers, and sweethearts mourned the loss of their dear ones. A runner was sent to El Paso del Norte and the citizens began to organize a punitive expedition at once, calling on Saragosa, Tres Jacales, Guadalupe, and San Ignacio for their quotas. These towns responded quickly and soon a hundred Mexicans were ready to take the field. A note was sent to Lieutenant Baylor at Ysleta requesting the rangers to go with the command. Baylor readily agreed to accompany the Mexicans, for he knew it was only a question of time before old Victorio would again be murdering and robbing on our side of the Rio

Grande. A detachment of Company C had been in one
Apache fight in Mexico and the Mexicans had a very
kindly feeling for us. Lieutenant Baylor's detachment
of ten rangers crossed the Rio Grande at Saragosa, a
little town opposite Ysleta, and joined the Mexicans
under Senor Ramos. We marched to the ranch of Don
Ynocente Ochoa until the volunteers from the other
towns came to Salamayuca Springs. When they arrived
the rangers moved down and our combined command
amounted to one hundred and ten men.

After organizing their force the Mexicans sent Senor
Ramos to inform Lieutenant Baylor that on account
of his experience as a soldier, and as a compliment to the
rangers, they had selected him to command the entire
party. The lieutenant thanked the messenger, but replied that as the campaign was on Mexican soil to rescue
or bury Mexicans, it would be more proper to appoint
one of their own men commander, and that he himself
would cheerfully serve under any leader so chosen.
Senor Ramos returned shortly and notified Lieutenant
Baylor that the Mexicans had selected Don Francisco
Escajeda of Guadalupe as commander-in-chief and
Lieutenant Baylor as second in command.

This solution of the leadership problem pleased us, as
there was an element among the Mexican party which
might have caused friction. Old Chico Barelo, the
pueblo cacique and principal commander of the mob
that had killed Judge Howard, Ellis, Atkinson, and
McBride at San Elizario, was with the expedition,
and we had at our Ysleta headquarters warrants for the
arrest of himself and many others; but we gave the old
fellow to understand we were now fighting a common
enemy and should act in harmony together. We did this

more willingly because we had learned that after killing
Judge Howard and the others the mob had wanted to
murder all the rangers barricaded in an old adobe house,
but had been dissuaded from this purpose by old Chico,
who had declared the rangers could only be killed after
he had first been slain.

Leaving one wagon at the Ochoa ranch and taking
three days' cooked rations and more in case of a siege,
we went out in the night to avoid Victorio's spies. Don
Francisco Escajeda and Lieutenant Baylor were at the
head of the column. I followed with eight rangers in Indian file, each ranger with a Mexican by his side, showing they looked on us as volunteers in the Mexican
service. We rode out along the hard sand road beyond
Salamayuca and sent spies ahead to locate the Apaches
if possible. Before we reached the Candelarias we halted
behind some mountains to await their report, but they
could learn nothing certain. It was a bitterly cold night
and a few of us made fires in the deep arroyos. We
moved on toward the mountains north of the Candelarias and reached them early next morning to find a
large fresh trail about two days old going in the direction of Lake Santa Maria, but, for fear of some stratagem, we divided our men. One party took the crest south
of the trail where the massacre took place, while the
other went to the right.

It was soon evident that the entire Apache band had
left, and that nothing remained for us but the sad duty
of collecting the bodies of the dead Mexicans for burial.
The second, or rescue party, had found the bodies of
their kinsmen killed in the first ambuscade and had col-
lected them and put them into a big crevice in the rocks.
When they began to cover the corpses with loose stones

Scouting in Mexico

the Indians, who had been watching them all the while, as a cat plays with a mouse before killing it, opened fire on the burial party and killed them to the last man. The saddest scene I ever witnessed was that presented as we gathered the bodies of the murdered men. At each fresh discovery of a loved friend, brother, or father, a wail of sorrow went up, and I doubt if there was a dry eye either of Mexican or Texan in the whole command.

While the immediate relatives were hunting for those who had scattered in trying to escape, we moved south to the main tank in the Candelarias. The ascent was up a winding path on the steep mountain-side to the bench where the tank, one of the largest in the West, was situated. The water coming down from a height, and big boulders, falling into the tank, had cut a deep hole in the solid rock in which the water was retained. Although Victorio's band of three hundred animals and two hundred or more Indians and our command had been using the water it could scarcely be missed.

We sent scouts to the left and right to make sure no trap was being set for us, for the cunning old chief, after sending his women and children off, could have hidden his warriors in the rough cliff which towered high above the tank of water and slaughtered all those below. We remained all day and night at this place. It was the most picturesque spot I had ever seen. We rangers rambled all over the Indian camp and found many of the Mexican saddles hidden in the cliffs, and several hats, each with bullet holes in it. We also discovered two Winchester rifles that had been hit in the fight and abandoned as useless. I saw a hundred or more old rawhide shoes that had been used to cover the ponies' feet, and dozens of worn-out moccasins. The Apaches had killed and eaten more than seventy-five head of horses and mules in this camp.

I followed a plain, well-beaten footpath to the topmost peak of the Candelaria or candle mountain, so called from the candle-like projection of rocks that shoot skyward from its top. The Candelaria is in an open plain fifty miles south of El Paso, Texas, and from its top affords one of the grandest views in northern Mexico. To the south one could see San José and Carbajal, to the north the mountains at El Paso del Norte; to the west the mountains near Santa Maria River and Lake Guzman were in plain view, while to the east the Sierra Bentanos loomed up, apparently only a few miles away. On this peak old Victorio kept spies constantly on the lookout, and it would have been impossible for a party of men to have approached without being seen by these keen-eyed watchers.

All the bodies having been recovered, they were buried in a crevice of the mountain where they had been killed. All were in a good state of preservation owing to the pure cold air of the mountains. It is a strange fact, but one beyond question, that no wild animal or bird of prey will touch the body of a Mexican. These corpses had lain on the ground nearly two weeks and were untouched. If they had been the bodies of Indians, negroes, or Americans the coyotes, buzzards, and crows would have attacked them the first day and night.

Nothing of interest occurred on our return trip. The rangers, as usual, ate their three days' rations at the first camp they made and got out of bread, but our Mexican allies divided with us. Don Ynocente Ochoa's major-domo or ranch boss gave us all the fresh beef we could eat and a supply of *carne seco* (dried beef) to take with us on the campaign. Quite a company had come out from Carrizal to see us and we returned sadly to the widows of the brave men who fell in this, probably the most wholesale slaughter ever made by Victorio's band. The citizens of Galena were nearly as unfortunate, but it was old Hu and Geronimo who massacred them. All the Saragosa men made for their church to offer up thanks for a safe return. Men, women, and children uttered their *"Gracias, senores,"* as the rangers rode through their town. We arrived safely in our adobe quarters at Ysleta and appreciated them after sleeping out-of-doors.

CHAPTER XIV

TREACHEROUS BRAVES, A FAITHFUL DOG, AND A MURDER

DURING the latter part of January, 1880, two mining engineers named Andrews and Wiswall from Denver, Colorado, appeared at the ranger camp in Ysleta. They had a new ambulance pulled by two good horses, and led a fine saddle pony. They were well fitted out for camping and had the finest big black shepherd dog I had ever seen. Andrews used a Springfield while Wiswall carried a Sharps sporting rifle, and besides these guns they had shotguns and six-shooters. These miners wanted to buy one hundred pack burros and, not finding what they sought in the Rio Grande Valley, decided to go over to the upper Pecos Valley near Eddy or Roswell, New Mexico, for pack animals. They consulted Lieutenant Baylor about the best route they should follow. He advised them to travel down the overland stage route to Fort Davis, thence by Toyah Creek and on up the Pecos, but the engineers thought this too much out of their way and concluded to travel by the old abandoned Butterfield stage route, which leads by Hueco Tanks, Alamo Springs, Cornudas Mountain, Crow Flat, and Guadalupe Mountain, and thence to the Pecos River. Lieutenant Baylor warned the men that this was a very dangerous route, without a living white man from Ysleta to the Pecos River, more than one hundred and fifty miles distant, and through an Indian country all the way.

Nevertheless, Andrews and Wiswall selected this latter route, and on the third day out from our camp

A Faithful Dog and a Murder

reached the old abandoned stage station at Crow Flat about noon. This was in an open country and from it one could see for miles in every direction. A cold north wind was blowing, so, for protection, the two men drove inside the old station walls, unhitched and hobbled their horses and pony, and were soon busily baking bread, frying bacon, and boiling coffee, not dreaming there was an Indian in the country, though they had been warned to look out for them. Like all men traveling in that country the two miners had appetites like coyotes and became deeply absorbed in stowing away rations. Unnoticed, the horses had grazed off some three or four hundred yards from the station and the two men were suddenly startled by a yelling and the trampling of horses' feet. Looking up, they saw ten or twelve Indians driving off their horses.

Seizing their guns, the two white men started after the thieves at top speed. Both being western men and good shots, they hoped, by opening on the redskins with their long-range guns, to get close enough to prevent them from taking the hobbles off the horses. But the animals made about as good time as if they had been foot-loose. This fact was well known to the rangers, who hobbled and side-lined also, and even then their horses, when stampeded, would run as fast as the guards could run on foot. The Apaches can be taught nothing about horse stealing—they are already past masters at the art. While some of the Indians halted and fought Andrews and Wiswall, the others ran the horses off and got away with them. The two miners returned to camp feeling very blue indeed.

A council of war was held and they were undetermined what course to pursue. To walk back one hundred miles to El Paso and pack grub, blankets, and water was no picnic; on the other hand, it was probably seventy-five miles to the Pecos. They finally decided to take the shortest way to assistance, which proved the traditional longest way. They determined to stay within the friendly adobe of the old stage stand until night. To keep up appearances they rigged up two dummy sentinels and put them on guard. They had no fear of an attack at night, especially as they had a dog to keep watch. They left the station at dark. Shep, the dog, wanted to go with them, but the men put a sack of corn and a side of bacon under the ambulance and made him understand he was to guard it. They then set out and followed the old stage route along a horrible road of deep sand. At daybreak they were near the point of the Guadalupe Peak, and having traveled on foot about twenty-five miles they were pretty well worn out.

The stage road here turns to the right and gradually winds around the mountain to get on the mesa land. It makes quite a circuit before getting to the next water, Pine Springs, but there is an old Indian trail that leads up the canyon and straight through. As Andrews and Wiswall were afoot and taking all the short cuts, they took this trail. It was late in the day when, in a sudden bend of the trail, they came in full view of an entire village of Indians coming toward them. The redskins were only two or three hundred yards off and discovered the white men at once.

Under such circumstances the two pedestrians had to think quickly and act at once. They could not hope to escape by running, for most of the Indians were mounted. Fortunately, to the south of the trail there was a sharp sugar-loaf peak, and for this Andrews and

A Faithful Dog and a Murder

Wiswall made with all speed. Reaching the summit, they hastily threw up a breastwork of loose rocks and as soon as the Indians came in sight they opened fire on them. The redskins returned the fire, but soon discovered they were wasting ammunition and ceased firing. The besieged, suspicious of some stratagem, kept a sharp lookout, and soon discovered the Indians were crawling upward to the barricade, pushing boulders before them to shelter their bodies. The two men decided to keep perfectly still, one on each side, and watch for a chance to kill a savage.

The watcher on the west side, where the fading light still enabled him to see, saw a mop of black hair rise cautiously over an advancing rock. He fired at once. The head disappeared and the boulder went thundering down the hill with the two white men running over the wounded warrior. As good luck would have it most of the attackers were on the east side, having taken it for granted that the men would try to escape in that direction. Before the astonished Apaches could understand just what was occurring, the men, running like old black-tailed bucks, were out of hearing, while the kindly night spread her dark mantle over them. Being good woodsmen, they had no trouble in shaping their course to Crow Flat again.

Worn out and weary after traveling more than fifty miles on foot and with not a wink of sleep for thirty-six hours, they made the old stage stand and found their dummy sentinels still on guard, with the faithful shepherd dog at his post. He was overjoyed at the return of his masters. Here they were in a measure safe, for they had water and grub and the walls of the stand, five feet or more high, would shelter them. Since no attempt had been made to kill the dog or rob the ambulance, the miners were satisfied that the Indians, after stealing their horses, had kept on their way to the Mescalero Agency, near Tularosa. This stage station was on the highway of these murderous, thieving rascals, who were constantly raiding Texas and Chihuahua. In these raids they had made a deep trail leading north from Crow Flat or Crow Springs, as some call it, toward the Sacramento Mountains.

After the fugitives had rested they decided they would start after dark for Ysleta. The fifty-mile walk over a rough country had pretty well worn out their shoes, so they used gunny sacks to tie up their sore and bleeding feet. Again giving Shep his orders, with heavy hearts they turned their faces to the Cornudas Mountains, with the next stage station twenty-five miles distant and not one drop of water on the way. They were so tired and footsore that they did not reach Cornudas until late the next day. Here they hid in the rocks, among the shady nooks of which they found cold water and sweet rest. After several days the two men dragged their weary bodies, more dead than alive, into Ysleta and to the ranger camp.

Lieutenant Baylor ordered me to take eight rangers, and with two mules, proceed to Crow Flat to bring in the ambulance Andrews and Wiswall had abandoned there. The first day we made the Hueco Tanks. Hueco is Spanish for tanks, and in the early days travelers spelled it Waco. Many wild adventures have occurred at these tanks—fights between the Mexicans and the Apaches. During the gold excitement this was the main immigrant route to California. Here, too, the overland stage route had a stand. The names of Marcy, General

A Faithful Dog and a Murder

Lee, and thousands of others could be seen written on the rocks. The Indians themselves had drawn many rude pictures, one of which was quite artistic and depicted a huge rattlesnake on the rock under the cave near the stage stand on the eastern side of Hueco.

Many times when scouting in the Sacramento and Guadalupe Mountains I have camped for the night in the Huecos. Sometimes the water in the tanks had all been used up by the travelers but there was always plenty of cool rain-water twenty-five feet above the main ground tanks. Often I have watered my entire command by scaling the mountain to these hidden tanks and, filling our boots and hats with water, poured it on the flat, roof-like rocks so it would run down into the tanks below. The city of El Paso, I am told, now has a fine graded road to these historic mountains, and many of its citizens enjoy an outing there.

Our next halt was at the Alamos, across the beautiful plains, at that time covered with antelope which could be seen scudding away with their swift change of color looking like a flock of white birds. Here we found some Indian signs at the flat above the springs, but it was at Cornudas that we again saw the old signs of the Apaches. This Cornudas is a strange conglomeration of dark granite rocks shot high in the air in the midst of the plains by some eruption of the earth in ages past. This was the favorite watering place of the Tularosa Agency Indians on their raids into Texas and Mexico.

From Cornudas to Crow Flat is a long, monotonous tramp of twenty-five miles, and we arrived in the night and were promptly challenged by the faithful sentinel, old Shep. Although we were strangers, the dog seemed to recognize us as Americans and friends. He went wild

175

with joy, barking and rolling over and over. The faithful animal had been there alone for nearly fifteen days. The side of bacon had been eaten and the sack of corn was getting very low. The rangers were as much delighted as if they had rescued a human being. The dog had worn the top of the wall of the old stage station perfectly smooth while keeping off the sneaking coyotes. Tracks of the latter were thick all around the place, but with the assistance of the dummy sentinels, Shep had held the fort. We found everything just as the owners had left it.

As was my custom, I walked over the ground where the Apaches and Andrews and Wiswall had had their scrap. Near an old dagger plant I found where an Indian had taken shelter, or rather had tried to hide himself, and picked up a number of Winchester .44 cartridge shells. We secured the ambulance and returned to camp without incident, having traveled two hundred miles in a week. Mr. Andrews presented Lieutenant Baylor with a beautiful Springfield rifle. I don't know whether Andrews or Wiswall is alive, but that Mexican shepherd dog is entitled to a monument on which should be inscribed, FIDELITY.

In the spring of 1880 two brick masons, Morton and Brown, stopped at our quarters in Ysleta on their way from Fort Craig, New Mexico, to San Antonio, Texas. They had heard that some freight wagons at San Elizario would soon return to San Antonio, and were anxious to travel back with them. These men spent two or three days in the ranger camp and seemed very nice chaps and pleasant talkers. One of them, Mr. Morton, owned one of the finest pistols I ever saw. It had a pearl

A Faithful Dog and a Murder

handle and was silver mounted. Our boys tried to trade for it, but Morton would not part with the weapon.

After the two men had been gone from our camp three or four days, word was brought to Lieutenant Baylor that two men had been found dead near San Elizario. The lieutenant sent me with a detail of three rangers to investigate. At San Elizario we learned that the bodies were at Collins' sheep ranch, four miles from town. On arriving there we found, to our surprise and horror, that the dead men were Morton and Brown, who had left our camp hale and hearty just a few days before. It was surmised that they had camped for the night at the sheep ranch and had been beaten to death with heavy mesquite sticks. They had been dead two or three days and were stripped of their clothing, their bodies being partly eaten by coyotes.

On repairing to his sheep ranch Mr. Collins had found the dead bodies of Morton and Brown, his shepherds gone, and his flock scattered over the country. Mr. Collins gave the herders' names as Santiago Esquibel and Manuel Molina. After beating out the brains of their unfortunate victims, the Mexicans had robbed the bodies and set out for parts unknown.

As the murderers were on foot and had been gone three or four days, I found it very difficult to get their trail, as loose stock grazed along the bosques and partially obliterated it. As there were a number of settlements and several little pueblos along the river, I knew if I did not follow the Mexicans' tracks closely I could never tell where they had gone, so I spent the remainder of the day trying to get the trail from camp. We were compelled to follow it on foot, leading our horses. We would sometimes be an hour trailing a mile.

Six Years with the Texas Rangers

On the following day I was able to make only ten miles on the trail, but I had discovered the general direction. I slept on the bank of the Rio Grande that night, and next morning crossed into Mexico and found that the murderers were going down the river in the direction of Guadalupe. I now quit the trail and hurried on to this little Mexican town. Traveling around a short bend in the road I came suddenly into the main street of Guadalupe, and almost the first man I saw standing on the street was a Mexican with Morgan's white-handled pistol strapped on him.

I left two of my men to watch the suspect and myself hurried to the office of the president of Guadalupe, made known my mission and told him I had seen one of the supposed murderers of Morton and Brown on the streets of his city, and asked that the suspect be arrested. The official treated me very cordially and soon had some police officers go with me. They found the two suspected Mexicans, arrested them, and placed them in the jail. The prisoners admitted they were Collins' sheep herders and said their names were Molina and Esquibel but, of course, denied knowing anything about the death of Morton and Brown. All my rangers recognized the pistol taken from the Mexicans as the weapon owned by Mr. Morton. The Mexican officers reported to the alcalde or town president that the suspects had been arrested. The latter official then asked me if I had any papers for them. I told him I had not, for at the time I left my camp at Ysleta we did not know the nature of the murder or the names of the parties incriminated. I declared I was sure the men arrested had committed the murder and that I would hurry back to Ysleta and have the proper papers issued for the prisoners' extradi-

A Faithful Dog and a Murder

tion. The alcalde promised to hold the suspects until the proper formalities could be complied with.

From Guadalupe to Ysleta is about fifty or sixty miles. I felt the importance of the case, and while my men and I were footsore and weary, we rode all night long over a sandy road and reached camp at nine o'clock the following morning. Lieutenant Baylor at once appeared before the justice of the peace at Ysleta and filed a complaint of murder against Manuel Molina and Santiago Esquibel, had warrants issued for their arrest, and himself hurried to El Paso, crossed the river to El Paso del Norte and, presenting his warrants to the authorities, asked that the murderers be held until application for their extradition could be made.

Within a week we learned, much to our disgust, that the two murderers had been liberated and told to vamoose. I doubt whether the warrants were ever sent to the alcalde at Guadalupe. A more cruel murder than that of Morton and Brown was never committed on the Rio Grande, yet the murderers went scot-free. This miscarriage of justice rankled in my memory and subsequently it led me to take the law into my own hands when dealing with another Mexican murderer.

CHAPTER XV

VICTORIO BECOMES A GOOD INDIAN

A S soon as the summer rains had begun in 1880 and green grass and water were plentiful, old Victorio again began his raids. He appeared at Lake Guzman, Mexico, then traveled east to Boracho Pass, just south of the Rio Grande. This old chief was then reported making for the Eagle Mountains in Texas. The Mexican government communicated this information to General Grierson at Fort Davis, Texas, and Lieutenant Baylor was asked to coöperate in the campaign to exterminate the wily old Apache.

General Grierson, on receipt of this information, at once put his cavalry in motion for Eagle Springs, and on August 2, 1880, Baylor left his camp at Ysleta with myself and thirteen rangers equipped for a two weeks' campaign. On August fourth our little band reached old Fort Quitman, eighty miles down the Rio Grande from El Paso, and Lieutenant Baylor reported to General Grierson by telegraph. His message was interrupted, for the Apaches had cut the wires between Bass Canyon and Van Horn's Well, but the general had previously ordered him by telegram to scout toward Eagle Springs until his command should meet the United States cavalry. We were to keep a sharp lookout for Indian trails, but we saw none until we reached Eighteen Mile Water Hole, where General Grierson's troops had had an engagement with Victorio. From here the Indians went south and around Eagle Mountains, so we continued down the road beyond Bass Canyon and found they had crossed the road, torn down the telegraph wire, carried off a long piece of it, and destroyed the insulators. They also dragged some of the telegraph poles two or three miles and left them on their trail. The signs indicated they had from one hundred and eighty to two hundred animals. After destroying the telegraph the raiders finally moved north toward Carrizo Mountains.

At Van Horn, Lieutenant Baylor could learn nothing of General Grierson or his movements. We thereupon took the general's trail leading north and overtook him in camp at Rattlesnake Springs, about sixty-five miles distant. Here we joined Company K, and Captain Nolan's company, both of the Tenth Cavalry. The cavalry camped at Carrizo Springs and our scouts found Victorio's trail the next day leading southwest toward the Apache Tanks. We left camp at dusk and rode all night and struck the redskins' trail next morning at the stage road where General Grierson had fought. The Indians crossed the road, but afterward returned to it and continued toward old Fort Quitman.

The overland stage company kept a station at this abandoned frontier post, situated on the north bank of the Rio Grande, eighty or ninety miles east of El Paso, Texas. On August 9, 1880, Ed Walde, the stage-driver, started out on his drive with General Byrnes, a retired army officer, occupying the rear seat of the coach. The stage, drawn by two fast-running little Spanish mules, passed down the valley and entered the canyon, a box-like pass with high mountains on either side,—an ideal place for an Indian ambuscade. Walde had driven partly through this pass when, at a short bend in the road, he came suddenly upon old Victorio and his band of one hundred warriors. The Indian advance-guard fired on the coach immediately, and at the first volley

General Byrnes was fatally wounded, one bullet striking him in the breast and a second passing through his thigh. Walde turned his team as quickly as he could and made a lightning run back to the stage stand with the general's body hanging partly out of the stage. The Apaches followed the stage for four or five miles, trying to get ahead of it, but the little mules made time and beat them into the shelter of the station's adobe walls.

It was a miracle that Walde, sitting on the front seat, escaped without a scratch and that both of the mules were unharmed. At old Fort Quitman I examined the little canvas-topped stage and found it literally shot to pieces. I noticed where a bullet had glanced along the white canvas, leaving a blue mark a foot long before it passed through the top. Three of the spokes of the wheels were shot in two and there were fifteen or twenty bullet marks on and through the stage. Lieutenant Baylor and his rangers buried General Byrnes near old Fort Quitman and fired a volley over his grave. Subsequently Walde joined Lieutenant Baylor's command and made an excellent ranger. It was from him that I obtained the particulars of the fight that resulted in the general's death.

En route the Apaches raided Jesus Cota's ranch, killed his herder, and drove off one hundred and forty head of cattle. In crossing the river forty of the animals mired in the quicksands. The heartless Indians thereupon pounced upon the unfortunate cattle and cut chunks of flesh out of their living bodies. Many of the mutilated animals were still alive when we found them. The redskins, with a freakish sense of humor, perpetrated a grim joke on the murdered herder. He was rendering some tallow when surprised and killed, so the murderers rammed his head into the melted tallow to make him a greaser!

After the fight at Quitman, Victorio and his band crossed into Mexico and there found temporary safety, as the United States troops were not permitted to enter that country in pursuit of Indians, though negotiations to permit such pursuit were even then pending between the two governments. Alone, we were no match for Victorio's hundred braves, so we returned to our camp.

Victorio, however, did not remain idle in Mexico. He made a raid on Don Saminiego's San José ranch and stole one hundred and seventeen horses and mules, besides killing two Mexican herders. Don Ramon Arranda, captain of the Mexican volunteers, invited the rangers to Mexico to coöperate with him in exterminating the Apaches, so, on September 17, 1880, Lieutenant Baylor with thirteen rangers, myself included, entered Mexico and marched to San Marcos de Cantarica, Don Arranda's ranch. Here we were joined by volunteers from the Mexican towns of Guadalupe, San Ignacio, Tres Jacales, Paso del Norte, and from the Texan towns of Ysleta, Socorro, and San Elizario, until our combined force numbered over a hundred men.

On the night of the nineteenth we crossed an Indian trail south of the Rancheria Mountains, but could not tell the number of redskins in the party, as it was then dark and the trail had been damaged by rain. The same night we saw Indian signal fires to the east of the Arranda ranch. Next morning, with a detail of five rangers and ten Mexican volunteers, I scouted in the direction of the fires but did not have time to reach the sign, as I was ordered to take and hold the Rancheria Mountains before old Victorio and his band should reach them.

At Lucero, the first stage stand, the Apaches were reported to be within a league of Carrizal. We made a night march with our rangers and seventy-three volunteers, but found the Indians had left, and, as a heavy rain had put out the trail, we struck east toward El Cobre Mountains. Here we again picked up the trail, and following it until night, we found a few loose horses of Saminiego's. The marauders now went west toward some tanks and we returned to Candelaria, where Victorio's entire band had crossed the Chihuahua stage road. Thence we marched back to San José and went into camp to await the arrival of General Joaquin Terrazas.

The Mexican general made his appearance on October third with two hundred cavalry and one hundred infantry. This general, a member of a well-known family of Chihuahua, was more than six feet in height, very dark, and an inveterate smoker of cigarettes. He used four milk-white horses, riding one while his aides led three. His cavalrymen, well armed with Remington pistols and carbines, were nicely uniformed and mounted on dark-colored animals of even size. The infantrymen were Indians from the interior of Mexico. They wore rawhide sandals on their feet and were armed with Remington muskets. Each soldier carried two cartridge belts, containing one hundred rounds of ammunition. I was impressed with the small amount of baggage and rations these infantrymen carried. On the march each man had a little canvas bag that held about a quart of ground parched corn, sweetened with a little sugar— and a tablespoonful of this mixture stirred in a pint cup

Victorio Becomes a Good Indian

of water made a good meal. Of course, when in a cattle country plenty of beef was furnished them, but when on the march they had only this little bag of corn. This lack of baggage and rations enabled them to move quickly and promptly. The infantry had no trouble at all in keeping up with the cavalry on the march, and in a rough country they could move faster than the horsemen.

With General Terrazas' three hundred soldiers and our hundred volunteers we could bring to bear against Victorio about four hundred men. From San José the combined command marched to Rebosadero Springs, twenty miles south of El Chaparro, on the new Chihuahua stage road. There we rested two days and then marched forty miles to Boracho Pass, where the Apaches had camped after killing General Byrnes and stealing Jesus Cota's stock. We crossed their trail twenty miles west of the pass and formed our line of battle, as we expected to find them encamped at some tanks there. They did not appear, so we camped at the pass to await supplies.

When the supply wagons arrived, General Terrazas sent an orderly to Lieutenant Baylor and invited him to send his men to draw ten days' rations. While I was standing in my shirtsleeves near the wagon one of the Mexican soldiers stole from my belt a fine hunting-knife which I had carried over ten thousand miles of frontier. I discovered the loss almost immediately and reported it to Lieutenant Baylor, who, in turn, mentioned it to General Terrazas. The general at once had his captains form their respective companies and had every soldier in camp searched, but the knife was not found. The thief had probably hidden it in the grass. The

Six Years with the Texas Rangers

Mexican volunteers remained with General Terrazas until after the defeat of Victorio, and one of them told me afterward that he had seen a Mexican soldier scalping Apaches with it. Just one year later an orderly of General Terrazas rode into the ranger camp at Ysleta and presented Lieutenant Baylor, then a captain, with the missing weapon and a note stating that Terrazas was glad to return it and to report that the thief had been punished.

While at Boracho we were joined by Lieutenant Shaffer, the Ninth United States Cavalry (negroes), Lieutenant Manney, Captain Parker, and sixty-five Apache scouts. These latter were Geronimo's Chiricauhaus, who later quit their reservation and wrought death and destruction in Arizona, New Mexico, and Mexico. From the first General Terrazas viewed these Indian allies with distrust, and as soon as we had scouted southeast from Boracho to Los Pinos Mountains, about seventy-five miles distant, and learned that Victorio's trail turned southwest toward Chihuahua, General Terrazas called Captain Parker and Lieutenants Baylor, Shaffer, and Manney to his camp and informed them that, as the trail had taken a turn back into the state of Chihuahua and was leading them away from their homes, he thought it best for the Americans to return to the United States. I was present at this conference and I at once saw my chance for a scrap with old Victorio go glimmering. However there was nothing to do but obey orders, pack up, and vamoose.

While on scouts after Victorio's band I met many United States officers, and often around the camp-fire we discussed the old chief. The soldiers all agreed that for an ignorant Indian Victorio displayed great military genius, and Major McGonnigal declared that, with the single exception of Chief Crazy Horse of the Sioux, he considered Victorio the greatest Indian general who had ever appeared on the American continent. In following this wily old Apache I examined twenty-five or more of his camps. He was very particular about locating them strategically, and his breastworks were most skillfully arranged and built. If he remained only an hour in camp he had these defenses thrown up. He had fought over two hundred engagements, but his last fight was now close at hand.

The very next morning after the United States troops, the Apache scouts, and the Texas Rangers turned homeward General Terrazas' scouts reported to him that Victorio with his entire band of followers was encamped at Tres Castillos, a small group of hills about twenty-five miles southwest of the Los Pinos Mountains. General Terrazas at once set his column in motion for that place. Captives afterward declared that Victorio's spies reported the presence of the Mexican cavalry early in the day, and thereafter kept him informed hour by hour as to the movements of the approaching enemy.

Victorio had just sent his war-chief, Nana, and fifty of his best young warriors away on a raid, so he had left in his camp an even hundred braves, some of them very old men. He also had ninety-seven women and children and about five hundred head of horses and mules, yet the remarkable old Indian made no move to escape. By nightfall General Terrazas had drawn near the Apache camp, where he surrounded the three hills as best he could and waited until morning before assaulting the enemy. During the night twelve of Victorio's warriors, with four women and four children, deserted the old chief and made their way back to the Eagle Mountains in Texas. Here they committed many depredations until they were exterminated three months later in the Diablo Mountains by Lieutenants Baylor and Nevill.

Early the following morning Victorio mounted a white horse and, in making some disposition of his braves to meet the expected onset of the enemy, exposed himself unnecessarily. The Mexicans fired a volley at long range and two bullets pierced his body. He fell from his horse dead—a good Indian at last.

The loss of Victorio and the absence of Nana demoralized the Apaches, and a vigorous assault by General Terrazas resulted in a complete victory for the Mexicans. Eighty-seven Indian warriors were killed and eighty-nine women and children were captured with a loss of only two men killed and a few wounded. The victory covered General Terrazas with glory. The Mexican government never ceased to shower honors upon him and gave him many thousands of acres of land in the state of Chihuahua. The general was so elated over the outcome of the battle that he sent a courier on a fast horse to overtake Lieutenant Baylor and report the good news. The messenger caught us in camp near old Fort Quitman. Every ranger in the scout felt thoroughly disgusted and disappointed at missing the great fight by only two days after having been with General Terrazas nearly a month.

The captured women and children were sent south of Mexico City into a climate wholly unnatural to them. Here they all died in a few years. When Nana heard of the death of Victorio and the capture of the squaws and children he fled with his fifty warriors to the Sierra

Victorio Becomes a Good Indian

Madre Mountains in the state of Sonora. There he joined forces with old Geronimo and massacred more people than any other small band of Indians in the world. To avenge himself on Terrazas for killing his friends and carrying away their wives and children, Nana and his band killed more than two hundred Mexicans before joining Geronimo. Nana, with his new chief, surrendered to General Lawton in 1886 and was carried away by our government to Florida, where he at last died.

On returning to camp at Ysleta Lieutenant Baylor found a commission as captain waiting him. Captain Neal Coldwell had been named quartermaster of the battalion, his company disbanded, and its letter, A, given to our company.

Though we missed the fight with Victorio it was not long before we were called upon to scout after the band of twelve warriors who had deserted the old chief on the night before the battle of Tres Castillos. However, we had first to clean up our company, for many undesirable recruits had seeped into it. This accomplished, we were ready to resume our Indian warfare.

CHAPTER XVI

SOME UNDESIRABLE RECRUITS

IN the early fall of 1880 two well-mounted and well-armed men appeared at the ranger camp at Ysleta and offered themselves to Captain Baylor for enlistment in his company. After questioning the applicants at some length the captain accepted them and swore them into the service. One gave his name as John (Red) Holcomb and the other as James Stallings. Unknown to us, both these men were outlaws, who joined the rangers solely to learn of their strength and their methods of operation. Holcomb was a rustler from the San Simon Valley, Arizona, a place long noted as a resort of outlaws and murderers, and was living under an assumed name. Stallings had shot a man in Hamilton County, Texas, and was under indictment for assault to kill.

These two recruits came into the service just before we started on our fall campaign into Mexico after old Victorio, and were with us on that long scout. Although one was from Texas and the other from Arizona, the two chummed together and were evidently in each other's confidence. Stallings had not been long in the company before he showed himself a trouble maker.

As orderly sergeant it was my duty to keep a roster of the company. Beginning at the top of the list and reading off the names in rotation, I called out each morning the guard for the day. We had in the company a Mexican, Juan Garcia, who had always lived in the Rio Grande country, and Captain Baylor had enlisted him as a ranger that he might use him as a guide, for Garcia

Some Undesirable Recruits

was familiar with much of the country over which we were required to scout. It so happened that Jim Stallings and Garcia were detailed on the same guard one day. This greatly offended Stallings, and he declared to some of the boys that I had detailed him on guard with a Mexican just to humiliate him and he was going to give me a damned good whipping. The boys advised him he had better not attempt it. I could see that he was sullen, but it was not until months afterward that I learned the cause.

After our return from our month's scout in Mexico, Captain Baylor received a new fugitive list from the adjutant general, and in looking over its pages my eyes fell on the list of fugitives from Hamilton County, Texas. Almost the first name thereon was that of James Stallings, with his age and description. I notified Captain Baylor that Stallings was a fugitive from justice. Baylor asked me what Stallings had been indicted for and I replied for assault to kill.

"Well, maybe the darned fellow needed killing," replied the captain. "Stallings looks like a good ranger and I need him."

Not many days after this I heard loud cursing in our quarters and went to investigate. I found Stallings with a cocked pistol in his hand standing over the bed of a ranger named Tom Landers, cursing him. I could see that Stallings had been drinking, and finally persuaded him to put up his pistol and go to bed. The next morning I informed Captain Baylor of the incident, and suggested that if we did not do something with Stallings he would probably kill someone. The captain did not seem inclined to take this view. In fact, I rather believe Captain Baylor liked a man who was somewhat "on the prod," as the cowboys are wont to say of a fellow or a cow that wants to fight.

John Holcomb soon found out as much about the rangers as he desired to know, and fearing he might be discovered, asked Captain Baylor for a discharge. After obtaining it he took up his abode in El Paso.

Not long afterward at breakfast one morning, while the twenty rangers were seated at one long table, Jim Stallings had a dispute with John Thomas, who was seated on the opposite side of the table and, quick as a flash, struck Thomas in the face with a tin cup of boiling coffee. Both men rose to their feet and pulled their pistols, but before they could stage a shooting-match the boys on either side grabbed them.

I at once went to Captain Baylor and told him that something had to be done. He seemed to be thoroughly aroused now and said, "Sergeant, you arrest Stallings, disarm, and shackle him. I'll send him back where he belongs."

I carried out the order promptly and Captain Baylor wrote to the sheriff of Hamilton County to come for the prisoner. Hamilton County is seven hundred miles by stage from El Paso and it took a week to get a letter through. There was no jail at Ysleta at that time, so we were compelled to hold this dangerous man in our camp.

Stallings was shrewd and a keen judge of human nature. We would sometimes remove the shackles from him that he might get a little exercise. Finally it came the turn of a ranger named Potter to guard him. Potter had drifted into the country from somewhere up north, and Captain Baylor had enlisted him. He knew very little about riding, and much less about handling firearms. Stallings asked Potter to go with him out into the

The Rangers at Home. From a photograph, taken in 1890, showing Captain Frank Jones at his mess, some visitors, and the cook.

Some Undesirable Recruits

corral. This enclosure was built of adobe and about five feet high. It was nearly dark and the prisoner walked leisurely up to the fence with Potter following close behind, Winchester in hand. Suddenly Stallings turned a handspring over the fence and hit the ground on the other side in a run. Potter began firing at the fugitive, which brought out all the boys in camp. Stallings had only about one hundred yards to run to reach the Rio Grande, and before anything could be done he was safe in Mexico. He yelled a good-bye to the boys as he struck the bank on the opposite side of the river. Captain Baylor was furious over the prisoner's escape and promptly fired Potter from the service and reprimanded me for not keeping Stallings shackled all the time.

Though we had lost the man we had his horse, saddle, bridle, and arms. Stallings at once went to Juarez and John Holcomb met him there. The fugitive gave his pal an order on Captain Baylor for his horse, saddle, and pistol, and Holcomb had the gall to come to Ysleta and present this order. He reached our camp at noon, while the horses were all in the corral. At the moment of his arrival I happened to be at Captain Baylor's home. Private George Lloyd stepped over to the captain's and said to me, "Sergeant, John Holcomb is over in camp with an order from Jim Stallings for his horse and outfit."

"Gillett, you go and arrest Holcomb and put him in irons and I'll see if I can find where he is wanted," ordered Captain Baylor, who had overheard what Lloyd said.

Holcomb, seeing Lloyd go into Captain Baylor's house, became suspicious, jumped on his horse, and left for El Paso in a gallop. I detailed three men to accompany me to capture him, but by the time we had saddled our horses and armed ourselves he was out of sight. We hit the road running and after traveling two or three miles and inquiring of people we met I became convinced that Holcomb had quit the road soon after leaving our camp and was striking for Mexico. I therefore turned back in the direction of camp and followed the bank of the river.

We had traveled perhaps a mile on our way home when we discovered Holcomb coming up the river toward us. He was about four hundred yards away and discovered us about the same time we saw him. Quickly turning his horse he made a dash for the river. Where he struck it the bank was ten feet high, but he never hesitated, and both man and horse went head first into the Rio Grande. The three men I had with me outran me, and when they reached the point where the fugitive had entered the water they saw him swimming rapidly to the Mexican side and began firing at him. I ran up and ordered them to cease, telling them not to kill Holcomb, as he was in swimming water and helpless. Just at this moment he struck shallow water and I ordered him to come back or I would shoot him.

"I'll come if you won't let the boys kill me," he called back.

I told him to hit swimming water quickly, which he did, and swam back to the American side. He was in his shirtsleeves and his hat was gone. His horse, meantime, had recrossed to our side of the river.

We all mounted and started back to camp, two of the rangers riding in front with Holcomb. I had not searched the prisoner because he was in his shirtsleeves. As we rode along he reached into his shirt-bosom and

Some Undesirable Recruits

pulled out an old .45 pistol and handed it to one of the boys, saying, "Don't tell the sergeant I had this." The rangers at camp gave him some dry clothes and dinner, then put him in chains and under guard.

Captain Baylor went on to El Paso, crossed the river to Juarez, and had Stallings arrested. In two days we had him back in camp and chained to Holcomb. The captain then wrote to Bell County, Texas, as he had heard John Holcomb was wanted there for murder. Holcomb had a good horse and he gave it to a lawyer in El Paso to get him out of his trouble. Of course we had no warrant for his arrest, and Judge Blacker ordered our prisoner brought before him. The county attorney made every effort to have Holcomb held, while his lawyer tried his best to have him released. The judge finally said he would hold Holcomb for a week and unless the officers should find some evidence against him during that time he would order him freed. It was nearly dark before we left El Paso on our return to Ysleta, twelve miles distant. Holcomb had, in some manner, got two or three drinks of whisky and was feeling the liquor. I had one ranger with me leading the prisoner's horse. The road back to camp followed the river rather closely and the country was very brushy all the way.

As soon as we had got out of El Paso, Holcomb sat sidewise on his horse, holding the pommel of his saddle with one hand and the cantle with the other, all the while facing toward Mexico. I ordered him to sit straight in his saddle, but he refused with an oath. We were riding in a gallop and fearing he would jump from his horse and try to escape in the brush, I drew my pistol and hid it behind my leg. Although Holcomb had the cape of his overcoat thrown over his head he discovered I had a pistol in my hand and began a tirade of abuse, declaring I had a cocked gun in my hand and was aching for a chance to kill him. I told him I believed from his actions he was watching for a chance to quit his horse and escape, and that I was prepared to prevent such a move. We reached camp safely and chained Holcomb to Stallings.

These men, although prisoners, were full of life, and laughed and talked all the time. Holcomb played the violin quite well. We held the two suspects several days and finally one night one of the rangers came to my room and said, "Sergeant, I believe there is something wrong with those prisoners. They are holloaing, singing, and playing the fiddle."

I was busy on my monthly reports and told him to keep a sharp lookout and before I retired I would come and examine them. On doing so I found that while Holcomb played the violin Stallings had sawed their shackles loose. They laughed when I discovered this and said that when the boys had all gone to bed they intended to throw the pack-saddle, which they used for a seat, on the guard's head and escape. We could get no evidence against Holcomb and the judge ordered his release.

While a prisoner, Holcomb swore vengeance against Prosecutor Neal and me. Mr. Neal heard of this threat, met Holcomb on the streets of El Paso afterward, and jerking a small Derringer pistol from his pocket, shot Holcomb in the belly. Holcomb fell and begged for his life. He was not badly hurt; as soon as he was well he quit El Paso and went to Deming, New Mexico, where he stole a bunch of cattle. He drove the stolen herd to the mining camp of Lake Valley and

Some Undesirable Recruits

there sold them. While he was in a saloon drinking and playing his fiddle the owner of the cattle appeared with a shotgun and filled him full of buckshot. As he fell, Holcomb was heard to exclaim, "Oh, boys, they have got me at last."

Jim Stallings was sent to Fort Davis and placed in jail, from which he and half a dozen other criminals made their escape.

A man named John Scott came to Captain Baylor, told a hard luck story, and asked to be taken into the service. Captain Baylor enlisted the applicant and fitted him out with a horse, saddle, and bridle, and armed him with a gun and pistol, himself standing good for the entire equipment. Scott had not been in the service two months when he deserted. I was ordered to take two men, follow him, and bring him back. I overtook him up in the brush near the line of New Mexico, and before I had even ordered him to halt he jumped down, sought shelter behind his horse, and opened fire on us with his Winchester. We returned the fire and killed his horse. He then threw down his gun and surrendered. We found that he had stopped in El Paso and procured a bottle of whisky. He was rather drunk when overtaken, otherwise he probably would not have made a fight against three rangers. Captain Baylor took away his saddle, gun, and six-shooter and kicked him out of camp, but he was compelled to pay $75 for the horse we had killed.

Another man, named Chipman, deserted our company and stole a bunch of horses from some Mexicans down at Socorro. They followed the trail in the direction of Hueco Tanks, where it turned west and crossed the high range of mountains west of El Paso. The pursuers overtook Chipman with the stolen horses on the boundary of New Mexico. The thief put up a fierce fight and killed two Mexicans, but was himself killed. Captain Baylor had a scout following the deserter, but the Mexicans got to him first and had the fight before our men arrived. However, they buried the body of Chipman where it fell. This man had made a good ranger and we all felt shocked when we learned he had stolen seven ponies and tried to get away with them single-handed.

Yet another San Simon Valley rustler, Jack Bond, enlisted in the company. A band of rustlers and cow thieves were operating in the brush country, eighteen miles above El Paso, about the time he joined the command. I did my best to break up this band and made scout after scout up the river, but without success. Finally, Captain Baylor learned that Bond and another ranger, Len Peterson, were keeping the thieves posted as to the rangers' movements. The captain dismissed these men from the company and within ten days I had captured Frank Stevenson, the leader of the gang, and broken up the nest of thieves. Stevenson was later sent to the penitentiary for fifteen years. Bond and Peterson went to El Paso where they stole Mayor McGoffin's fine pair of carriage horses and fled to New Mexico. Subsequently Bond was killed at Deming by Deputy Sheriff Dan Tucker in an attempted arrest.

Captain Roberts, Captain Coldwell, or Lieutenant Reynolds would never have let such a bunch of crooks get into their companies, for they insisted on knowing something about a man before they would enlist him. However, there was some excuse for Baylor at the time he was on the Rio Grande. It was a long way from the

Some Undesirable Recruits

center of population and good men were hard to find. Then, too, it looked as if all the criminals in Texas had fled to New Mexico and Arizona, from which places they would ease back into the edge of Texas and join the rangers. Captain Baylor was liberal in his views of men: all looked good to him until proved otherwise. If there was a vacancy in the company any man could get in; if he lacked equipment, the captain would outfit him, deducting the cost from the man's first three months' pay. However, Baylor generally had to pay the bill himself. The captain also liked to keep his company recruited to the limit and this made enlistment in his command easy.

In all the years I was with Captain Baylor I never knew him to send a non-commissioned officer on a scout after Indians. He always commanded in person and always took with him every man in camp save one, who was left to guard it, for he liked to be as strong as possible on the battlefield.

Captain Baylor never took much interest personally in following cattle thieves, horse thieves, murderers, and fugitives from justice. He left this work almost entirely to me. Sometimes we would have as many as six or eight criminals chained up in camp at one time, but the captain would never come to see them, for he could not bear to see anyone in trouble. His open, friendly personality endeared him to the Mexicans, from El Paso down the valley as far as Quitman. They were all his *compadres* and would frequently bring him venison, goat meat, and mutton. Always they showed him every courtesy in their power.

CHAPTER XVII

LAST FIGHT BETWEEN RANGERS AND APACHES

DESPITE General Terrazas' great victory at Tres Castillos, he did not destroy all the Apaches that had been with old Victorio. Nana and fifty warriors escaped, and finally joined Geronimo in his campaign of murder and destruction. On the night preceding the battle in which Victorio was killed and his band of warriors exterminated twelve braves with four squaws and four children deserted the old chief and made their way to those rough mountains that fringe the Rio Grande in the vicinity of Eagle Springs. At once this band began a series of pillages and murders that has no parallel, considering the small size of the party.

The little band of Apaches soon appeared at Paso Viejo and began their depredations by an attack on Lieutenant Mills and his cavalry. Paso Viejo is a gap in the mountains which parallel the Rio Grande from the Eagle Mountains on the west to Brites's ranch on the east, and is situated ten or twelve miles west of the present little town of Valentine, Texas. The tribe of Pueblo Indians has lived at the old town of Ysleta, El Paso County, Texas, for more than three hundred years. They have always been friends of the Americans and inveterate enemies of the Apaches. It was customary, therefore, for the United States troops at Fort Davis to employ the Pueblos as guides during the Indian disturbances along the border. In 1881 Bernado and Simon Olgin, two brothers, were the principal chiefs of this

Last Fight with the Apaches

tribe. Bernado was the elder, and looked it. Both chiefs dressed in the usual Indian fashion, wore moccasins and buckskin leggins, and had their long black hair braided and hanging down the back. Simon was a very handsome Indian, and he, with four of his tribe—all nephews of his,—were employed by General Grierson during the troublesome times of 1880-1881.

Simon and his four aides had been detailed to make scouts down on the Rio Grande with Lieutenant Mills, commander of a detachment from the Tenth United States Cavalry (colored). On their way out the troops reached Paso Viejo early in the evening, and after they had eaten supper Simon advised the lieutenant to move out on the open plains three or four miles north of the pass, where they would be safe from attack. Olgin said that because of the fine water and good grass Paso Viejo was a favorite camping-place for the Indians going to and returning from Mexico, and if one of these bands reached the pass during the night and found it occupied by soldiers they would attack at daylight and probably kill some of them.

Lieutenant Mills, fresh from West Point, replied that he was not afraid of Indians and did not propose to move. During the night the little band of twenty Apaches reached the pass, just as Olgin had prophesied, and hid themselves in the rocks. The next morning the soldiers had breakfast, packed their mules, and were standing by their horses ready for the order to mount, when a sudden fusillade of bullets was fired into their midst at short range. Other volleys came in quick succession. At the very first volley that grand old Indian, Simon Olgin, was killed, as were five or six of the negro cavalry. The remainder of the soldiers there-

201

upon fled, but the four Pueblo scouts took to the rocks and fought until they had routed the Apaches and saved the bodies of their uncle and the soldiers from falling into the hands of the attackers to be mutilated.

Repulsed at Paso Viejo, the twenty Apaches next appeared at Bass Canyon, a gap in the mountains on the overland stage road about twelve or fourteen miles west of Van Horn. Here they waylaid an emigrant train on its way to New Mexico. At the first fire of the Indians a woman of the party, Mrs. Graham, who was walking, jumped upon the tongue of the wagon and reached for a Winchester, but was shot and killed. A man named Grant was killed at the same time, while Mr. Graham had his thigh broken. From Bass Canyon the Indians turned south, passed around the east end of the Eagle Mountains, and again entered Mexico, where for a time they were lost to view.

The next appearance of the band was at Ojo Caliente, some hot springs on the Rio Grande southwest of the Eagle Mountains. A captain of cavalry in command of some colored troops near old Fort Quitman detailed a sergeant and seven men to scout down the river as far east as Bosque Bonita, with instructions to keep a sharp lookout for Indian signs and report back to camp in one week. The scout was made, and on the return journey the soldiers camped for the night at Ojo Caliente. Next morning at daybreak they were preparing to cook breakfast when the Apaches fell upon them, killing all but one at the first assault. The single survivor made his escape on foot, and after two days in the mountains without food finally reached camp and reported to his captain. The Indians had evidently located the detachment the evening before the attack and waited until

Last Fight with the Apaches

daylight to massacre their victims. The redskins captured all the equipment and baggage of their victims, including seven horses and two pack-mules. Before resuming their journey they took six stake-pins made of iron and about twenty inches long, which were used by the soldiers in fastening their horses, and drove one through each soldier's corpse, pinning it firmly to the earth. The captured stock was killed and eaten, for the soldiers' animals were fat while most of the ponies and little mules of the Apaches were worn out by constant use in the mountains.

About two months after the massacre of the soldiers the warriors fell upon the stage at Quitman Canyon and killed the driver, Morgan, and his passenger, a gambler named Crenshaw, concealing their bodies so that they were never found. The reports about this stage-robbery and murder were so conflicting, and the impression that the driver and the passenger had themselves robbed the stage and made Indian signs to avert suspicion was so strong, that Captain Baylor deemed it best to go down to the canyon and investigate the matter for himself. Accordingly, he made a detail of fourteen privates and one corporal, and with ten days' rations on two pack-mules left Ysleta on January sixteenth to ascertain if possible whether the stage had been robbed and the driver and passenger killed by Indians or by white men, and to punish the robbers if they could be caught. To repress disorder and violence at El Paso in his absence, Captain Baylor left me and a detail of three men in our camp at Ysleta.

At Quitman, Captain Baylor learned that the trail of the stage robbers bore southeast to Ojo Caliente, and as the foothills of Quitman Mountains are very rough, he went down the north bank of the Rio Grande, since he felt quite certain he would find signs of the marauders in that direction. About twenty-five miles below Quitman he struck the trail of a freshly-shod mule, two barefooted ponies, and two unshod mules, and within fifty yards of the trail he found a kid glove which was thought to have belonged to Crenshaw. The trail now bore down the river and crossed into Mexico, where the Indian band made its first camp. Captain Baylor followed, and the next day found the second camp near the foothills of the Los Pinos Mountains, where we had left General Terrazas the fall before. Here all doubts about the Indians were dispelled, as the rangers found a horse which had been killed for food, and a pair of old moccasins. Moreover, the camp had been located on a high bare hill after the custom of the Indians. The same day Captain Baylor found another camp and a dead mule, and on the trail discovered a boot-top which was recognized as that of Morgan, the driver. Here, also, was the trail of some fifteen or twenty mules and ponies, quite fresh, coming from the direction of the Candelaria Mountains with one small trail of three mules going toward the Rio Grande. The rangers passed through some very rough, deep canyons and camped on the south side of the Rio Grande, this being their second night in Mexico.

Next morning the trail crossed back into Texas. While proceeding toward Major Carpenter's old camp above the Bosque Bonita the scouting party found a camp where the Indians had evidently made a cache, but Captain Baylor tarried here only a short time and followed on down the river a few miles, when he found that the Apaches had struck out on a bee line for the Eagle

Mountains. The captain felt some hesitation about crossing the plains lying between the Eagle Mountains and the Rio Grande in the daytime for fear of being seen by the Indians, but as the trail was several days old he took the risk of being discovered. He camped within three or four miles of the mountains and at daybreak took the trail up a canyon leading into the peaks. Suddenly he came upon a camp which had been hastily deserted that morning, for the Indians had left blankets, quilts, buckskins, and many other things useful to them. They had killed and piled up in camp two horses and a mule, the blood of which had been caught in tin vessels. One mule-tongue was stewing over a fire, and everything indicated that the redskins were on the eve of a jolly war dance, for the rangers found a five-gallon can of mescal wine and a horse skin sunk in the ground that contained fifteen or twenty gallons more. They also found the mate to Morgan's boot-top and a bag which had been made from the legs of Crenshaw's pantaloons, besides express receipts, postal cards, and other articles taken from the stage. The night before had been bitterly cold and the ground had frozen hard, so that the rangers could not get the trail, though they searched the mountains in every direction, and the three Pueblo Indians, Bernado Olgin, Domingo Olgin, and Aniccto Duran, looked over every foot of the ground. The party now turned back toward Mexico to scout back on the west side of the Eagle Mountains around to Eagle Springs in search of the trail.

At Eagle Springs, as good luck would have it, Captain Baylor learned that Lieutenant Nevill and nine men had just gone toward Quitman to look for him. As soon as Lieutenant Nevill returned to the Springs he informed Baylor that he had seen the trail six miles east of Eagle Springs and that it led toward the Carrizo Springs or Diablo Mountains.

Captain Baylor's rations were exhausted and Lieutenant Nevill had only enough to supply the combined force five days, but the two commanders trusted either to catch the Indians or reach the vicinity of the Pecos settlements within that time. The Apaches made pretty good time across the plain in front of Eagle Springs, and did not seem to recover from their scare until they reached the Diablo Mountains. Here they killed a horse and cooked the meat and melted snow with hot rocks to obtain water.

The trail led northward by Chili Peak, a noted landmark to be seen from Eagle Station. Here the rangers quit the trail and went into the Diablo Mountains to camp at Apache Tanks, where General Grierson had cut off Victorio from the Guadalupe Mountains the summer before. Next morning Captain Baylor followed the trail north and camped on the brow of some cliffs overlooking Rattlesnake Springs. The sign now led to the edge of the Sierra Diablo, where the Indians camped and slept for the first time since leaving Eagle Mountains. They were still watchful, as they were near a horrible-looking canyon down which they could have disappeared had the scouting party come upon them. Their next camp was about ten miles farther on, and Captain Baylor saw that they were getting more careless about camping. On the twenty-eighth he came upon another horse and fire where the Apaches had eaten some meat. The legs of the horse were not yet stiff, and blood dropped from one when picked up. The chase was becoming exciting, and Captain Baylor and

Last Fight with the Apaches

his men felt that their opportunity to avenge the many outrages committed by this band was now near at hand.

The trail led off north as though the redskins were going toward the Cornudas in New Mexico, but turned east and entered the Sierra Diablo Mountains. In a narrow gorge the rangers found where the Indians had eaten dinner, using snow to quench their thirst, but their horses had no water. From this camp the Apaches made for the cliffs on the northeast side of the Devil Mountains. The rangers now felt sure that the Indians were near by, as they were nearly all afoot. The danger of being discovered if they passed over the hills during the daytime was so apparent that the rangers decided to make a dry camp and pass the mountain's brow before dawn the next morning. All the signs were good for a surprise; the trail was not over two hours old, and a flock of doves passing overhead, going in the direction of the trail, showed that water was near by.

On the morning of January twenty-ninth the rangers were awakened by the guard, and passed over the brow of the mountain before daylight. There was some difficulty in picking up the trail, though Captain Baylor, Lieutenant Nevill, and the Pueblos had been up the evening before spying out the land. By stooping down with their faces close to the ground the Pueblos got the trail, which led north along the crest of the mountains. Soon the guides said in low voices: *Hay estan Los Indios,* and Captain Baylor perceived their camp-fires not over half a mile distant.

Leaving a guard of five men with the horses, the rangers advanced stealthily on foot. By taking advantage of the crest of the mountain they crept within two hundred yards of the camp, supposing the Indians were camped on the western slope of the hill. The Apaches, however, had been cautious enough to put one tepee on the eastern slope, overlooking the valley and the approaches from that direction. Captain Baylor thereupon ordered Sergeant Carruthers of Lieutenant Nevill's company with seven men to make a detour to the left and attack that wigwam, while Lieutenant Nevill and himself with seventeen men advanced on the western camp. Sheltering themselves behind some large Spanish dagger plants and advancing in Indian file, the attackers got within one hundred yards of the Indians, who, apparently, had just left their beds, for it was now sunrise. Halting, the men deployed to the right and left and then, kneeling, poured upon the astonished Indians a deliberate volley. At the second fusillade they broke and fled, the rangers charging after them with a Texas yell.

Sergeant Carruthers executed his orders in gallant style. The Apaches on his side, alarmed and surprised by the fire of Captain Baylor's force, huddled together and three were killed within twenty yards of their campfire. The redskins made no resistance, but ran like deer, each man for himself. As they fled they were thickly peppered by the rangers and all but two or three out of the party of sixteen or eighteen left spots of blood along their trail.

One Indian, whom the rangers dubbed Big Foot because of his enormous track, ran up the mountain in full view for four hundred yards; although no less than two hundred shots were fired at him, he passed over the hill. Sergeant Carruthers and several men pursued him for a mile and a half and found signs of blood all the way. Another warrior was knocked down and lay as

though dead for some time, but finally regained his feet
and disappeared over the hills to a running accompani-
ment of Springfield and Winchester balls. One brave
stood his ground manfully, and was shot in the head
early in the action.

The women, of course, were the principal sufferers.
As it was a bitterly cold, windy morning and all ran
off with blankets about them, the rangers found it difficult to distinguish braves from squaws and in the confusion of the battle two women were killed and a third
mortally wounded. Two children were killed and another was shot through the foot. One squaw, with three
bullets in her hand, and two children were captured.
Seven mules and nine horses, two Winchester rifles, one
Remington carbine, one United States cavalry pistol
and one .40 double-action Colt's, six United States
cavalry saddles taken from the troops killed at Ojo
Caliente, besides clothing and other articles fell as spoil
to the victors. All the Indians' camp equipage was
burned.

The victorious rangers breakfasted on the battle-
ground, as they had eaten nothing since dinner the day
before. Some of the men found horse meat good, while
others feasted on venison and roasted mescal. The victors could not remain long at this camp for water was
very scarce. They had forty head of stock to care for,
and the Indians, in their flight, had run through the
largest pool of water, dyeing it liberally with their blood.
The rangers found enough good water for their own
use, but the horses had to wait until the force reached
Apache Tanks, thirty miles distant. But for this
scarcity of water Captain Baylor could have added three
or four more scalps to his trophies. The return march

Six Years with the Texas Rangers

was begun, and at Eagle Station Lieutenant Nevill and Captain Baylor separated. The captured squaw and the two children were sent to Fort Davis to be turned over to the post commander for medical attention, since the rangers had neither a surgeon nor a hospital.

On their return from the battle of the Diablos, Captain Baylor's Pueblo Indian scouts suddenly halted about a mile from Ysleta, unsaddled and unbridled their tired little ponies, and went into camp. This was their custom after a successful campaign against their Apache enemies, so that their comrades might come out and do honor to the returning heroes. For three days and nights a feast and a scalp dance were held by the whole of the Pueblo tribe of Ysleta. They feasted, wined, and dined their returning warriors, and invited the rangers to the festivities. This celebration was the last scalp dance the Pueblo Indians ever had, for the destruction of the Apaches in the Diablos exterminated the wild Indians and there were no more of them to scalp.

CHAPTER XVIII

AN INTERNATIONAL EPISODE

THE American citizens of Socorro, New Mexico, held a church festival during Christmas week of 1881, Mr. A. M. Conklin, editor of the Socorro *Sun,* conducting the exercises. Two Mexicans, Abran and Enofre Baca, appeared at the church under the influence of liquor. Their talk and actions so disturbed the entertainment that Mr. Conklin went to them and requested them to be more quiet, telling them they were perfectly welcome in the church but that they must behave. The brothers, highly indignant, invited Mr. Conklin to fight, but he declined and again assured them that they were welcome, but must act as gentlemen. Abran and Enofre at once retired from the church.

After the social had ended Mr. Conklin was passing out of the church door with his wife at his side when Abran Baca caught Mrs. Conklin by one arm and jerked her away from her husband. At the same instant Enofre shot and killed the editor on the church steps.

This foul murder aroused great indignation in the little town of Socorro, and scouting parties were sent in all directions in pursuit of the murderers. However, the two Bacas managed to elude their pursuers and escaped to Mexico. The governor of New Mexico at once issued a proclamation offering $500 for their capture, while the citizens of Socorro offered a like amount for them, dead or alive. The proclamation, with a minute description of the two Bacas, was sent broadcast over the country, and, of course, the rangers at Ysleta received several of the circulars.

Six Years with the Texas Rangers

The county judge of El Paso County at that time was José Baca, an uncle of the two murderers. He was also a merchant at Ysleta, then the county seat. Captain Baylor's company of rangers was quartered in the west end of Ysleta, about one-half mile from the public square. On receiving the governor's proclamation I set a watch over the home and store of Judge Baca and kept it up for nearly a month, but without success. We finally concluded that the Baca boys had not come our way and dismissed the incident from our minds.

One morning in the latter part of March, however, Jim Fitch, one of our most trustworthy rangers, hurried back to camp from Ysleta and informed me that he had seen two well-dressed Mexicans, strangers to him, sitting on the porch of Judge Baca's home. With a detail of four men I at once rounded up the Baca home and captured the two strangers. Believing them to be the Baca brothers, I set out for New Mexico with my prisoners.

Before we reached El Paso on our journey we were overtaken by Judge Baca, who had with him an interpreter. He asked me to halt, as he wished to talk with the prisoners. After a short conversation with the boys, the judge asked me what was the reward for the capture of Abran Baca. I replied, "Five hundred dollars."

"If you will just let him step out in the bosque and get away I will give you $700," Judge Baca finally said with some hesitation.

Subsequently he raised the bribe to $1,000, but I informed him there was not enough money in El Paso County to buy me off, so he returned to Ysleta and I continued my journey to New Mexico, feeling assured I had captured at least one of the Conklin murderers.

An International Episode

On arriving at Socorro I learned that I had Abran all right, but my second prisoner was Massias Baca, a cousin of the murderers, but not involved in the crime.

I was treated royally by the citizens and officers of Socorro. They were delighted that one of the murderers had been captured, and promptly counted out to me $250 as their part of the reward offered for his apprehension. Colonel Eaton, deputy sheriff of the county, gave me a receipt for the body of Abran Baca delivered inside the jail of Socorro County, New Mexico. This receipt, forwarded to the governor of the territory, promptly brought me a draft for $250 and a letter of thanks from his Excellency.

About a month after the capture of Abran Baca, I learned from Santiago Cooper, a friend who lived in Ysleta, that he had seen a man at Saragosa, Mexico, whom, from the description, he believed to be Enofre Baca. I told Cooper I would give him $25 if he would return to Saragosa and find out to a certainty whether the person he had seen was Enofre Baca. A week later he came to me and said the man at Saragosa was Baca, and that the murderer was clerking in the one big store of the town. This store was a long adobe building situated against a hill with the front facing so that one riding up to the front of it would bring his saddle skirts almost on a level with the building because of the terraces in front of it made necessary by the slope of the hill. Enofre was of florid complexion with dark red hair, which made it easy to identify him.

I kept this information about the murderer to myself for nearly a week while I pondered over it. I was anxious to capture Baca, yet I well knew from previous experience that if I caused him to be arrested in Mexico the authorities there would turn him loose, especially when the influence of wealthy relatives was brought to bear. Knowing Captain Baylor would follow the law to the letter, I could not take him into my confidence. Saragosa, a town of about five hundred inhabitants, is situated about four miles southwest of Ysleta. It is only about a mile from the Rio Grande as the crow flies, yet, because of the many farms and big irrigation ditches, it was possible to enter or leave the town only by following the public road between Ysleta and Saragosa. It has always been the delight of border Mexicans to get behind an adobe wall or on top of an adobe house and shoot to ribbons any hated gringo who might unfortunately be caught on the Mexican side of the river. I knew only too well from my own experience that I could not go into Saragosa, attempt to arrest a Mexican, stay there five minutes, and live, yet I determined to take the law into my own hands and make the attempt.

I took into my confidence just one man, George Lloyd. If ever there was an ace in the ranger service he was one. When I unfolded my plans to him, he said, "Sergeant, that is an awful dangerous and risky piece of business and I will have to have a little time in which to think it over." The next day he came to me and said, "Sergeant, I will go anywhere in the world with you." But although willing to accompany me I could see he doubted our ability to execute the project.

I planned to attempt the capture of Baca the next morning and sent Cooper back to Saragosa to look over the situation there once more. He informed me on his return that Baca was still clerking in the store. I now told Lloyd to keep our horses up when the animals were turned out to graze next morning. This move caused no especial comment, for the men frequently would keep their horses to ride down town. As soon as we had crossed the Rio Grande into Mexico I planned to quit the public road, travel through the bosques, pass around on the west side of Saragosa, and ride quickly up to the store in which our man was working. Lloyd was to hold the horses while I was to dismount, enter the store, and make the arrest. Then, if possible, I was to mount Baca behind Lloyd and make a quick get-away.

Our plans were carried out almost to the letter. We reached Saragosa safely, and while Lloyd held my horse in front of the store I entered and discovered Baca measuring some goods for an old Mexican woman. I stepped up to him, seized him by the collar, and with drawn pistol ordered him to come with me. The customer promptly fainted and fell on the floor. Two other people ran from the building, screaming at the top of their voices. Baca hesitated about going with me, and in broken English asked where he was to be taken. I informed him to Paso del Norte, and, shoving my pistol against his head, ordered him to step lively. When we reached our horses I made him mount behind Lloyd. I then jumped into my saddle and, waving my pistol over my head, we left Saragosa on a dead run. Our sudden appearance in the town and our still more sudden departure bewildered the people for a few minutes. They took in the situation quickly, however, and began ringing the old church bell rapidly, and this aroused the whole population.

As I left Saragosa I saw men getting their horses together and knew that in a few minutes a posse would be following us. When we had gone two miles almost at top speed I saw that Lloyd's horse was failing, and we lost a little time changing Baca to my mount. We had yet two miles to go, most of the way through deep sand. I could see a cloud of dust, and shortly a body of mounted men hove in view. It was a tense moment. Lloyd thought it was all off with us, but we still had a long lead and our horses were running easily. As our pursuers made a bend in the road we counted nine men in the group. When they had drawn up within six hundred yards they began firing on us. This was at long range and did no damage. In fact, I believe they were trying to frighten rather than to wound us, as they were just as likely to hit Baca as either of us. We reached the Rio Grande at last, and while it was almost one hundred yards wide it was flat and shallow at the ford. We hit the water running, and as I mounted the bank on good old Texan soil I felt like one who has made a home run in a world-series baseball game. Our pursuers halted at the river, so I pulled off my hat, waved to them, and disappeared up the road.

We lost no time in reaching camp, and our appearance there with a prisoner and two run-down horses caused all the boys in quarters to turn out. Captain Baylor noticed the gathering and hurried over to camp.

"Sergeant, who is this prisoner you have?" he asked, walking up to me.

I replied it was Enofre Baca, the man who had murdered Mr. Conklin. The captain looked at the run-down horses, wet with sweat, and asked me where I had captured him.

"Down the river," I replied, trying to evade him.

"From the looks of your horse I would think you had

just run out of a fight. Where down the river did you capture this man?"

I saw that he was going to corner me and I thought I might as well "fess up." I told him I had arrested Baca at Saragosa and kidnapped him out of Mexico. Captain Baylor's eyes at once bulged to twice their natural size.

"Sergeant, that is the most imprudent act you ever committed in your life! Don't you know that it is a flagrant violation of the law and is sure to cause a breach of international comity that might cause the governor of Texas to disband the whole of Company A? Not only this, but it was a most hazardous undertaking and it is a wonder to me that the Mexicans did not shoot you and Lloyd into doll rags."

Captain Baylor was plainly out of patience with me.

"Gillett, you have less sense than I thought you had," he declared, heatedly. "If you have any explanation to make I would like to have it."

I reminded him of the tragic fate of Morgan and Brown, and how the authorities at Guadalupe had turned loose their murderers, Esquibel and Molina. I declared that had I had Baca arrested in Mexico, with his rich and influential friends to help him, he would have gone scot-free. Baylor replied that two wrongs did not make one right, and said I should have consulted him. I finally told him frankly that I had been in the ranger service six years, in which time I had risen from the ranks to be orderly sergeant at a salary of only $50 a month. I pointed out that this was the highest position I could hope to get without a commission, and while one had been promised me at the first vacancy yet I could see no early hope of obtaining it, as every captain in the battalion was freezing to his job. This remark seemed to amuse Captain Baylor and somewhat eased his anger.

I went on to say that I not only wanted the $500 reward offered for Baca, but I wanted the notoriety I would get if I could kidnap the murderer out of Mexico without being killed in the attempt, for I believed it would lead to something better than a ranger sergeancy.

"Sergeant, you can go with your man," Captain Baylor finally said, "but it is against my best judgment. I ought to escort him across the Rio Grande and set him free."

I lost no time in sending a ranger to the stage office at Ysleta with instructions to buy two tickets to Mesilla, New Mexico, and one to El Paso. The stage was due to pass our quarters about twelve o'clock, so I did not have long to wait. I took Lloyd as a guard as far as El Paso and there turned him back, making the remainder of the journey to Socorro alone with the prisoner. I reached the old town of Mesilla, New Mexico, at dark after a rather exciting day. I was afraid to put Baca in jail at that place, as I had no warrant nor extradition papers upon which to hold him and I feared the prison authorities might not redeliver him to me next morning. The stagecoach from Mesilla to Rincon did not run at night, so I secured a room at the hotel and chaining Baca to me we slept together.

On the following day we reached Rincon, then the terminus of the Santa Fé Railroad. I had wired the officers of Socorro from El Paso that I had captured Baca and was on my way to New Mexcio with him. Baca's friends had also been informed of his arrest, and they lost no time in asking the governor of New Mexico

An International Episode

to have me bring the prisoner to Santa Fé, as they feared mob violence at Socorro. When I reached San Marcial I was handed a telegram from the governor ordering me to bring Baca to Santa Fé, and on no account to stop with him in Socorro.

Because of delay on the railroad I did not reach Socorro until late at night. The minute the train stopped it was boarded by twenty-five or thirty armed men, headed by Deputy Sheriff Eaton. I showed Eaton the governor's telegram, but he declared Baca was wanted at Socorro and that was where he was going. I remonstrated with him and declared I was going on to Santa Fé with the prisoner. By this time a dozen armed men had gathered around me who declared, "Not much will you take him to Santa Fé." I was furious, but I was practically under arrest and powerless to help myself. Baca and I were transferred from the train to a big bus that was in waiting. The jailer entered first, then Baca was seated next to him, and I sat next the door with my Winchester in my hand. The driver was ordered to drive to the jail.

It was a bright moonlight night and we had not traveled far up the street when I looked out and saw at least a hundred armed men. They came from every direction. The men swarmed around the bus and three or four of them grabbed the horses by the bridle reins, while others tried to force open the doors. I asked the jailer if I could depend on him to help me stand the mob off, but he replied it would do no good. I was now madder than ever, and for the first time in my life I ripped out an oath, saying, "God damn them, I am going to stand them off!"

As the doors were forced I poked my Winchester

out and ordered the mob to stand back or I would shoot. The men paid no more attention to my gun than if it had been a broomstick. A man standing beside the bus door seized the muzzle and, with a quick jerk to one side, caused it to fly out of my hand and out upon the ground. Another man grabbed me by the collar and proceeded to pull me out of the bus. I spread my legs and tried to brace myself, but a hard and quick jerk landed me out on the ground, where one of the men kicked me. I was tame now, and made no effort to draw my pistol. One of the crowd said to me, "What in hell do you mean? We do not wish to hurt you but we are going to hang that damned Mexican right now!"

I then informed the mob of the nature of Baca's arrest and told them that the hanging of the prisoner would place me in an awkward position. Then, too, the reward offered by the territory of New Mexico was for the delivery of the murderer inside the jail doors of Socorro County. The leaders of the crowd consulted for a few minutes and then concluded I was right. They ordered me back into the bus, gave me my Winchester, and we all started for the jail. As soon as Baca had been placed in prison Deputy Sheriff Eaton sat down and wrote a receipt for the delivery of Baca inside the jail doors.

By this time day was beginning to break and I tried to stay the hanging by making another talk. The mob interpreted my motive and invited me to step down a block to their community room where they would talk with me. I started with them but we had gone only a hundred yards when the whole mob broke back to the jail. I started to go with them but two men held me, saying, "It's no use; they are going to hang him."

An International Episode

The men took Baca to a near-by corral and hanged him to a big beam of the gate. The next morning Baca's relatives came to me at the hotel with hats in their hands and asked me for the keys with which to remove the shackles from the dead man's legs. As I handed them the keys I felt both mortified and ashamed. A committee of citizens at Socorro waited on me just before I took the train for home, counted out $250 as their part of the reward, and thanked me for capturing the two murderers. They assured me they stood ready to help me financially or otherwise should I become involved with the federal government over the capture and kidnapping of Baca.

I presume the relatives of young Baca reported his kidnapping to our government, for a few weeks after his capture Mr. Blaine, Secretary of State, wrote a long letter to Governor Roberts regarding a breach of international comity. Governor Roberts wrote Captain Baylor for a full explanation of the matter. Captain Baylor, while never countenancing wrongdoing in his company, would stand by his men to the last ditch when they were once in trouble. He was a fluent writer, and no man in Texas understood better than he the many foul and outrageous murders that had been committed along the Rio Grande, the perpetrators of which had evaded arrest and punishment by crossing over into Mexico. Baylor wrote so well and so to the point that nothing further was said about the matter. However, he received an order never again to allow his men to follow fugitives into Mexico.

Soon afterward the Safety Committee of Socorro wrote to Captain Baylor saying: "We are informed by a reliable party that José Baca of Ysleta, Texas, has hired a Mexican to kill Sergeant Gillett. Steps have been taken to prevent this. However, he would do well to be on the lookout." Baylor at once went to Judge Baca with this letter, but the jurist emphatically denied any knowledge of the reported plot. Also, there was a report current in both Ysleta and El Paso that a reward of $1,500 had been offered for the delivery of my body to the Mexican authorities at El Paso del Norte. Upon investigation I found that no such offer had been made, but for safety's sake I kept out of Mexico for several years.

CHAPTER XIX

LAST SCOUTINGS

DURING the summer of 1881 Captain Baylor's company made several scouts to the Sacramento and Guadalupe mountains. These were reported to the adjutant general as scouts after Indians, but there were no more redskins in Texas, for the rangers had done their work effectively. These expeditions were, therefore, more in the nature of outings for the boys. It was pleasant to get away from camp in the hot Rio Grande Valley and scout in these high mountains covered with tall pine timber that teemed with game, such as deer, bear, and wild turkey. The plains between the Guadalupe Mountains and Ysleta contained hundreds of antelopes, thus affording the rangers the best of sport.

On one of these hunting expeditions we had with us George Lloyd, who had been a ranger under Lieutenant Tays when his company was first mustered into service in El Paso County. We camped at Las Cornudas, where Lloyd had had an engagement with Indians. He went over the ground and gave us an interesting account of the fight. He said there were but twelve men in the scout, including Lieutenant Tays. In marching from Crow Springs to Las Cornudas, a distance of thirty miles, six of the rangers were riding nearly a mile ahead of the others and on approaching Las Cornudas made for some *tinajas* (water holes) up in these mountains. They rode around a point of rocks and met face to face some ten or twelve Indians coming out from the water. Indians and rangers were within

223

forty feet before they discovered each other's presence, and paleface and redskin literally fell off their horses— the Indians seeking cover in the rocks above the trail while five of the rangers turned somersaults into a friendly gully.

A ranger who was said to be a Russian nobleman and nihilist was killed early in the fight and buried on the spot where he fell. A headboard was placed to mark the grave, but the Indians soon defaced it by hacking at it with their knives whenever they passed the spot. Though he could have had splendid cover, the Russian stood upright according to the etiquette prevailing among British officers in the Transvaal and was shot through the brain.

In dismounting, Lloyd held on to the end of a thirty-foot stake-rope that was tied around his horse's neck. Four of the scouts wriggled their way down the creek and got away. In reloading his Winchester after shooting it empty Lloyd unfortunately slipped a .45 Colt's pistol cartridge into the magazine of his .44 Winchester and in attempting to throw a cartridge into his gun it jammed, catching him in a serious predicament. However, taking his knife from his pocket the fearless ranger coolly removed the screw that held the side plates of his Winchester together, took off the plates, removed the offending cartridge, replaced the plates, tightened up the screw, reloaded his gun, and began firing. It takes a man with iron nerve to do a thing like that, and you meet such a one but once in a lifetime. When I was casting around for a man to go into Mexico with me to kidnap Baca I naturally selected Lloyd out of the twenty men in camp.

Seeing that the Russian was dead and his companions

gone, Lloyd crawled back down the arroyo, pulling his horse along the bank above until he was out of danger. The five rangers' horses, knowing where the water was, went right up into the rocks, where they were captured, saddles, bridles, and all, by the Indians.

As soon as Lloyd was gone, the redskins came out of hiding, took the Russian's Winchester and pistol, and left. Lloyd was the only man of the six to save his horse, for the Indians with their needle guns, high up in the rocks, held Lieutenant Tays and the remainder of his force at bay.

In the latter part of the summer of 1881 Captain Baylor moved his company of rangers from Ysleta to a site three miles below El Paso. While camped there the captain was warned by the sheriff of Tombstone, Arizona, to be on the lookout for four San Simon Valley rustlers, supposed to be a part of Curley Bill's gang. The robbers' names were given as Charley and Frank Baker, Billy Morgan, and a fourth person supposed to be Curley Bill himself. These outlaws had stolen sixteen big work mules and four horses at a wood camp some twelve miles from Tombstone. They had also robbed a store and, assaulting the proprietor with pistols, left him for dead. A $500 reward was offered for the capture of the desperadoes and the stolen stock. The robbers' trail led down into New Mexico and it was believed Curley Bill and his gang were headed for western Texas, where they would try to dispose of the stock at some of the railroad grading camps near El Paso.

Captain Baylor at once ordered me to take seven men and five days' rations and scout up the Rio Grande to the line of New Mexico for the bandits' trail, and, if I found it, to follow it up. I worked up the river but found no trail. Neither could I learn anything about any strange men driving stock through the country. My time was nearly up and I concluded to return to camp through a gap in the Franklin Mountains, some thirty or forty miles north of El Paso. We left the Rio Grande late in the evening, passed out through the gap, and made a dry camp on the plains east of the mountains.

Early the following morning we rode to a watering place known as Monday's Springs and stopped for breakfast. Here the boys discovered some horse and mule tracks. At first we thought nothing of this, supposing the trail had been made by some loose stock grazing near the water. From Monday's Springs a dim road led along the east side of the mountains to El Paso and we took this route home. Before we had traveled very far we noticed that some of the stock was traveling the same road, though even then I did not suspect that these tracks might be the trail of the bandits for whom we were scouting. Finally, we came to footprints made by some men as they adjusted their saddles or tightened their packs. Here it dawned on me that the tracks might have been made by the parties we wanted.

I thereupon followed the trail carefully and it led me through what is today the most beautiful residential portion of the city of El Paso. The tracks led to a big camp yard where now stands the $500,000 federal building and postoffice. In the description of the stolen stock we were told that one of the mules carried a small Swiss stock bell. As I neared the wagon yard I heard the tinkle of this bell and felt sure we had tracked our quarry. We dismounted, and with our Winchesters cocked and ready for action, our little party of rangers slipped quickly inside the large corral gate and within ten feet of it we came upon three heavily armed men bending over a fire cooking their breakfast. Their guns were leaning against the adobe fence near at hand, so the surprise was complete.

The outlaws rose to their feet and attempted to get their guns, but my men held their cocked Winchesters at their breasts. I told them that we were rangers ordered to arrest them, and demanded their surrender. The robbers were undecided what to do; they were afraid to pull their pistols or seize their guns, yet they refused to hold up their hands. Finally, one of the Baker brothers turned slightly toward me and said they would rather be shot down and killed than give up—surrender meant death anyway. I thereupon answered that we had no desire to hurt them, but declared that the least attempt to pull a gun would mean instant death to them all, and again ordered them to raise their hands. They slowly obeyed. I stepped up to them, unbuckled their belts, and took their weapons.

In looking over their camp I found four saddles and Winchesters, but I had captured only three men. I mentioned this fact to the prisoners and they laughingly said one of their number had stepped down town to get a package of coffee, and had probably noticed our presence and lit out. The two Baker boys and Billy Morgan were the men captured, and I asked if the missing man was Curley Bill himself. They replied it was not, but refused to tell who he was. As we had no description of him and he was on foot in a town full of armed men we had no means of identifying him and he was never captured.

From the captured robbers we learned that, having run out of provisions, they had risen early and come into El Paso for breakfast. They declared it was a good thing for us that they had built their camp-fire so near the gate, for had they been thirty feet from it they would have put up a fight we should have remembered for a long time. I replied that the eight of us could have held our own no matter where they had camped.

These robbers were held in our camp some ten days or more until the proper extradition papers could be had from the State Capitol at Austin, as they refused to be taken back to Arizona without the proper authority. They owned horses, which they gave to some lawyers in El Paso to prevent their being taken back to the scene of their crimes. We secured all the stolen stock —sixteen mules and four horses. The owners came and claimed them and paid the rangers $200, and the Arizona sheriff paid us a like amount for the capture of the rustlers.

Our rangers became well acquainted with these thieves while we held them in our camp. They admitted they were going under assumed names and said they were Texans, but refused to say from what part of the state they came. The three of them were taken back to Arizona, tried for assault to kill and the theft of the horses at Tombstone, and sent to the prison at Yuma for twenty-five years. They frequently wrote to our boys from there and seemed to hold no grudge against us for capturing them. The scout to capture these men was the last one of importance I took part in, for my work with the rangers was now drawing toward its close.

In the fall of 1881 Captain Baylor received word from Israel King of Cambray, New Mexico, that a band of thieves had stolen a bunch of cattle from him and at last reports was headed toward El Paso with them. With a detail of four men I was ordered to make a scout up the river and into the thickets to intercept the rustlers. After traveling some ten miles up the Rio Grande we crossed the river into New Mexico to get on more even ground. Some eighteen miles above El Paso we found the trail of the stolen stock and followed it back across the Rio Grande into Texas.

While working our way along the trail through almost impassable brush we entered a small glade and came upon the stolen animals quietly grazing. On the opposite side of them a Mexican with a Winchester stood guard, while his horse grazed near by. The guard fired on us as he ran to his horse, and we were compelled to run around the cattle to get to the thief. We fired our guns as we ran and this sudden noise frightened the loose pony so that the fugitive was unable to mount. He was then forced to dive into the brush on foot. Knowing we could make no headway through the heavy tornilla bosque, we dismounted and charged it on foot. The fleeing Mexican undertook to run through a muddy slough formed by back water from the Rio Grande. Here he bogged, but extricating himself, he backed out the way he had entered and found safety in the friendly brush. In running to where he was last seen we found his gun abandoned in the mud. Some twenty or thirty shots were fired at him and while none found the mark we captured his Winchester, his pony, and thirty-six head of stolen cattle and gave him a scare that he will remember as long as he lives. The cattle were returned to Mr. King, who presented us with a reward of $200 for their recovery.

We learned later that Frank Stevenson, a notorious rustler, whose rendezvous was in this brush, had stolen these cattle and had left the Mexican in charge of them while he had gone into El Paso to effect their sale. As described in a previous chapter, I finally captured Stevenson and he was sent to the penitentiary for fifteen years for horse stealing. His capture and imprisonment broke up the Canutillo gang; today, the upper Rio Grande Valley is almost an Eden on earth with its fine apple and peach orchards, its alfalfa fields, big dairy herds, and elegant homes. It is one of the beauty spots adjacent to the now fine city of El Paso. The Santa Fé Railroad traverses this valley, and I sometimes travel over it. As I sit in an easy seat in the Pullman and look out over the country, I always reflect on the past and wonder how many of its present inhabitants know what a wilderness and what a rendezvous it once was for cutthroats, cattle thieves, and murderers.

While the rangers were camped near El Paso during the fall of 1881 I met Captain Thatcher, then division superintendent of the Santa Fé Railroad. He told me, because of the stage and train robberies in New Mexico and Arizona, the railroad and the Wells-Fargo Express companies feared that their trains would be held up near El Paso. They had decided, therefore, to place an armed guard of three men on the main line of the Santa Fé to run between Deming and Las Vegas, New Mexico, and a similar guard on the branch from El Paso, Texas, to Rincon, New Mexico. Captain Thatcher had known me as a ranger, and my kidnaping of Enofre Baca out of Mexico had won me no little notoriety, so he now offered me a position with the railroad company as captain of the guard at a salary of $150 per month. I would be allowed to select my own men for guards and would be responsible for their acts.

Last Scoutings

I requested time to consider the proposition. While the position as captain of the railroad guard might not be permanent—might not hold out more than six months—yet the salary attached was exactly three times what I received as sergeant of rangers. I discussed Thatcher's offer with Captain Baylor and finally prevailed upon him to give me my discharge. On December 26, 1881, after serving as a ranger for six years and seven months, I laid down my Winchester with the satisfied consciousness that I had ever done my duty. My term of service embraced one of the happiest portions of my life, and recollections of my ranger days are among my most cherished memories.

The personnel of Captain Baylor's company changed rapidly, so that at the time of my discharge there was scarcely a man in the company who had served longer than six months. There was, therefore, no wrenching or straining of strong friendship ties when I left the command, save only for my leaving of Captain Baylor. To part from him did, indeed, make me feel sad. My farewell and departure were simple and unimpressive. I sat down with my comrades for a last ranger dinner of beans, bacon, bread, and black coffee. After the meal I rose from the table, shook hands with Captain Baylor and the boys, mounted my horse, and rode away from the ranger camp forever.

CHAPTER XX

FRUITS OF RANGER SERVICE

EARLY in the spring of 1881 the old town of El Paso awoke out of her Rip Van Winkle sleep to find that four grand trunk railroad lines were rapidly building toward her and were certain to enter the town by the end of the year. Situated, as it was, many hundreds of miles from any other town, it was a foregone conclusion that El Paso had the making of a great city and was a fine field for investment. Bankers, merchants, capitalists, real-estate dealers, cattlemen, miners, railroad men, gamblers, saloon keepers, and sporting people of both sexes flocked to the town. They came in buggies, hacks, and wagons, on horseback, and even afoot. Hotel accommodations were utterly inadequate, so people slept and ate as best they could. El Paso Street, the only business thoroughfare, was flooded with crowds.

At night there was not enough room for people on the sidewalks and they filled the streets. A saloon was opened on almost every corner of the town, with many in between. Each drinking place had a gambling house attached, where the crowds played faro bank, monte, roulette, chuck-a-luck, stud poker, and every other gambling game on the calendar. If one wished a seat at the gambling tables he had to come early in the evening or he could not get within thirty feet of them. Two variety theaters, the Coliseum, operated by the Manning Brothers,—the largest in the southwest—and Jack Doyle's, were quickly opened.

An election was called in El Paso and the city was

Fruits of Ranger Service

duly incorporated and a mayor and board of aldermen installed. George Campbell was elected city marshal and was given one assistant, Bill Johnson. The new marshal had come to El Paso from Young County, Texas, where he had been a deputy sheriff. He had done some good detective work and was a good and efficient officer, but his assistant was much below ordinary.

The marshal soon found that with but one man to aid him he had the biggest kind of a job on his hands, with something doing every hour in the twenty-four. Campbell decided he was not getting enough pay for the work he had to do and asked for a raise in salary, but the city council refused it. He at once resigned and left Bill Johnson to hold the town. Campbell was very friendly with the sporting element in El Paso, especially with the Manning Brothers, who were running two saloons and a big variety theater. Campbell and his friends decided to use strategy to force the council to increase his salary and planned to shoot up the town, thinking this would cause the city fathers to reinstate him in his old position with a substantial increase in pay. At two o'clock one morning the town was shot up, some three or four hundred shots being fired promiscuously and with no attempt to make arrests.

The following morning Mayor McGoffin sent a hurry call to Captain Baylor at Ysleta and asked that a detachment of rangers be sent to El Paso to help police the town. At that time I had not severed my connection with the rangers, so I was ordered to make a detail of five men, issue them fifteen days' rations, and have them report at once to the mayor of El Paso.

The peace-loving citizens of the town welcomed the rangers, secured good quarters for them, and furnished them with a stove on which to cook their meals. They had been doing police duty about a week when there appeared in the town from New Mexico the famous Dallas Stoudenmire. The newcomer was six feet two inches in height and weighed one hundred and eighty-five pounds. He had a compelling personality and had been a Confederate soldier, having served with General Joe Johnston at Greensboro, North Carolina. He applied for the position of city marshal, and having good references was duly appointed.

George Campbell now saw his chance for reinstatement as an officer in El Paso go glimmering. Marshal Stoudenmire called on Bill Johnson for the keys of the city jail, but the latter refused to surrender them. Thereupon Stoudenmire seized the recalcitrant assistant, shook him up, and took the keys from his pocket, thereby making his first enemy in El Paso.

About ten days after the new marshal had been installed it was reported in El Paso that two Mexican boys had been found murdered some ten or twelve miles from town on the Rio Grande. The rangers stationed in the city went out to the ranch to investigate. The bodies were brought to El Paso and a coroner's inquest was held in a room fronting on El Paso Street. Johnnie Hale, manager of Manning's little ranch, was summoned to appear before the coroner, and it was believed by the rangers that Hale and an ex-ranger named Len Peterson had committed the double murder.

The inquest, being held in such a public place, attracted a crowd of onlookers. Besides the rangers, Marshal Stoudenmire, ex-Marshal Campbell, and Bill Johnson were present. Gus Krimpkau, an ex-ranger, who had come from San Antonio to El Paso County

Fruits of Ranger Service

with Captain Baylor, acted as interpreter. The trial dragged along until the noon hour and the proceedings were adjourned for dinner. The rangers went at once to their quarters to prepare their meal, though there was still a crowd standing about the scene of the inquest. Krimpkau came out of the room and was accosted by John Hale, who had become offended at the way he had interpreted the evidence. After a few hot words Hale pulled his pistol and shot Krimpkau through the head, killing him instantly. Marshal Stoudenmire ran up and shot at Hale, but missing him, killed a Mexican by-stander. At the second shot from the marshal's pistol, however, Hale fell dead. George Campbell had pulled his pistol and was backing off across the street when Stoudenmire suddenly turned and shot him down. Four men were thus killed almost in the twinkling of an eye.

Stoudenmire was held blameless by the better class of citizens for the part he had played, but a certain sporting element—mostly friends of Campbell—was highly indignant at him for killing Campbell, and declared the latter had been murdered. The Manning Brothers were especially bitter against the marshal, as he had killed their ranch foreman, Hale, and their friend, Campbell. The friends of the latter sought to take the life of Stoudenmire, and they used as their instrument Bill Johnson, a man of simple mentality. They furnished him with plenty of free whisky and when they had made him drunk they told him Stoudenmire had had no right to catch him by the collar and shake him as if he were a dog. Johnson finally agreed to kill the marshal. One night, armed with a double-barrel shotgun, he stationed himself behind a pile of bricks in San Antonio

Street where it enters El Paso, and lay in wait for his intended victim.

Stoudenmire was then down at Neal Nuland's Acme saloon, and it was well known that he would soon make his round up the street. Shortly afterward he was seen coming, and when he had approached within twenty-five feet of the brick pile Bill Johnson rose to his feet and fired both barrels of his shotgun. Unsteady with drink, Johnson's fire went over the marshal's head and left him unharmed. The marshal pulled his pistol and with lightning rapidity filled Johnson full of holes. At the same moment Campbell's friends, posted on the opposite side of the street, opened fire on Stoudenmire and slightly wounded him in one foot, but he charged his attackers and single-handed put them to flight.

From that day Marshal Stoudenmire had the roughs of El Paso eating out of his hand. There was no longer any necessity for the rangers to help him police the town and they were withdrawn. Stoudenmire's presence on the streets was a guarantee of order and good government. He was a good man for the class of people he had to deal with, yet he knew there were those in El Paso who were his bitter enemies and always on the alert for a chance to take his life. This caused him to drink, and when under the influence of liquor he became mean and overbearing to some of his most ardent supporters, so that by the spring of 1882 he was asked to resign. In a dramatic and fiery speech Stoudenmire presented his resignation, declaring he had not been treated fairly by the city council and that he could straddle them all.

Immediately on leaving the rangers I had accepted a position as captain of guards on the Santa Fé Railroad, under my friend, Captain Thatcher. I did not remain long in the railroad's employ, however, resigning after a few months to become assistant city marshal under Mr. Stoudenmire. On his resignation as marshal I was appointed to succeed him. On my appointment he walked over, took me by the hand, and said, "Young man, I congratulate you on being elected city marshal, and at the same time I wish to warn you that you have more than a man's size job on your hands."

Stoudenmire at once secured the appointment as United States deputy marshal of the Western District of Texas, with headquarters at El Paso. He always treated me with the greatest consideration and courtesy, giving me trouble on only one occasion. I reproduce here a clipping from an El Paso paper of the time:

"Last Thursday night a shooting scrape in which ex-Marshal Stoudenmire and ex-Deputy Page played the leading parts occurred at the Acme saloon. It seems that early in the evening Page had a misunderstanding with Billy Bell. Stoudenmire acted as peacemaker in the matter. In doing so he carried Page to Doyle's concert hall, where the two remained an hour or so and got more or less intoxicated. About midnight they returned to the Acme and soon got into a quarrel. Stoudenmire drew his pistol and fired at Page; the latter, however, knocked the weapon upward and the ball went into the ceiling. Page then wrenched the pistol from Stoudenmire and the latter drew a second pistol and the two combatants were about to perforate each other when Marshal Gillett appeared on the premises with a double-barrel shotgun and corralled both of them. They were taken before court the following morning and fined $25 each and Stoudenmire was placed under bond in the sum of $250 to keep the peace."

Six Years with the Texas Rangers

My election as marshal I attribute solely to my training as a ranger, and to the notoriety my kidnaping of Baca out of Mexico had given me, so that the marshalship of the town was one of the direct fruits of my ranger service.

I was an officer of El Paso for several years. Soon after my acceptance of the marshalship Captain C. L. Nevill, with whom I had served in Lieutenant Reynolds' company, resigned his ranger command and became sheriff and tax collector of Presidio County, Texas. The Marfa country was now seen to be a very promising cattle section, so Captain Nevill and I formed a partnership and embarked in the cattle business. This did not interfere with our duties as sheriff and marshal, respectively, and we soon built up a nice little herd of cattle.

In the spring of 1885 General Gano and sons of Dallas formed a company known as the Estado Land and Cattle Company. The new concern arranged to open a big ranch in Brewster County and General Gano wrote to Captain Nevill, asking him to secure a good cattleman as ranch manager for the new company. Nevill at once wrote me and advised me to accept this position. In his letter he jokingly remarked:

"Jim, you have had a quart cup of bullets shot at you while a ranger and marshal, and now that you have a chance to quit and get something less hazardous I advise you to do it. Besides, you will be near our own little ranch and can see your own cattle from time to time."

I considered the proposition seriously, and on April 1, 1885, I resigned from the police force of El Paso and became a cowboy again. In accepting the marshalship I had reaped the fruits of my ranger service; now, in resigning from that position I severed all connection

James B. Gillett. From a photograph taken in 1925.

Fruits of Ranger Service

with the ranger force and all that it had brought me. Henceforth my ranger days and ranger service were to be but a memory, albeit the happiest one of my life.

I managed the Estado Land and Cattle Company's ranch for nearly six years and during that period the herd increased from six to thirty thousand head. When I resigned the managership it was that I might attend to my own ranch interests, which had also grown in that period. Though today I own a large and prosperous ranch in the Marfa country, and though my business interests are many and varied, I still cherish the memory of my ranger days and am never too busy to see an old ranger comrade and relive with him those six adventurous, happy, and thrilling years when I was a member of the Frontier Battalion of the Texas Rangers.

INDEX

Index

Index

243

Index

Index

Index

Dublin, Dell, criminal career, 88-89; escapes rangers, 91-92; captured, 103-104.

Dublin, Jimmie, father of outlaws, 87; son-in-law captured, 102.

Dublin, Richard, criminal career, 87-89; killed, 92-95.

Dublin, Role, swears vengeance against rangers, 95; captured, 103-104.

Dunbar, Levi, slain, 13.

Duncan, Jack, captures bandit, 85.

Duran, Aniceto, in campaign against Apaches, 200-210.

Durham, Paul, on scout against Indians, 33-45.

EAGLE Ford, train robbed, 115.

Eagle Mountains, objective of Victorio, 180; Indian atrocities 188; Indians pass, 202; pursued by rangers, 205.

Eagle Pass, rendezvous of filibusters, 71.

Eagle Springs, route via, 146; rangers scout toward, 180; Indian raiders near, 200; pursued by rangers, 205-206.

Eagle station, rangers at 210.

Eaton, Colonel ——, assumes custody of murderers, 213, 219-220.

Egan, W. F., employs Sam Bass, 108.

Eighteen Mile Water Hole, fight with Indians at, 180.

El Cobre Mountains, operations against Victorio, 184.

Ellis, ——, slain in Salt Lake War, 138.

Ellis, Wess, as cattleman, 14, 23.

Elm Creek, game killed on, 57; rangers camp, 67.

El Paso, residents in Salt Lake War, 136-140; mail route to, 146; stage-drivers slain, 148; road from, to mountains, 175; activities of outlaws, 198; route via, 218; rangers camp, 225; criminals captured, 226-227; boom, 232; disorders, 232-237.

El Paso del Norte, former name for Juarez, 161; citizens march against Apaches, 164-168, 183.

Escajeda, Don Francisco, leads scouting party against Apache raiders, 165-168.

Esquibel, Santiago, murders Americans, 177-180.

Estado Land and Cattle Company, organized, 238; Gillett employed by, 238-239.

FABIN'S Station, Indian raid near, 151.

Feuds, in Mason County, 46-52; Horrell and Higgins families, 69-80; between Horrells and Mexicans, 76.

Index

Index

Index

Harrison, Dick, on scout for criminals, 89-91.

Hawkins, James B., heads scouting party of rangers, 29-32; in scout for Indians, 33-45; captures Mexican boy, 48; retained as ranger, 53.

Hawkins Station, Indians raid near, 151-152.

Head, Dick (Richard), in journey to El Paso County, 141-148; on scout after Apaches, 151-160.

Heffridge, Bill, career as outlaw, 109-113.

Herndon, ——, criminal career, 115-116.

Higgins, Pink, in Horrell-Higgins feud, 77-80.

Hill, Frank, retained as ranger, 53.

Hitsons, John, as cattleman, 10.

Hoard's Creek, cattlemen on, 7.

Hogg, Governor, pardons J. W. Hardin, 87.

Holcomb, John, career as ranger, 190-196.

Hondo River, as refuge of Horrell gang, 76.

Honey, wild, found, 31-32.

Honey Creek, Indian raid on, 33.

Horrell, Ben, in Horrell-Higgins feud, 73-80.

Horrell Brothers, in cattle business, 9.

Horrell, John, killed, 73.

Horrell, Mart, in Horrell-Higgins feud, 73-80.

Horrell, Merritt, in Horrell-Higgins feud, 73-80.

Horrell, Sam characterized, 73.

Horrell, Tom, in Horrell-Higgins feud, 73-80.

Houston, Masonic gathering in, 67.

Houston, Sam, organizes rifle troop, 15.

Howard, Charley (Judge), in Salt Lake War, 136-139.

Howard's Draw, Indians raid wagon train, 145.

Howard's Well, rangers camp, 133; Indians raid wagon train, 145.

Hu, massacres whites, 169.

Hueco Tanks, route via, 170, 197; described, 174-175.

Hughes, George, joins Lieut. Reynolds' company, 82.

Hughes, Lowe, joins Lieut. Reynolds' company, 82.

INDEPENDENCE Creek, objective of rangers, 59.

Indians, attack cattlemen, 9-10; steal horses, 12; policy of government toward, 16-17; rangers' service against, 18-19; raid Texas settlements, 29; John Gamble ranch, 33; in Kimble County, 100-102; rangers pursue, 29-32, 33-40, 58-59; battles with, 41-45, 223-225; murder Dowdy chil-

Index

dren, 129-130; destroy wagon train, 145. See also Apaches, Tonkawas, Lipans, and Kickapoo.

JACKSON, Frank, criminal career, 115-128.

Jennie, pack-mule, slain, 39, 44.

Jim, Tonkawa guide, 64-66.

Jim Ned Creek, cattlemen on, 7.

Johnson, Arkansas, criminal career, 115-116.

Johnson, Bill, as assistant marshal of El Paso, 233-234; plot to kill Stoudenmire, 235; killed, 236.

Johnson's Fork, rangers traverse, 69.

Johnston's Run, rangers traverse, 59; seek outlaws, 132-133.

Jones, Major John B., appointed to command rangers, 17; ends Mason County War, 49-52; orders mules restrained, 56; leads scout for Indians, 58-60; escort company, 61; career sketched, 62; Masons honor, 67; cleans up Kimble County, 69-70; made adjutant general, 71; receives confession of criminal, 103; in overthrow of Sam Bass gang, 115-127; investigates Salt Lake feud, 138.

Juarez, route via, 154.

Junction City, rendezvous of rangers, 69; road via, 96;

raiders near, 100; present status, 105.

KENDALL, T. J. T., kills Billy Brown, 106-107.

Kerr County, rangers scout in, 59; Indians raid, 129-130.

Kickapoo Indians, rangers scout for, 59-60; raid settlers, 130.

Kickapoo Springs, rangers camp, 36.

Kimble County, cattlemen's activities in, 10, 13; as rendezvous of outlaws, 69-70, 87-88; Indians raid, 100; Dublin gang captured, 102-103; cleared of outlaws, 105; prosperity, 105.

Kimbrough, William, on scout against Indians, 33-45.

King, Israel, cattle stolen, 228; recovered, 229.

Krimpkau, Gus, in journey to El Paso County, 141-148; killed, 235.

LAKE VALLEY, John Holcomb killed, 196-197.

Lampasas, Horrells defeat rangers, 74.

Lampasas County, cattlemen's activities in, 13; seat of Horrell-Higgins feud, 70-80; search for criminals in, 107; N. O. Reynolds sheriff, 134.

Lampasas River, residence of Horrell brothers on, 77.

250

Index

Index

McCarthy, Tim, on scout for criminals, 89-91; slain, 91.

McCollum, Bob, teamster, 7.

McGee, Henry, joins Lieut. Reynolds' company, 82; promoted, 84; career, 85; on scout for criminals, 89-91; in capture of Sam Bass gang, 122-126.

McGoffin, Mayor ——, appeals to Captain Baylor for rangers, 233.

McGonnigal, Major ——, opinion of Victorio, 187.

McKavett, Fort, route via, 35, 146; rendezvous of criminals, 70.

Maltimore, Henry, on scout for Indians, 33-45; retained as ranger, 53; joins Lieut. Reynolds' company, 82; transferred, 134; on journey to El Paso County, 141-148.

Maltimore, Kit, retained as ranger, 53.

Manney, Lieut. ——, in campaign against Victorio, 186.

Manning Brothers, o p e r a t e theater, 232; relations with Marshal Campbell, 233; plot against Stoudenmire, 235-236.

Marfa, as cattle raising country, 238.

Marsh, Capt. ——, rangers transferred to company, 134.

Marsh, Billy, resents surrender of rangers, 139.

Martin, Jack, retained as ranger,

53; nicknamed, 57; joins Major Jones's company, 61; Lieut. Reynolds' company, 81; hears rangers pass, 122.

Mason, Jim Pope, escapes rangers, 92.

Masons, Major Jones's connection with, 67.

Mason County War, 46-52.

Mason, Fort, Indian raid near, 33; route via, 146.

Mattimore, Sergeant, ——, slain, 138.

Maverick County, filibusterers in, 71.

Mead, Tom, retained as ranger, 53.

Means, John, teamster, 77.

Mejia, Pablo, brings news of Indian raid, 151; carries message, 154.

Melville, Andrew, killed, 74.

Menard, objective of rangers, 70, 146.

Menard County, cattlemen's activities in, 11-13; criminals captured, 92.

Menardville, Gillett visits, 13, 23; rangers near, 14, 26, 54; Indian raiders sought, 34.

Mescalero Agency, Indians from, raid whites, 161, 173.

Mesilla, route via, 218.

Mesquite Station, train robbed, 115.

Mexicans, war with Horrell gang, 76; rangers adopt costume, 83; in Salt Lake War,

252

Index

136-140, 149-150; Indians raid, 151-153, 164-169; join rangers against Indians, 154-160; corpses shunned by wild animals, 168; murder Americans, 168, 177-180, 197-198; murdered, 234; affray at inquest over, 235; friendship for Captain Baylor, 199. See also Mexico.

Mexican War, service of James S. Gillett, 2.

Mexico, filibustering project against, 71; rangers pursue Apaches into, 164-168, 207; murderer kidnapped from, 213-216. See also Mexicans.

Miles, General Nelson A., testimonial to rangers, 20.

Mills, Lieut. ——, battle with Apaches, 200-202.

Mitchell, Bob, in Horrell-Higgins feud, 77-80.

Molina, Manuel, murders Americans, 177-180.

Monday's Springs, rangers camp, 226.

Moore, Morris, in capture of Sam Bass gang, 121-124; shot, 124.

Morgan, ——, killed by Apaches, 203.

Morgan, Billy, capture of, 225-228.

Morton, ——, murder of, 176-177; murderers taken, 177-178; released, 179.

Mourland, Millard, joins Lieut. Reynolds' company, 82.

Mules, Spanish, on mail route, 147.

Murphy, Jim, criminal career, 115-127.

Murray, Sergt. Plunk, instructions concerning Indian raiders, 34; retained as ranger, 53.

NANA, leads Apache raid, 187-188; joins Geronimo, 189, 200; General Lawton captures, 189.

Neal, ——, affray with John Holcomb, 196-197.

Negroes, in fight with rangers, 90-91.

Nevill, Lieut. Charles L., retained as ranger, 53; buys rifles, 56; joins Major Jones's company, 61; Lieut. Reynolds' company, 81; promoted, 84; fails to capture bandit, 90-91; captures criminal, 102; in capture of Sam Bass gang, 122-126; commands ranger company, 133-134; destroys Apache raiders, 188; in campaign against Apaches, 205-206; leaves rangers, 238; partner of Gillett, 238.

New Mexico, Horrell gang seeks refuge in, 75-76; resort of criminals, 199.

Nicholls, ——, as cattleman, 13.

253

Index

Index

255

Index

Index

Index

on scout after Apaches, 151-160.

Sydnor, Kate, sister of Mrs. Baylor, 141.

Sydnor, Sallie Garland, wife of George W. Baylor, 144-145.

TARRANT County, Sam Bass frequents, 116.

Tays, John B., leads rangers in Salt Lake War, 138-140; battle with Indians, 223-225.

Terrazas, General Joaquin, campaign against Victorio, 184-188; victory, 200.

Territ, Fort, as rendezvous, 29.

Terry, General Con, leads rangers, 16.

Texas Pacific Railroad, train robbed, 115.

Thatcher, Captain ——, engages Gillett as railroad guard, 230.

Thomas, Henry, joins Lieut. Reynolds' company, 82; guards bandit, 86.

Thomas, John, on scout after Apaches, 151-160; quarrel with James Stallings, 192.

Tinnins, ——, wounded feudist carried to home of, 77.

Tombstone, horses stolen near, 225.

Tom Green County, cattle thieves in, 91.

Tonkawa Indians, activities described, 64-66.

Toyah Creek, route via, 170.

Trail Drivers' Association, old time, reunion of, 44.

Tres Castillos, battle with Apaches, 187-188, 200.

Tres Jacales, citizens march against Apaches, 164-168, 183.

Trout, Jim, on scout against Indians, 33-45; retained as ranger, 53.

Tucker, Dan, kills criminal, 198.

Tularosa, Mescalero Indian agency near, 174.

Turner, Ben, in Horrell-Higgins feud, 75-80.

UNDERWOOD, Henry, criminal career, 115.

Underwood, John, criminal career, 109-113.

Union Pacific Railroad, train robbed, 109-113.

Uvalde County, cattle driven to Dakota, 108.

VAN HORN'S Well, Indian raiders near, 180.

Victorio, leads raid into Mexico, 161-169; band exterminated, 180-189.

WACO, Sam Bass gang in, 118.

Walde, Ed, stage-driver, attacked by Indians, 181-182.

Ware, Charles, in capture of Eli Wixon, 130-131.

Ware, Dick, joins Lieut. Reynolds' company, 81; later

Index